CHOOSE TO BE
happy

By the same author
GoodStress: The life that can be yours
FearLess: Your guide to overcoming anxiety

CHOOSE TO BE
happy

your step-by-step guide

revised edition

WAYNE FROGGATT

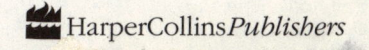

HarperCollins*Publishers*

National Library of New Zealand Cataloguing-in-Publication Data

Froggatt, Wayne.
Choose to be happy : your step-by-step guide / Wayne Froggatt.
Rev. ed.
Previous ed.: 1993.
Includes bibliographical references and index.
ISBN 1-86950-495-X
1. Self-actualization (Psychology) 2. Rational-emotive
psychotherapy. I. Title.
158.1—dc 21

First published 1993
Second edition 2003
Reprinted 2004

HarperCollins*Publishers (New Zealand) Limited*
P.O. Box 1, Auckland

Copyright © Wayne Froggatt 1993, 2003

Wayne Froggatt asserts the moral right to be identified as the author of this work.

All rights reserved. No part of this publication may be reproduced, stored in a retrieval system or transmitted in any form or by any means, electronic, mechanical, photocopying, recording or otherwise, without the prior written permission of the publishers.

ISBN 1 86950 495 X

Designed and typeset by Chris O'Brien/PagesLP
Set in ITC Garamond and Rotis Semi Sans
Printed by Griffin Press. Australia, on 79 gsm Bulky Paperback

Publisher's note

This publication is designed to provide accurate and authoritative information on the subject matter covered. It is sold with the understanding that the publisher is not engaged in rendering psychological, financial, legal, or other professional services. If expert assistance or counselling is needed, the services of a competent professional should be sought.

Acknowledgements to the first edition

Of the people who have contributed to this book, many will remain anonymous. They are the clients who have shared with me their thoughts about the self-help methods I have taught them. In this way, they have in turn taught me how to refine these methods to the point where they are ready to be presented to a wider audience.

There are colleagues who have spent many hours reading drafts and providing constructive comment. My special thanks to Terri Smith and Stefan Thevessen, who met with me regularly and helped me set the direction for the book, and encouraged me when the task began to seem dauntingly long-term; to Audrey Adams, for her support and the help she gave me on the writing process; to Linda Kennington and Judy Wilford, who have edited the book in its entirety, providing extensive comments both from the point of view of the professional social worker and the professional editor; and to David Ramsden and Dr Tom Flewett, for feedback and guidance on specific chapters relating to their fields of expertise.

Perhaps the person who knows the book best is my wife, Glenys, who has edited each chapter so many times she can almost recite them from memory. I owe a great debt to my family for the way they have kept the home running over the years I have been locking myself away to write.

Finally, this book owes much to the work of two people whom I have met only through their writings: Drs Albert Ellis and Aaron Beck. It is to Dr Beck I owe my understanding of the ways in which human beings distort reality; and to Dr Ellis that crucial insight into how we apply personal meanings to our interpretations of reality. I hope that my book, in the way it has attempted to integrate their thinking, has done justice to the parallel but related systems of psychotherapy they have so elegantly developed over the past four decades.

Wayne Froggatt, 1992

Acknowledgements to the second edition

Many people, without realising they were doing so, have contributed to this new edition of *Choose to be Happy*. Readers have shared those parts of the first version they found especially helpful; colleagues have asked: 'Why don't you add such and such?' and, finally, there are the teachers from whom I have learned so much more about cognitive-behavioural psychotherapy over the past 10 years. Drs Ellis and Beck are still in practice and contributing to the literature on CBT. As well as Dr Ellis, I have received stimulating training from such people as Janet Wolfe, Ray DiGiuseppe and Michler Bishop from the Albert Ellis Institute in New York, and Rob Dawson and Monica O'Kelly from the Australian Institute for Rational Emotive Therapy. I am especially indebted to Professor Stephen Palmer from the UK Centre for Rational Emotive Behaviour Therapy, for his support in the development of REBT in my own country and his encouragement to maintain a scientific, evidence-based approach — which, I trust, this book continues to reflect.

Wayne Froggatt, 2003

Contents

Acknowledgements to the first edition   7
Acknowledgements to the second edition   8
Foreword to the first edition   12
Foreword to the second edition   13

Part I **Self-understanding and the tools for change**

1 Who controls you?   **16**
2 Taking back your power   **27**
3 What is irrational thinking?   **33**
4 Distorting reality   **44**
5 Demanding: turning wants into needs   **51**
6 Catastrophising: making mountains out of molehills   **59**
7 People-rating: are you living down to your label?   **64**
8 Rational Self-Analysis   **73**
9 Learning self-analysis: practice exercises   **97**

Part II **Applying self-analysis to life's common problems**

Introduction   **118**
10 What are you really afraid of?   **120**

11	Give up guilt: you don't need it	137
12	Climbing out of the black hole: no more depression	147
13	Anger: who's in charge?	162
14	You don't need approval	180
15	How to get more of what you want and less of what you don't	193
16	Are you trying to be perfect?	208
17	What do you really want out of life?	220
18	Changing your circumstances	231
19	Managing stress	238
20	Putting it all together: twelve principles for rational living	244
21	Overcoming blocks to change	252
22	Getting help	261

Further reading 265

Index 277

Foreword to the first edition

Why another book applying rational-emotive behaviour therapy (REBT) and cognitive-behaviour therapy (CBT) to self-help procedures? Aren't there enough already?

In a word: No.

As the father of REBT and the grandfather of CBT, I am an old hand at self-help books myself, having written many of them, including *How to Live with a 'Neurotic'* (Wilshire, 1957), *A New Guide to Rational Living* (Wilshire, 1975) and *How to Stubbornly Refuse to Make Yourself Miserable About Anything — Yes, Anything!* (Lyle Stuart, 1988). So I know how important it is to state the principles and practices of REBT in a highly readable, understandable and usable form.

Wayne Froggatt has done exactly this. Although REBT is at times subtle and complex — especially when it teaches people how to accurately rate and measure their acts and performances while refraining from inefficiently and self-defeatingly rating their self, their being or their personhood — the author of the present book has included its main concepts, has lucidly explained them, and has nicely shown his readers how to apply them effectively in their own lives.

In Part I of his book, Froggatt has outlined the general theory and practice of rational-emotive therapy and cognitive-behaviour therapy, including useful exercises that readers can employ on their own. In Part II he applies REBT and CBT methods to some of the most common specific disturbances, such as worry, guilt, depression, rage, the need for approval, unassertiveness and perfectionism. It is amazing how he covers so much ground in so little space and with such clarity. This book is hardly a cure-all for every conceivable emotional and behavioural problem. But, used with energetic application, it can greatly help!

Albert Ellis, PhD, President
Institute for Rational-Emotive Therapy
New York, 1992

Foreword to the second edition

What has changed over the past 10 years that would warrant a new edition of a book already acceptable, as it is, to so many people? The basic premise of its underlying theory, cognitive-behaviour therapy (CBT), remains the same — namely, that we create our own reactions to what life throws at us, and we have the potential to change those reactions if we choose to do so.

The main difference is that there are now more ways to make this choice: new strategies and techniques that can aid the process of personal change and development. The revised edition of *Choose to be Happy* reflects these advances.

For example, the instructions for analysing self-defeating thinking have been expanded. In particular, there are new strategies for disputing irrational beliefs, and additional behavioural approaches for going beyond rethinking to action. The chapter on managing anxiety has been expanded to reflect new learning about the usefulness of behavioural techniques in helping people overcome their fears.

In response to the current world-wide interest in stress, especially as it relates to the workplace, there is a completely new chapter on the subject of stress management. There is also a new chapter, summarised from my 1997 book *GoodStress*, presenting the 'Twelve Rational Principles'. Having received a great deal of positive feedback from people who have found them useful, it seemed appropriate to include these principles in this new edition of *Choose to be Happy*. They bring together and sum up material on rational thinking from different parts of the book.

Previous readers will notice a few changes in terminology. For example, 'ratings' are now referred to as 'evaluations'. These revisions are will help provide consistency with the terms readers will come across in other CBT-based books.

There are some things in this new edition that have not changed.

In particular, the people are still here, sharing their stories so that others may identify with them. It is my hope that new readers will take encouragement from these accounts as they work towards the same positive changes in their own lives.

Wayne Froggatt
Hastings, 2003

Part I

Self-understanding and the tools for change

1 Who controls you?

Most people want to be happy. They would like to feel good, avoid pain and achieve their goals.

For many, though, happiness seems to be an elusive dream. In fact, it appears that we humans are much better at disturbing and defeating ourselves. Instead of feeling good, we are more likely to worry, feel guilty and get depressed. We put ourselves down and feel shy, hurt or self-pitying. We get jealous, angry, hostile and bitter, or suffer anxiety, tension and panic.

On top of feeling bad, we often act in self-destructive ways. Some strive to be perfect in everything they do. Many mess up relationships. Others worry about disapproval and let people use them as doormats. Still others compulsively gamble, smoke and overspend — or abuse alcohol, drugs and food. Some even try to end it all.

Look at the evidence. Around 60 per cent of people in countries such as Britain, America and New Zealand have had an identifiable mental-health problem at some time in their lives. Anxiety heads the list: one in every three people has suffered from it. Fifteen per cent have had a significant episode of depression. Over 30 per cent have experienced a sexual dysfunction. One in every three has had problems with alcohol. High numbers of people drink at hazardous levels — with a huge cost to their country in work-related problems.[1]

These are discomfiting figures. But the strange thing is, most of this pain is avoidable. We don't have to do it to ourselves. Humans can, believe it or not, learn to *choose* how they feel and behave.

You may be surprised to hear that — many people are. 'I don't get it,' they say. 'Surely you can't choose the way you feel? Feelings just happen. Or they're caused by your circumstances.' But feelings don't just happen. Every emotion and every behaviour has a cause. And that cause is *within us*. Externals — circumstances, other people or the past — do not control our reactions. This means that you and I have the potential to change the reactions we don't want.

To feel and act differently, the secret is to work on *yourself* (internal change). Even if you want to change your external circumstances, you are better off dealing first with any internal blocks that disable you. Get rid of the insecurity that traps you in a dead-end job or relationship. Deal with the resentment that keeps you grumbling about injustices rather than changing them. Shake off the guilt that makes you an easy target for others to exploit.

Judith knows what it is like to be disabled. A person who has always believed that others should come first, she married a man who drank to excess, neglected his business, deprived the family of money, and communicated only with verbal abuse. But she wouldn't leave him. She used to justify this by saying that the children needed a father. But when the children left home, Judith stayed on. She thought it would devastate her husband if she left — which meant she would never be able to live with herself.

What kept Judith in her dead-end, joyless marriage? Guilt was the trap. She had been brought up to believe that her role as a woman was to attend to her family's needs and look after their interests, denying her own. Though Judith wanted to leave, she believed that she 'shouldn't'. She created her own guilt trap — in the same way that we all cause ourselves to feel and behave as we do in response to life's events and circumstances.

As you think, so you feel

'People feel disturbed not by things, but by the views they take of them.' Ancient words, from a first-century philosopher named Epictetus — but they are just as true now.

Events and circumstances don't cause your reactions — these result from what you tell yourself about the things that happen. Put simply, *thoughts cause feelings and behaviours* — or, more precisely, *events and circumstances trigger thoughts*, which then create *reactions*. These processes are intertwined.

Look around. Clearly, different people react differently to the same thing. The circumstance doesn't cause the variation — so what does?

'Our past,' you might say. 'Surely it's all to do with the way we were brought up, things that happened to us as children, how other people treated us.'

Let's assume for the moment you are right (even though we know that people with similar backgrounds often handle life differently as adults). How is it, then, that things which happened in the past (and are thus no longer present) can influence our reactions *now*?

'Well,' you respond, 'I guess our past experiences leave us with certain ways of looking at life that we keep and carry round with us in the present.'

Now we're getting there. The past is significant — but only insofar as it leaves us with our *current* attitudes and beliefs. External events — whether in the past, present or future — cannot influence the way you feel or behave until you become aware of and begin to think about them.

Test this out for yourself. Explain to someone that you would like their help to check out a theory. Point a pencil at them, and ask how they would feel if the pencil were a gun. Most people will probably say they would be afraid, or something similar. Then ask how they would feel if they didn't know what it was you were holding. You will most probably get a different reaction — curiosity, for example. Now ask how they would feel if they didn't even notice you were pointing something at them. They will probably say that they wouldn't feel anything.

This shows that to fear something (or to react in any other way) you have to be *thinking* about it. The cause is not the event — it is what we tell ourselves about the event.

The ABCs of feelings and behaviours

American psychologist Dr Albert Ellis, the originator of *Rational Emotive Behaviour Therapy*, was one of the first to show systematically how beliefs determine the way human beings feel and behave. He developed the *ABC* model to demonstrate this.

A is whatever starts things off — a circumstance, event or experience, or just thinking about something which has happened. This triggers thoughts (*B*), which in turn create a reaction — feelings and behaviours (*C*).

To see this in operation, let's consider Alan. A young man who had always tended to doubt himself, Alan imagined that other people didn't like him and that they were only friendly because they pitied him. Made redundant when his government department was restructured, he decided to retrain as a computer technician. At polytechnic he met another trainee who as well as sharing his shyness also had similar interests. The two developed a friendship. One day, this other person passed Alan in the street without returning his greeting, to which Alan reacted negatively.

Here is the event, Alan's beliefs and his reaction in the *ABC* format:

A What started things off
Friend passed me in the street without speaking to me.

B Beliefs about A
1. He's ignoring me. He doesn't like me.
2. I could end up without friends for ever.
3. That would be terrible.
4. For me to be happy and feel worthwhile, people must like me.
5. I'm unacceptable as a friend, so I must be worthless as a person.

C Reaction
Feelings: worthless, depressed.
Behaviour: avoiding people generally.

Note that *A* doesn't cause *C*. *A* triggers *B*. *B* then causes *C*.

You may be thinking, 'Why didn't Alan just speak to his friend and avoid all this pain?' But people often don't do what is in their interests. Alan had always believed that he was only worthwhile if he had friends who liked and approved of him. Because he thought no one wanted him, he began to avoid people generally. This made things worse. Because he was not having contact with others, he saw this as proof that no one wanted him. This, in turn, 'proved' that he was worthless. Irrational thinking often consists of vicious circles of this kind.

Now, someone who thought differently about the same event would react in another way:

A What started things off
Friend passed me in the street without speaking to me.

B Beliefs about A
1. He's ignoring me. He doesn't like me.
2. I've been wanting to end this relationship for a while now.
3. If he doesn't like me, then I don't have to find a way to end it.
4. This has worked out better than I hoped.

C Reaction
Feelings: relief.

Someone else could have different thoughts again. This would lead to a third possible reaction:

A What started things off
Friend passed me in the street without speaking to me.

B Beliefs about A
1. He didn't ignore me deliberately. He may not have seen me.
2. He might have something on his mind.
3. I'd like to help if I can.

C Reaction
Feelings: concerned.
Behaviour: went to visit friend to see how he was.

These examples show how different ways of viewing the same event can lead to different reactions. The same principle operates in reverse: when people react alike, it is because they are thinking in similar ways.

Not only does thinking create feelings, it keeps them going. Alan felt hurt because he told himself his friend deliberately rejected him, meaning he was worthless. He will continue hurting for as long as he keeps thinking this way. But by changing what he tells himself, he could feel better — even if he wasn't able to sort things out with his friend.

Furthermore, Alan doesn't have to tell the other person how he feels in order to feel better. Many people think there are only two choices in dealing with strong emotions — either to express the feelings outwardly or to suppress them inwardly. But as we have just seen, there is a third option — change the thoughts that keep the feelings going.

Let's say that I'm bitter because I think someone is rotten and should behave better. I don't have to express my anger to deal with it, nor do I have to bottle it up inside. I can choose, instead, to get rid of my rage by changing what I think. I can remind myself, for instance, that other people don't have to behave to suit me. I can also learn to see that labelling them as rotten won't change their behaviour. Then, instead of hostile anger, I can substitute less disabling emotions such as disappointment and annoyance.

Thinking can be subconscious too

No doubt you can recall occasions when you know you thought yourself into a bad feeling. But what about the times you reacted, seemingly, without thinking at all? Many people are confused about this until they discover that thinking goes on at more than one level of awareness.

Conscious thoughts are those you are aware of. They are the thoughts in the forefront of your mind. You can hold only a small number of thoughts in your conscious mind at any one time.

Subconscious thoughts, on the other hand, are beneath your awareness. You may be only partly aware of them, sometimes hardly at all. It is in our subconscious memory systems, too, that we hold our attitudes and beliefs — those lasting ideas about how we want ourselves, others and the world to be, such as 'I must get love from others in order to feel good about myself' or 'Children should never speak back to their parents.' We can call these underlying beliefs *core beliefs* or *rules for living*. They guide the way we react to the events and circumstances we face in everyday life, and one or more of them can be triggered by a specific event.

This underlying belief system explains why people often react instantly to events. We already have, in our memory stores, rules about many of life's recurrent happenings. An event or experience simply 'plugs in' to an existing rule.

Take, for example, the fear of dogs — a growing problem with the number of fierce dogs now found in urban areas. When some people see a large dog, they don't consciously think, 'Is this dangerous?' They already have an existing rule, which they select, subconsciously, to fit what is happening — something like: 'Large dogs are always dangerous and I must avoid them at all costs.' As a result, whenever they sight a large dog, they instantly feel afraid and try to avoid it.

Consider the many things you 'automatically' respond to — spiders, authority figures, gangs, noises in the night, relationships, disobedient children and so on. What type of permanent beliefs do you hold about these things?

Why do we do it?

When you look at the irrational beliefs that disrupt your life and happiness, you could well ask, 'Why? After all, it doesn't make sense. Why would I choose to create misery for myself?'

The short answer is — because you are a human being. Human beings naturally and normally think irrationally. We appear to have a built-in tendency to exaggerate, view life in negative and absolute terms, and judge ourselves and others in a simplistic fashion. This bias, apparently, is to be found in all cultures and historical periods. Some evidence suggests it may be passed on genetically. Research has shown that tendencies toward unhappiness, for example, appear to run in families (even when members are raised apart).[2] Also, our brains seem to favour simplistic modes of thought.

This 'biological' susceptibility, though, is only a *tendency*. Its influence is modified by what happens to us throughout life — and through conscious learning and effort. We can increase our own happiness no matter what genes we have inherited.[3]

We also learn irrational ways of thinking from our parents, teachers, friends, the media and other sources. Many irrational ideas are taught to achieve social control. For example, children (and adults, too) are often told they 'should' or 'must' behave in certain ways and are 'rated' negatively when they don't. We take on many of our irrational beliefs in childhood. Because our ability to criticise is not yet fully matured, that is when we are most suggestible and receptive to the teaching of authority figures.

We keep learning throughout life, adding to our store of irrational beliefs. Every life experience that results in bad feelings may reinforce the belief that external events (*As*) cause internal reactions (*Cs*), and will lead to 'awfulising' and demands that such things not happen. We may also discover that changing some *As* can lead to temporary relief, which can further reinforce the idea that circumstances we dislike should not or must not exist.

Irrational thinking becomes a habit. Let's say that when you were a child others said you were useless. By hearing this often enough you gradually came to believe it. It is as though you made a tape recording in your head that you could replay over and over again. Every time someone says something critical or you think that you have failed, you reach for the 'play' button.

Psychological gains of a kind may also reinforce irrational thinking. By awfulising we can get attention and sympathy for our woes or avoid difficult situations. We can try to control others with demands. We can avoid taking responsibility for our own wants by pretending they are needs. Rating or labelling others may be another way to manipulate them.

Often, however, these gains are more apparent than real. Why not work out your reasons for holding onto irrational thinking and ask yourself, 'Is it worth it?'

Myths about what controls you

Not everyone finds it easy to accept that they cause their own feelings and behaviours. There are a number of myths about external control that can confuse the issue:

- *My past controls me.* This myth claims that past events, especially those of childhood, cause the way you feel and behave in the present. The past, though, is just that — the past. It has gone. What happened yesterday, last year or 30 years ago is no longer present. Past experiences helped to form your belief system, but it is beliefs you hold *now* (wherever they came from) which cause your reactions in the present. It is your choice to maintain old beliefs or to change them, and while you cannot alter the past, you can change what you tell yourself about it.

- *Other people cause my reactions.* This myth suggests that others have direct control over your feelings and actions. It is as though there is a button on your nose that others can press, and away you go. What other people say or do, though, can only affect you if you let it — in other words, if you *tell yourself* something about their behaviour. This doesn't mean that people should be robots who never react to anyone else, but you can learn to respond in different ways — as and how you choose.
- *My circumstances control me.* This is a version of the 'button-on-the-nose' theory. It suggests that your reactions result from the neighbourhood you live in, your employment, your state of physical health, your bank balance, the share market or the economy. But what this assumption doesn't explain is just how *external* circumstances can cause things to happen *inside* a person, or why other people often react differently to the same things. It is rational to feel negative about something you dislike, but you can learn to avoid extreme, disabling emotions and responses that are out of proportion and may only make your situation worse.
- *This is just the way I am.* Again, this myth suggests that you cannot help the way you are. But how do you get to be the way you are? How is it that others get to be the way they are — different from you? Most people would say, 'I was brought up this way', or propose a similar version of the first myth. Saying 'I'm just the way I am' is simply stating the obvious.

Responsibility doesn't mean blame

These myths all serve the same purpose: they block us from taking responsibility for ourselves. It isn't surprising they are so popular. As one person put it: 'Since I've been having therapy I feel even worse. Before, I didn't think I caused the way I felt. Now it sounds as though I am to blame for my feelings.'

Many people make the mistake of confusing blame and responsibility. Blame is moralistic, unnecessary — and unhelpful. Why? Because it carries a moral stigma. It suggests that not only did you cause something to happen, but you should also be condemned and punished for it. No one wants to feel like that, so it is tempting to deny all accountability. As a result, blame retards personal growth. If you operate according to a blaming philosophy, you won't want to admit to any need for change.

Responsibility, on the other hand, is a useful concept. To see yourself as responsible (in a practical sense) for what you cause will motivate you to set about changing yourself — not because you 'should', but because you want to achieve a happier existence.

So why not simply view the fact that you create your own emotions and behaviours as just that — a fact? Don't make it into a moral issue. Remember: blame and responsibility are simply ways of thinking. Which one you adopt is your choice.

Internal or external control?

To take responsibility for and gain control over your emotions and behaviours, change what you tell yourself about their cause.

External control	Internal control
She makes me sick.	I make myself sick by the way I view her behaviour.
You made me angry.	I got angry because of what I told myself about you.
I can't help the way I feel.	I can help myself feel differently by changing my views.
I'm like this because I was put down in childhood.	I'm like this because I keep repeating those childhood put-downs to myself.
How can I feel good when everyone treats me so unfairly?	I can't change the way others act, but I can change the way I view their actions.

External control	*Internal control*
Crowds scare me.	I make myself scared by what I tell myself about crowds.
How dare he make me feel embarrassed in public!	I made myself feel embarrassed by the view I took of his behaviour.
How can you be happy when you're fifty, redundant, and there are no jobs out there?	I don't have to like being made redundant, but how I feel inside depends on what I tell myself, not on the state of the economy.
I can't help overeating.	One of the reasons I overeat is because I tell myself I'm helpless, and that if I *want* something I *must* have it.
She made me hit her.	I *chose* to hit her. I could choose not to in future.
I'm just the way I am.	True — but I could choose to be different and make the effort to change.

As many others already have, you can gain internal control over the way you think, feel and behave. This will involve some work. You need to understand the types of thinking that cause your problems and how you can change them. The rest of the book aims to provide this knowledge. The first step, though, is to accept that you can be responsible for yourself, your feelings and your actions. Once you have done that, you will be well on the way.

References

1. Statistical sources quoted here are:
   (i) McDonnell, B., (1982). *Employee Alcohol Impairment.* Wellington: Alcoholic Liquor Advisory Council.
   (ii) Wells, J.E., et al. (1989). Christchurch psychiatric epidemiology study. *Australian and New Zealand Journal of Psychiatry*, 23, 315–26.
2. Swanbrow, D., (1989). The paradox of happiness. *Psychology Today* (Jul.–Aug.), 37–9.
3. Myers, D.G., (1992). *The Pursuit of Happiness: Who is happy — and why.* New York, N.Y.: William Morrow.

2 Taking back your power

Our reactions, as we have seen, are the result of what we believe. Once we accept that, we are ready to start building a more useful philosophy and to help ourselves to better feelings and ways of behaving. Let's begin by seeing that change is possible and dealing with some of the blocks.

People often wonder whether it is possible to do much about the way they feel. After all, they say, aren't we influenced by our circumstances and our physical make-up? Up to a point, they are right. To say that thoughts cause feelings does not mean that what happens around you — or inside you — is irrelevant.

What about our circumstances?

While As (events or circumstances) don't cause Cs (feelings and behaviours), they are still important in that they act as *triggers* to Bs (your thoughts about As). Without A to trigger B, you are less likely to experience C.

It isn't hard, for instance, to see a link between such events as increasing unemployment and greater numbers of people developing mental-health problems or, alternatively, engaging in criminal activity. But to say that unemployment causes mental ill health or crime leaves out an important fact: most unemployed people do not commit crimes or need psychiatric treatment. What causes the differences between people facing similar external circumstances is how they view those circumstances. Some unemployed people see their situation as catastrophic, unbearable or hopeless and become overly anxious or depressed. Others accept it and find ways of achieving what happiness they can under the circumstances. Yet others see it as a challenge to develop a new career.

This book emphasises changing your thoughts — not because the

As in your life don't matter, but because you often need to deal with irrational beliefs before you can do much about them.

You won't always be able to influence what happens to you, but the thoughts you have about these events are under your control. By taking charge of your thoughts, you cover both options: you are in a better position to change what you can, and to live with what you cannot.

Do biochemical changes affect our emotions?

I often meet people who believe their emotional problems have a medical cause, so they cannot see why their doctor has referred them for psychotherapy. I can understand their confusion. It isn't hard to see that physical changes influence our moods.

Various chemicals can affect the way we feel. Toxic substances such as weedkillers and other poisons may dramatically affect mood. Many illegal drugs are taken for the purpose of getting a high. The most popular drug of all — alcohol — is a depressant. Drugs prescribed for many physical conditions have side effects that influence mood. Psychiatric drugs, such as tranquillisers and antidepressants, are expressly designed to alter the user's emotional state. Commonly used stimulants such as caffeine — and even one's diet generally — can influence feelings. Hormonal changes can affect moods to varying degrees and for varying lengths of time, and can be triggered by such things as physical exercise, menstruation and childbirth.

Biochemical changes like these, however, are still often influenced by what we think and believe. Let's say that I feel a little low in the morning, for no obvious reason. I interpret this as meaning I'm 'depressed' and tell myself that it's terrible and is going to get worse. As a result, my mood drops even further. But I could choose to see my low mood in a different light. I could, for instance, decide it is a temporary condition. If I then got myself involved in some interesting task, I would most probably soon feel better.

Even the effects of mind-altering drugs are often influenced by thoughts. A person who uses alcohol, for example, can become hostile in one situation and overly friendly in another. To some extent, this depends on the way they interpret the situation they are in.

What we think can affect our physical wellbeing. As Dr John Raeburn of the Auckland Medical School argues in a paper on the prevention of health problems, an individual's overall health depends on how that person perceives their own competence and control.[1] The link between one's approach to life and specific health problems, such as heart disease, is now well documented. There is some promising research into the same link with certain forms of cancer.

It is also possible to modify the effects of conditions that have a mainly physical cause. This is shown by research carried out at the University of Melbourne on premenstrual syndrome.[2] PMS is a problem faced by many women in their reproductive years. Symptoms include restlessness, headaches, depression, aggression, tiredness, and loss of concentration and sexual interest. Evidence suggests that biochemical changes are a significant factor.

Researcher Carol Morse and her team set up a course of group treatment to see if the symptoms of PMS could be relieved beyond what medication usually achieved. They used a blend of cognitive psychotherapy (on which this book is based) and relaxation training. Those taking part learned how to understand and take charge of their symptoms and deal better with external stresses. This led to improvements in both psychological and physical symptoms. Most importantly, the participants were able to maintain these gains in the long term without the help of a therapist.

Other studies show that thinking can influence many functions of the body that we used to see as 'automatic', such as breathing, heart beat and pain.[3] With training, you can alter these processes. You can learn, for example, to raise or lower your pulse, or reduce the amount of pain you feel.

Overcoming obstacles

While change is possible it isn't easy — mainly because of a very human tendency known as *low discomfort tolerance*. Most of us want to be physically and emotionally comfortable, but personal change means giving up some old habits of thinking and behaving and 'safe' ways of approaching life.

Whereas before you may have blamed others for your problems, now you start to take responsibility for yourself and what you want. You risk new ways of thinking and acting. You step out into the unknown. This can increase your stress and emotional pain — temporarily. In other words, you may well feel worse before you feel better.

Telling yourself that you 'can't stand it' can lead you to avoid change. You might decide to stick with the way things are, unpleasant though this is. You know you would be better off in the long run, but you choose to avoid the extra pain now.

Alternatively you might look for a quick solution. Do you hope that somewhere there is a fancy therapy that will cure you straightaway, without your having to do anything? I meet many people who try therapist after therapist, but never stay with one approach long enough to learn anything that will help. They still live in hope, though, and often get a brief boost from meeting new therapists or therapy groups.

As well as fearing discomfort, you may also worry that you 'won't be a real person'. You think that you will end up 'pretending' to feel and behave in new ways, and imagine yourself as false or phoney. Somehow, it seems, to choose how you feel seems 'less than human'.

You are, though, already choosing your reactions — even though you may not be fully aware of it. Using conscious choice is what sets humans apart from instinct-bound animals. It is also what makes you a unique person, different from every other. So give up the notion that it is false and machinelike to use your brain to avoid bad feelings. Getting depressed, worried and desperate doesn't make you more human.

You might worry that learning self-control will make you cold and unemotional, with no feelings at all. This common fear is quite misguided. The opposite is true: if you learn how to handle strong feelings, you will be less afraid of them. This will free you to experience a fuller range of emotions than before.

While self-improvement may be hard, it is achievable. The blocks I have described are all self-created. They are nothing more than beliefs — ideas you can change using the techniques you will learn from this book.

The techniques of change

How does one actually set about achieving self-control and choice? The best place to start is by learning how to identify the thoughts and beliefs that cause your problems. The next chapter explains the two main kinds of thinking involved in any reaction: *interpretation* and *evaluation*. Chapters 4 to 7 will help you understand the types of irrational thinking characteristic of each: in the case of interpretations, *distorting reality*; in the case of evaluations, *demanding, catastrophising* and *people-rating*. Later, you will learn to recognise the roles these play in your particular problem areas.

Next, you need to learn how to apply this knowledge by analysing specific episodes when you feel and behave in the ways you would like to change. It is most effective to do this in writing. Chapter 8 will teach you a structured technique for doing this — *Rational Self-Analysis*. The analysis will help you bring everything together. You can connect whatever started things off, your reaction, and the thoughts that came in between. You can then check out those thoughts and change the irrational ones. Rational Self-Analysis uses the *ABC* method described in chapter 1, extended to include steps for changing beliefs and then acting on those changes.

Which brings us to the final step. You will get there faster when you put into action what you have changed in your mind. Let's say you decide to stop feeling guilty when you do something for yourself. The next step is to do it. Spend an hour a day reading a novel. Purchase some new clothes. Have coffee with a friend or a weekend away without the family. Do the things you would previously have regarded as 'undeserved'. The rest of this book will give you many ideas for action, and as time goes on you will come up with more of your own.

Rational Self-Analysis is not just academic theory. People from a wide range of social and educational backgrounds have already used it successfully. This book represents that experience brought together in one place.

In the previous chapter we saw human beings described as entities who start life with a biological predisposition to irrational thinking, to which they then usually add by learning new and harmful ways of behaving and viewing life. There is, though, a positive side to human nature: we also have the ability to think about our beliefs and change the dysfunctional ones.

What about problems you cannot sort out on your own? A little outside help may be a useful supplement to this book. For guidance about professional assistance see chapter 22. Whether or not you seek such help, though, taking responsibility for your feelings and actions will be the key to success. Also required will be some hard work and perseverance — but, happily, all these things can be under your control.

References

1. Raeburn, J., (ca. 1986). Health and the poor: strategies for prevention. Auckland: unpublished paper.
2. Morse, C., et al. (1989). The effects of Rational-Emotive Therapy and relaxation training on premenstrual syndrome. *Journal of Rational-Emotive and Cognitive-Behavior Therapy*, 7:2, 98–110.
3. (i) Shapiro, D., et al. (1970). Control of blood pressure in man by operant conditioning. *Circulation Research*, 26, 127–32.
   (ii) Budzynski, T.H., et al. (1973). EMG biofeedback and tension headache: a controlled outcome study. *Psychosomatic Medicine*, 35, 484–96.
   (iii) Fried, R., (1990). *The Breath Connection: How to reduce psychosomatic and stress-related disorders with easy-to-do breathing exercises.* New York, N.Y.: Plenum.
   (iv) Goleman, D., & Gurin, J., (eds.), (1993). *Mind Body Medicine.* New York, N.Y.: Consumer Reports Books.

3 What is irrational thinking?

There are countless ways of looking at life — how can you know which help and which hinder? Fortunately, there are some guidelines. It is probably most useful to start by learning how to recognise irrational thinking.

Why bother with problem thoughts? This is what distinguishes Rational Self-Analysis from so-called positive thinking: instead of rushing to tell yourself positive ideas, you first uncover and dispute the irrational ones. Otherwise, they remain untouched — and thus able to disturb you in the future.

What does *irrational* mean? To describe a belief as irrational is to say:

1. It *distorts reality* (i.e. it is a misinterpretation of what is happening); or it involves some illogical ways of *evaluating* yourself, others and the world around you — demanding, catastrophising and people-rating.
2. It is *dysfunctional* for you: it blocks you from achieving your goals and purposes; it creates extreme emotions which persist, distress and immobilise; and it leads to behaviours that harm you, others and your life in general.

The rules we live by

Dr Albert Ellis, whom we met in chapter 1, suggests that a small number of core beliefs underlie most unhelpful emotions and behaviours.[1] Here are 12 of the more common irrational beliefs:

1. I need love and approval from those significant to me, and I must avoid disapproval from any source.
2. To be worthwhile as a person I must achieve, succeed at whatever I do, and make no mistakes.

3. People should always do the right thing. When they behave obnoxiously, unfairly or selfishly, they must be blamed and punished.
4. Things must be the way I want them to be, otherwise life will be intolerable.
5. My unhappiness is caused by things that are outside my control, so there's little I can do to feel any better.
6. I must worry about things that could be dangerous, unpleasant or frightening, otherwise they might happen.
7. I can be happier by avoiding life's difficulties, unpleasantnesses and responsibilities.
8. Everyone needs to depend on someone stronger than themselves.
9. Events in my past are the cause of my problems, and they continue to influence my feelings and behaviours now.
10. I should become upset when other people have problems and feel unhappy when they're sad.
11. I shouldn't have to feel discomfort and pain. I can't stand them and must avoid them at all costs.
12. Every problem should have an ideal solution, and it's intolerable when one can't be found.

Everyone has a set of core beliefs or 'rules' of this kind. Some are rational, others are similar to those above. Each person's set is different.

Mostly subconscious, the rules we hold determine how we react to life. When an event triggers a train of thought, what we *consciously* think depends on the general rules we *subconsciously* apply to the event. Say you hold the core belief 'To be worthwhile, I must succeed at everything I do', and you happen to fail an examination. This event, coupled with your rule, will lead you to conclude, 'I'm not worthwhile.'

Again, suppose you believe 'I can't stand discomfort and pain, so I must avoid them at all costs', and you lose a filling in a tooth. You know that going to the dentist would be painful, hence you conclude, 'I'll leave the dentist for now.'

Core beliefs are generalisations: one rule can apply to many situations. If you believe, for example, 'I can't stand discomfort and pain and must avoid them at all costs', you might apply this not just to the dentist, but also to work, relationships and life in general.

Why be concerned about your core beliefs? While most will be valid and helpful, some will be irrational — and faulty beliefs lead to faulty conclusions. Take the rule 'If I am to feel OK about myself, others must like and approve of me.' Let's say your boss tells you off. You may (rightly) think, 'He is angry with me' — but you may wrongly conclude, 'This proves I'm a failure.' Furthermore, changing the situation (for instance, getting your boss to like you) would still leave the underlying rule untouched. It would remain, ready to bother you whenever some future event triggered it.

Interpretations and evaluations

How do we identify these underlying core beliefs? We have to go beyond the surface *interpretations* we make to our *evaluations* or *personal meanings*.

In everyday life, events and circumstances trigger two kinds of thinking: *interpreting* and *evaluating*. First, we attempt to *interpret* things in some way. That is, we make guesses or inferences about what's 'going on' — what we think has happened, is happening or will happen. Interpretations are statements of 'fact' (or at least what we think are the facts — they can be true or false).

For example, John's wife says she is feeling unhappy in herself and would like to go and stay with friends in another city for a few weeks to sort herself out. John immediately jumps to the conclusion that she wants to leave him. This is his *interpretation*.

However, we still don't know what it means to John that his wife may be leaving. As well as interpreting things that happen, we also *evaluate* them in terms of what they *mean to us*. Evaluations go beyond 'facts': they are the *meanings* that we attach to what we *interpret* as the facts.

What personal meaning does John attach to the prospect that his wife might leave? If he wanted the marriage to end, he might regard it as a good thing. But in fact he evaluates it as a catastrophe that will lead to misery and prove he's a failure. He reacts accordingly, by feeling hopeless and putting himself down.

Note that John is not directly evaluating what has happened — his wife saying she is unhappy — rather, he is evaluating his *interpretation* of what has happened. Using the *ABC* model, we can summarise the chain of events as follows:

A John's wife says she is unhappy.

B John *interprets* what is going on: 'She's thinking of leaving.'
John *evaluates* his interpretation in terms of what this *means to him*: 'This is a catastrophe'; 'I'll be miserable for the rest of my life'; 'I'm a failure.'

C John feels hopelessness.

Note, too, that interpretations can be true or false, and evaluations can be rational or irrational. You can, of course, both interpret and evaluate something quite rationally. Unfortunately, you can also get things wrong twice over. Say, for instance, your boss wants to see you. You can start by misinterpreting this by guessing that he must be upset with you when in fact he wants to offer you a raise. You can then go on to evaluate it irrationally, concluding 'It's awful', 'I can't stand it', 'I'm useless' and 'He shouldn't treat me like this.'

It is also possible to get one right but the other wrong, e.g. interpret something correctly (the boss is out to get you) but then rate it irrationally ('I can't stand it', etc.).

Here are some more examples to show the differences between events, interpretations and evaluations.

Event/Situation	Interpretation	Evaluation
Son won't do his homework.	He'll end up uneducated.	This would make me a failure as a parent.
Saw crash, one car had a young driver.	The young driver caused the accident.	These kids shouldn't be allowed on the road.
Woke up feeling anxious.	I have five clients to visit.	I can't stand it, so I'll have to take the day off.
Saw a cake.	That cake would be delicious.	I must have it.
He was really angry.	I caused it.	I'm a bitch.
Read that violent crime is on the increase.	Soon it won't be possible to walk the streets alone.	The government should bring back the death penalty.

What to look for

When considering unwanted reactions, we are concerned mainly with identifying the irrational beliefs, the ones that cause our problems. These are of three kinds:

1. Interpretations
2. Evaluations
3. Core beliefs

Interpretations

Irrational interpretations consist of *distortions of reality*, of which there are several kinds:

1. Black-and-white thinking
2. Filtering
3. Overgeneralising
4. Mind-reading
5. Fortune-telling
6. Emotional reasoning
7. Personalising

Interpretations are usually conscious, though not always.

Evaluations

Irrational evaluations consist of:

1. *Demanding*: using 'shoulds' or 'musts'
2. *Catastrophising*: seeing something as 'awful', 'horrific', 'unbearable' or 'intolerable'
3. *People-rating*: labelling or evaluating your total self (or someone else's)

These are described in chapters 5, 6 and 7 respectively.

Your evaluation of something may include either or both of the circumstances and the people involved. In other words, you can demand of, catastrophise about, or rate both situations ('I can't stand it', 'It should/must not happen', 'Things should be a certain way') and people ('It's awful that people are like this', 'I should have done better', 'People shouldn't behave like that', 'I'm a hopeless case', 'She's a bitch').

Evaluations are sometimes conscious but often beneath awareness. You can uncover them by asking yourself, 'If my interpretation is true, how do I evaluate what is going on?' or 'What does it mean to me?' Let's say, for example, your interpretation of news reports is that people are getting more violent. How do you evaluate this? What does it mean to you? You could rate it as 'terrible' (awfulising), as 'intolerable' (can't-stand-it-itis), as meaning that the people concerned should be locked up (demanding), or as proving that they are 'animals' (people-rating).

Note that when you ask 'How am I evaluating this' or 'What does this mean to me?', you may first come up with another interpretation, or sometimes a chain of them, as follows: 'Things are going to get worse'. . . 'Sooner or later someone is going to break into our home' . . . 'We'll be attacked' . . . 'We'll be killed'. Finally, you arrive at the evaluations: 'This would be awful. These people are animals. They should be locked up.'

How do you know when you have got to the irrational evaluation that is the real cause of your unwanted reaction? When you examine your reaction, you will see that you have uncovered demanding, catastrophising or people-rating.

Core beliefs

Core beliefs, as we saw earlier, are the underlying rules that guide how we react to life. How you interpret *specific events* and then evaluate them depends on the *general rules* you apply. The examples on page 36 reflect rules such as:

'If I fail at something important to me, this proves I'm a failure as a person and therefore not worthwhile.'
'People should always behave correctly, and must be condemned and punished when they don't.'
'It's easier to avoid responsibilities than to face them.'
'I must have whatever I want and I can't stand the discomfort of being deprived.'

'I am responsible for other people's feelings, so I deserve to be condemned if I do anything that hurts or upsets them.'
'Violent people do not deserve to live.'
Note that each of the examples given on page 36 represents a *general* rule applied to a *specific* situation. For example:

> *Interpretation*: The young driver caused the accident.
> *Evaluation*: These kids shouldn't be allowed on the road.
> *General rule*: People should always behave correctly and must be punished when they don't.

Most irrational core beliefs are a variation of one or other of the 12 irrational beliefs listed on pages 33–34. It will be worth your while to study this list carefully, even memorise it.

Putting it all together

To summarise, people view themselves and the world around them on three levels: interpretations, evaluations and core beliefs. Your main aim is to get at the underlying, semipermanent, general rules that are the continuing cause of your unwanted reactions. Here are some more examples (using the *ABC* model) to show how it all works:

A Your daughter is three hours late home from a date.

B You *interpret* what has happened: 'They might have had an accident and she's been hurt.'
You *evaluate* your interpretation: 'This would be awful. I should never have allowed her to go out with that boy.'
Your evaluation comes from the underlying *core belief* 'I must worry about things that could be dangerous, unpleasant or frightening, otherwise they might happen.'

C You feel anxious.

A Your neighbour phones and asks if you will baby-sit for the rest of the day. You have already planned to catch up with some gardening.

B You *interpret* what will happen: 'If I say no, she will think badly of me.'

You *evaluate* your interpretation: 'I couldn't stand to have her disapprove of me and see me as selfish.'
Your evaluation comes from the underlying *core belief* 'I can't stand disapproval and must avoid disapproval from any source.'

C   You say yes.

A   You receive an offer of a more interesting and better-paid job.

B   You *interpret* what will happen: 'There will be more responsibility and risk involved, and in today's economic situation I may not get another job if the new one fails.'
You *evaluate* your interpretation: 'I couldn't stand the feeling of uncertainty and the risk of being unemployed.'
Your evaluation comes from the underlying *core belief* 'I can be happier by avoiding life's difficulties, dangers and responsibilities.'

C   You turn down the new job.

A   Another driver changes lanes in front of you without warning.

B   You *interpret* what happened: 'He didn't even bother to look.'
You *evaluate* your interpretation: 'He should be put off the road.'
Your evaluation comes from the underlying *core belief* 'People should always do the right thing. When they behave obnoxiously, unfairly or selfishly, they must be blamed and punished.'

C   You get angry.

Rational thinking: in touch with the real world

Rational thinking presents a vivid contrast to its illogical opposite:

1. It is *based on reality*: it emphasises seeing things as they really are, preferring rather than demanding, keeping events and circumstances in perspective, and acceptance of one's self and others.
2. It is *functional* for you: it helps you achieve your goals and purposes; it creates emotions you can handle; and it helps you behave in ways that promote your aims and survival.

We are not talking about so-called positive thinking. Rational thinking is *realistic* thinking. It is concerned with facts — the real world — rather than subjective opinion or wishful thinking.

Realistic thinking leads to realistic emotions. Negative feelings aren't always bad for you, neither are all positive feelings beneficial. Feeling happy when someone you love has died, for example, may hinder you from grieving properly; or to be unconcerned in the face of real danger could put your survival at risk. Realistic thinking avoids exaggeration of both kinds, negative and positive.

The rest of the book examines many new and more functional ways of viewing life. The next four chapters will help you understand distorting reality, demanding, catastrophising and people-rating. Because these kinds of thinking underlie almost all emotional/behavioural problems, it is worth spending some time learning how to recognise and replace them.

12 irrational beliefs and 12 rational alternatives

In the left-hand column are the 12 irrational beliefs presented earlier in this chapter. Beside each is a rational alternative.

Irrational beliefs	*Rational alternatives*
I need love and approval from those significant to me, and I must avoid disapproval from any source.	Love and approval are good things to have, and I'll seek them when I can, but they're not necessities. I can survive (albeit uncomfortably) without them.
To be worthwhile as a person I must achieve, succeed at whatever I do, and make no mistakes.	I'll always seek to achieve as much as I can, but unfailing success and competence is an unrealistic ideal. Better I just accept myself as a person, separate from my performance.
People should always do the right thing. When they behave obnoxiously, unfairly or selfishly, they must be blamed and punished.	It's unfortunate that people sometimes do bad things. But humans aren't yet perfect, and upsetting myself won't change that reality.

Irrational beliefs	Rational alternatives
Things must be the way I want them to be, otherwise life will be intolerable.	There is no law that says things have to be the way I want. It's disappointing, but I can stand it — especially if I avoid catastrophising.
My unhappiness is caused by things that are outside my control, so there's little I can do to feel any better.	Many external factors are outside my control. But it's my thoughts, not the externals, which cause my feelings, and I can learn to control my thoughts.
I must worry about things that could be dangerous, unpleasant or frightening, otherwise they might happen.	Worrying about things that might go wrong won't stop them happening. It will, though, ensure I get upset and disturbed right now!
I can be happier by avoiding life's difficulties, unpleasantnesses and responsibilities.	Avoiding problems is only easier in the short term — putting things off can make them worse later on. It also gives me more time to worry about them!
Everyone needs to depend on someone stronger than themselves.	Relying on someone else can lead to dependent behaviour. It's OK to seek help as long as I learn to trust myself and my own judgement.
Events in my past are the cause of my problems, and they continue to influence my feelings and behaviours now.	The past can't influence me now. My current beliefs cause my reactions. I may have learned these beliefs in the past, but I can choose to analyse and change them in the present.
I should become upset when other people have problems and feel unhappy when they're sad.	I can't change other people's problems and bad feelings by getting myself upset.
I shouldn't have to feel discomfort and pain. I can't stand them and must avoid them at all costs.	Why should I in particular not feel discomfort and pain? I don't like them, but I can stand them. Also, my life would be very restricted if I always avoided discomfort.

Irrational beliefs	Rational alternatives
Every problem should have an ideal solution, and it's intolerable when one can't be found.	Problems usually have many possible solutions. It's better to stop waiting for the perfect one and get on with the best available. I can live with less than the ideal.

References

1. Ellis, A., (1994). *Reason and Emotion in Psychotherapy*, rev. edn. New York, N.Y.: Carol Publishing.

4 Distorting reality

We constantly interpret what goes on around us — what others do or say, events we observe, and things we read in the newspaper or see on TV. We also interpret things that have happened in the past, or which may happen in the future. In addition, we interpret our own actions, and even the physical sensations and emotional changes happening inside us.

By *interpreting*, I mean that we *draw conclusions* about what we think is happening. Sometimes our interpretations are correct, but often they are wrong.

Seven ways to get things wrong

Psychiatrist Aaron Beck has studied and listed the ways in which people can get things out of perspective. His research shows that our feelings are in proportion to how we *describe* events and situations, rather than to the actual intensity of events and situations themselves. The main ways in which we misinterpret things that happen, adapted from Dr Beck's list, are presented here.

Black-and-white thinking
People often see things in extremes, with no middle ground — good or bad, perfect versus useless, success or failure, right against wrong, moral versus immoral, and so on. By doing this, they miss the reality that things rarely are one way or the other but usually somewhere in between. In other words, there are shades of grey. Another name for this distortion is *all-or-nothing thinking*. It involves self-talk like:

> 'People are either honest or crooked.'
> 'If it's not perfect, it's useless.'
> 'If it's not right, it must be wrong.'

'If you don't love me, you must hate me.'
'There are only two sorts of people in the world.'
'Either I succeed or I'm a total failure.'
'This is my one and only chance.'
'If I mess up this part, I may as well give up the whole thing.'
'There's only one way to . . .'

Filtering

If you tend to see all the things that are wrong but ignore the positives, you are filtering. Here are some examples:

'I've got nothing at all going for me.'
'I can't see anything good about my situation.'
'I don't have any good points.'
'There's no hope.'
'I've achieved nothing worthwhile at all with my life.'
'All I get is pain.'

People mostly filter in a negative direction, but it can also work in reverse — if you ignore negatives and fail to attend to important realities:

'She'll be right.'
'If I just ignore this [court summons, warning from my wife about the state of our marriage, noise in the car engine, etc.], it will go away.'
'It's better to keep the peace, so I won't say no to my son now. Plenty of time for discipline in the years ahead.'

Do you ever find yourself seeing all that's going wrong in your life but ignoring the things that are going right? It's easy to take positives for granted that are part of everyday life. What about, for instance, the fact that you are capable of reading this book? What other positives can you bring to mind that are so basic you wouldn't normally be conscious of them?

Overgeneralising
This distortion is to do with the way people tend to build up one thing about themselves or their circumstances and end up thinking that it represents the whole situation. In other words, they make a universal issue out of an isolated event. For example:

'Everything's going wrong.'
'Nothing I do ever turns out right.'
'I'm a bitch because of what I said.'
'Everyone thinks I'm stupid.'

Mind-reading
There are various ways in which we can jump to a conclusion without enough evidence. One of these is mind-reading — making guesses about what other people are thinking:

'She ignored me on purpose.'
'You don't really love me.'
'He's mad with me.'
'They think I'm boring.'
'You're only saying that because . . .'

Fortune-telling
Another way of jumping to a conclusion is to treat beliefs about the future as though they are realities rather than just predictions:

'I'll always be a failure.'
'I'll never get another job.'
'Things can only get worse.'
'I'm going to go crazy.'
'There's no hope.'

Emotional reasoning
Yet another way to leap to a conclusion is to tell yourself that because you *feel* a certain way, this is how it really is:

DISTORTING REALITY

'I feel like a failure, so I must be one.'
'If I'm angry, you must have done something to make me so.'
'I wouldn't be worrying if there wasn't something to worry about.'
'Because I feel unattractive, I must be.'

Emotional reasoning can, for example, keep you thinking anger is 'justified', sustain a vicious circle of self-downing, or make worrying feed on itself.

Personalising

You can also jump to a conclusion by thinking that something is directly related to you:

'Everyone is looking at me.'
'That criticism was meant for me.'
'It must have been me that made her feel bad.'
'It's because of me that they're all fighting.'
'He didn't return my greeting. What did I do?'

Personalising can make you feel self-conscious, guilty, or responsible for events you may not have caused, including other people's problems and emotions.

Why do we do it?

As we have seen, distorting reality can lead to many unwanted consequences. So why do we do it? Exaggerated thinking appears to be based on a combination of learning, taking the easy way, and subconscious gains.

As children, we model ourselves on our parents. From our earliest years we hear them overgeneralising, saying 'You're a bad child!', rather than specifying the behaviour: 'That was a bad thing to do.' Then take the media. To attract attention, they sensationalise much of the news. Certain aspects, usually the negative, are built up out of proportion. Pick up any major newspaper and see what makes the headlines: the successful rehabilitation of a murderer isn't news, but a ghoulish murder may stay on the front page for days and the subsequent trial fill the inside pages for months. Whereas only a small proportion of crimes involve the use of violence, it is these that receive by far the most extensive coverage by the press and other media, while the majority of criminal acts go unremarked. This is negative filtering applied to the marketplace. It isn't surprising that we grow up to dwell on negatives and view life mainly in extremes.

'Lazy brains' may be part of the problem. Humans prefer simplistic ways of thinking about themselves and the world. Black-and-white thinking, for example, is easier than looking at the many subtleties of a complex situation or issue. Likewise, by jumping to conclusions we can avoid checking out all the facts. Moralists who won't recognise that shades of grey exist, and people with fixed 'convictions', have often closed their minds and stopped thinking.

Finally, there may be subconscious gains. We can use emotional reasoning to blame others for our bad feelings. Overgeneralisations such as 'It's hopeless/useless/pointless' may be a way to avoid the pain of personal change.

Keeping in touch with reality

How can you stop distorting reality?

- *For a start, catch yourself doing it.* Know the cues to watch for: looking at things in extremes, only seeing negatives, building up the bad points in a situation (be it past, present or future), 'reading' other people's minds, predicting the future, assuming that what you feel is reality, and relating everything back to yourself.
- *Watch especially for rigid thinking.* When you find yourself resisting other ways of viewing something, this could be a sign that you are locking yourself into a narrowed, distorted viewpoint.
- *Stop using words that exaggerate,* such as *always, forever, totally, all, everything, everybody, nothing, nobody, never.*

- *Get things back into balance* by looking for the side of the picture you have been filtering out. Make a list, for example, of the positives and the negatives in your life. If you cannot find both, you know you are distorting reality: few things are either one way or the other — so keep listing.
- *Develop the habit of sticking to the facts* as far as you can unearth them. When you think you might be jumping to conclusions, ask yourself, 'What evidence do I have for assuming this? Is it the most likely explanation of the facts available? Are there any others which may be just as valid?'
- If you are worrying about something, *rate the likelihood of it happening* on a scale of, say, 0–100 per cent. Being this specific will help you clarify vague predictions.
- Finally, whenever possible, *check out your interpretation* of something you are concerned about and see how it compares with reality. There are some suggestions for how to do this in chapter 8.

Getting things back into perspective

Take a look at the list of typical distortions below. Alongside each, to show 'in-perspective' thinking, is a more realistic alternative.

Distorted thinking	Realistic thinking
Everything's wrong.	I'm facing some problems at present.
It's got to be done perfectly or not at all.	I'd prefer to get it just right, but less than perfect will do.
This is totally wrong.	I disagree with some aspects of this.
She made me angry.	I don't like what she did, but I made myself angry by the way I viewed it.
She did it because she hates me.	I don't know why she did it. There's more than one possible explanation.

Distorted thinking	Realistic thinking
Everyone will think I'm stupid.	Some people may be critical of me.
I'll never be happy again.	Sure, things aren't so good now. But how do I know what the future holds?
All I get is pain.	I get a lot of pain. But good things also happen — if only I were prepared to notice them.
If my partner is unhappy, it must be because of me.	It may be a good idea for me to take a look at my behaviour, but to suspend judgement on myself until I've checked it out.

Sometimes it is hard to know for sure just what is going on. You won't always have enough information to be certain. But it is important at least to recognise there may be more than one way to interpret a given situation. By doing so you can avoid jumping to erroneous and possibly harmful conclusions.

That could be the best way to avoid distorting reality: retain a healthy scepticism about it.

5 Demanding: turning wants into needs

As well as *interpreting* the events and circumstances we are exposed to, we also *evaluate* them. That is, we decide whether they are pleasant, unpleasant, good, bad, tolerable or intolerable, whether they should or shouldn't be happening, or whether they prove something about us or about others. In other words, we decide *what they mean to us*.

Irrational evaluations involve *demanding, catastrophising* or *people-rating*. Because demanding is the most significant and is often basic to the other two, we will deal with it first.

The pressure of 'must'

You have your preferences, I have mine. We would all like the world to be a certain way. If we just left it at that, there would be no problem. Unfortunately, though, we often go beyond wanting. We turn desires into *needs*. Preferences become musts, and guidelines become unbending rules.

Jenny knows what demanding can mean. Back with her old firm after maternity leave, she was keen to resume her career. She had been able to obtain a good childcare arrangement, but still felt guilty over a conflict between paid employment and her role as a mother. What caused the guilt? Jenny was operating on a 'should' message about motherhood — a rule turned into a demand. She was finding it hard to break away from the old stereotype of a woman as someone who doesn't need a career, whose role in life is to run the home and bring up the children while her husband provides the income.

Countless people, both men and women, are under pressure from their own rules. Many, like Richard, find that sooner or later the pressure gets to them. Usually efficient, self-assured and in command of an expanding business, Richard's veneer of control had begun to develop some cracks. He had always suffered a degree of tension but was now having severe anxiety attacks two or three times a week. His problem was his constant striving for perfection. He wanted everything he did to be of the highest possible standard. A worthy aim — but Richard carried it too far. He made it into an absolute *necessity* — a demand.

We can direct our demands at others as well as ourselves. Take John and Marie. They were looking at parenthood, but things were not too well between them. John held the view that Marie's main role was to satisfy his needs, and expected to have sex whenever he felt like it. As a result, Marie felt put off. John thought that Marie had the problem: in his view, sex had to be spontaneous. For lovemaking to be 'natural', you should be able to have it when you felt like it.

Probably most people would prefer to have sex whenever they felt like it. But John was turning his want into a *need*. His demand, though, achieved the opposite of what he desired — he ended up with nothing at all.

Many others are like John and miss out entirely. Michelle, at twenty-nine, felt left on the shelf. It seemed that whenever she got involved with a male, she tried too hard and ended up putting him off. What was the problem? Her belief that 'we all need someone'. This led her to think that she couldn't face the prospect of being single all her life. Hence she discovered the paradox that often typifies demanding: the more her want became a need or must, the less likely she was to fulfil it.

As suggested earlier, demanding may be the most basic of the three types of evaluative thinking. It seems to create the other two types. You are more likely to catastrophise about something if you think that it 'shouldn't' be as it is. And you are only likely to rate your total self if you believe that you 'shouldn't' be as you are.

What is demanding?

Demanding is a way of thinking, with two variations: *moralising* and *musturbation*.

Moralising refers to the way humans turn guidelines — which may be reasonable and helpful — into absolute requirements. When we say that something 'should' or 'ought' to be a certain way, it implies that there is a 'Law of the Universe' that humans should never fail to observe. Moralising often leads to people-rating: when we (or others) do not behave as we (or they) 'ought to', this means we (or they) are bad, immoral or evil.

Musturbation is taking a want or desire and turning it into an absolute need or must. We think that because we want to be liked, we 'must' be liked; or because we want to avoid pain, we 'must' avoid it at all costs. Catastrophising usually accompanies a must — we believe it would be awful or intolerable if our 'need' were not met.

Demands are exaggerated preferences

Rules and wants are an everyday fact of life. They can be helpful or unhelpful. A particular rule for living may be relevant to our current circumstances or it may be out of date. A want can be achievable or impossible. Whether or not our rules and wants are appropriate, though, they are unlikely to do us any harm if we hold them as *preferences*.

The problem is that we often inflate our preferences into *needs*. Because we want the world to be a certain way, it 'should' be so. If we desire something, we 'must' have it. This is the heart of demanding — the exaggeration of a preference into a necessity.

What demanding costs

In real life, things are often different from how we would like them to be. By turning our wants into demands, we set ourselves up to be frustrated by reality. In fact, demanding is the underlying cause of many human problems.

Take anxiety. We often catastrophise about what will happen if a 'need' isn't met or a rule is broken. We get anxious by demanding rigid standards, especially when we think we might feel guilty or put ourselves down if we don't match up. Performance demands can make us so uptight that our achievement levels drop. Men become sexually impotent, perfectionists set themselves up for failure.

Demanding can lead to obsessive or compulsive behaviours, such as reading a boring book right through, finishing a meal when already full, overchecking the locks at night to ensure security, repeatedly washing one's hands to avoid infection, or vacuuming the house twice a day. People often keep on with things that aren't in their interests because they think they have no choice.

Demanding is the main cause of hostile anger. We get angry when our 'needs' aren't met, or when people don't behave as we think they 'should'. We can direct this anger onto ourselves, too, and become depressed.

Because 'shoulds' conflict with wants, we can find it hard to make decisions, to ask others for what we want, or to act according to our own wishes. We might do things we dislike out of a sense of duty but still feel frustrated or resentful.

If we think that we 'need' love, sex, attention, consideration and affection, our demands can turn people off. We can also become resentful or jealous when others don't behave as they 'ought to', or when they treat us 'unfairly'.

Why do human beings demand?

Given that demanding is so unhelpful, why do we do it? To begin with, we are taught to. From our earliest days we are surrounded by 'shoulds' and 'should nots'. Most people communicate with others in these terms.

Demanding may serve subconscious purposes. It can be a convenient way to justify our wants. John, for instance, found it easier to tell himself and others that he 'needed' sex rather than admit he just wanted it. This also enabled him to put pressure on his wife: 'I need it so you should give it to me.' It is tempting to deny responsibility for our wants and demand that others give to us because they 'should' or because it is their 'duty'.

Demanding is a way to avoid thinking. Instead of working out for ourselves why we might want things to be a certain way, it is simpler to fall back on 'It should be that way.' We can also use this to push our values onto other people without having to justify them. You cannot argue with a 'Law of the Universe'.

Demanding may arise from fear. As we saw in the previous chapter, human beings desire physical and emotional comfort. This is fine if desire remains just that — something we would like. Unfortunately, though, we often tell ourselves that discomfort is awful and intolerable; so, to avoid it, we demand certain things 'must' or 'must not' happen. In effect, we are afraid of our own feelings.

Many people believe that demanding helps motivate them. They use self-talk such as 'I should get up earlier in the morning', 'I must get that project finished tonight' or 'I have to make a good job of it', thinking this will help them get moving. The trouble is, it often has the opposite effect. It is as though one part of you says, 'I should do this', but another part says, 'I won't be bossed around!' As a result, you resist your own 'should'. Trying to motivate other people with demands often has the same effect — it turns them off.

From demands to preferences

You don't need the pain that demanding creates. Fortunately there is a solution. Richard discovered it: he decided that he still wanted to do things to a high standard, and that he would, generally, try to do the best he could; but such an accomplishment was no longer a *need*. When he couldn't get it perfect, too bad — he could live with it.

What is a need?

While there are many things we might want, there are, in reality, few things that are absolute necessities. To survive we need air, food, clothing and shelter. We do not *need* success, love, approval or friends — no matter how much we may *want* them. Our lives will be better if we have these things, but we can survive without.

Realising this is what helped Richard. He didn't give up desiring excellence — he just stopped demanding it. It became a preference instead of a necessity.

John chose to do the same. He adopted the view that while

spontaneous sex was great, he and his marriage could survive when it didn't happen that way.

As for Jenny, she came to view full-time parenthood as appropriate for those who wish it, but not as an overriding rule for every mother.

Michelle, too, while continuing to regard a long-term relationship as desirable, realised that it wasn't an absolute need without which the rest of her life would be miserable.

You don't have to give up your values

To get rid of your demands doesn't mean you have to give up what is important to you. Hold onto your ideas and values, but hold them as *preferences*.

Stop moralising about what is 'right' or 'wrong'. Take a more practical approach. Focus on the *results* of rules, behaviours or decisions. Ask yourself questions like the following:

- Is this behaviour or rule helpful or unhelpful, and in what ways?
- Will it advance or hinder me in achieving my goals?
- Does it create emotions I can handle, or does it leave me distressed and immobilised?
- Does it promote my own and others' aims and survival, or does it lead me to act in harmful ways?
- Does it help me keep in touch with the real world, or does it entail misinterpreting, demanding, catastrophising, or rating myself or others?
- Is it flexible, i.e. does it allow for exceptions when appropriate?

I hope by now it is obvious I am not suggesting an attitude of anarchy or 'I don't care.' Guidelines are important. To check out those you took on as a child, and to review them as circumstances change, is to show respect for the importance of guiding principles in your life. Furthermore, a flexible, 'preferring' philosophy is not a self-centred one. It is in your own long-term interest to consider the goals, wants and concerns of other people — that is, *their* preferences — along with your own.

A helpful value is one you have chosen to adopt and which serves some useful purpose. It helps you and others achieve what is important to you both. Above all, it is a preference rather than a must.

Acceptance

Holding preferences instead of demands means accepting yourself, others and the world around you.

People often misunderstand the idea of acceptance. They think that to accept something means you have to agree with it and give up trying to change it, but that is not what it means at all. To accept something is to recognise two things:

1. That it exists.
2. That there is no universal law that says it should not exist.

You may not like it. You might want to do something to change it, and perhaps plan to. But you avoid *demanding* that it not be as it is.

This is important for several reasons. First, if you tell yourself that something should not be the way it is, you are really saying that reality should not exist. Have you ever heard people say, for instance, 'You can't do that' about something which someone has already done?

Second, it is helpful to say that you don't like something and would prefer to change it. It can motivate you to take action, whereas demanding a reality not exist is more likely to create disabling feelings such as despair or hostile anger.

Finally, if you avoid hurting yourself over current realities, you will be better equipped to start changing them.

Getting demands back to preferences

Get those musts back into perspective. Here are some examples of demands turned into preferences:

Demand	*Preference*
I need to feel good and avoid physical and emotional pain at all times.	I'd prefer to feel good and avoid pain, but demanding this will guarantee that I get uptight!

Demand	*Preference*
Everything I do must be to a high standard.	High standards are desirable but not always essential. Seeing them as musts will only make me anxious and probably inhibit my performance.
Difficulties and handicaps should not exist.	Difficulties and handicaps do exist. Demanding they don't won't make them go away. Better to change them if possible, otherwise learn to live with them.
I must have love and approval from everyone who is significant to me.	Love and approval are good to have, but they're not essential to my survival. As I won't always get them, it's better I learn to depend on them less.
If you want something badly enough, it's a need.	The 'need' exists in my head. If I believe it, I'll upset myself when it isn't met.
Other people must always behave in a correct and proper fashion for life to be bearable.	In real life, people don't always behave 'correctly'. There is no reason why they should, though there are many reasons why I'd prefer them to.
Other people, and the world generally, should always treat me with justice and fairness.	Justice and fairness are worth striving for, but they don't always prevail in the real world. Demanding they exist won't achieve anything except disable me with anger.
My circumstances must always be right for me to be happy.	My circumstances aren't always going to suit me. Better to change what I can and accept what I can't.

6 Catastrophising: making mountains out of molehills

Negative experiences and circumstances are a part of the real world. Every one of us dislikes certain things. While it is mostly helpful to have a positive outlook, it is also appropriate and rational to recognise the *bad* things that exist, to feel sad about them and to regret them. Unfortunately, though, we all too commonly exaggerate the badness of the negative things in our lives — that is, we *catastrophise*.

Two ways to catastrophise

We tend to exaggerate badness in two ways:

1. By viewing things as much worse than they are — *awfulising*.
2. By thinking of them as unbearable — *can't-stand-it-itis*.

Awfulising

How often do you rate something as awful, terrible or horrible? Sometimes we use such words in a superficial sense: 'Wasn't that a terrible movie?', 'Look at that awful outfit she's wearing', and the like. But often we attach a significant meaning to them. We imply to ourselves that something is a source of terror, the worst that could ever happen, or that it is the end of the world.

We awfulise about things that have happened in the past, that are happening now, and that may happen in the future. Typical self-talk involves this kind of thing:

'I feel terrible.'
'It would be awful if . . .'
'This is the worst thing that could ever happen.'
'It's the end of the world.'

Can't-stand-it-itis

Do you ever tell yourself that you cannot stand, tolerate or endure something? You can make it harder to cope with unpleasant situations when you have thoughts such as:

'I can't stand it any longer.'
'I can't bear . . .'
'It's intolerable . . .'
'I'd never be able to live with myself if . . .'

Usually, awfulising and can't-stand-it-itis go together: 'It's awful and I just can't bear it.'

It is important to note that what we are often afraid of is not the situation itself, but rather the *unpleasant feelings* we associate with it. In other words, we anticipate feeling bad (e.g. putting ourselves down, becoming anxious, feeling rejected or hurt) and tell ourselves we simply cannot stand the discomfort this entails. This in turn leads to the demand 'Because I can't stand experiencing such discomfort, I *must not.*' Unfortunately, such a combination of awfulising and demanding makes us even more uptight.

This common tendency is known as *low discomfort tolerance*. It is a significant cause of many of the emotional and behavioural problems that afflict human beings. We shall meet it again and again throughout the book.

Why do we do it?

Why do human beings catastrophise when it is so unhelpful? One key reason is that, increasingly in modern industrialised societies, we expect to feel good all the time. Human beings have always preferred to feel happy rather than upset. It seems, though, that feeling good has become something of an obsession in modern times.

This is probably a result of two trends. First, we enjoy higher levels of material welfare and freedom from physical danger than our ancestors did. Understandably, we would like to match this with emotional welfare.

Second, medical science has been increasingly able to help people avoid physical and emotional pain with medications. This development, coupled with the relative success of the psychotherapies that emerged in the second half of the twentieth century, has encouraged the belief that anything is possible.

There is nothing wrong with such an expectation in itself. Unfortunately, though, human beings tend to go beyond wanting something to *demanding* it. We have come to see emotional comfort not just as desirable, but as a *must* or *need*. This leads us to consider it disastrous or intolerable when we don't get that comfort. We may also seek immediate relief from our pain in ways that create long-term distress: many of those prescribed mood-changing benzodiazepines become addicted to them. Our demand for happiness, paradoxically, makes it more likely we will end up unhappy.

Catastrophising can also be maintained because it appears to provide some gains. We may exaggerate to attract attention to our woes. Telling someone we feel 'awful', for example, is more likely to get their attention than simply saying we are ill. We can also avoid the discomfort of difficult situations — and personal change — by telling ourselves that we 'can't stand it'.

All things in moderation

Could you 'stand' a life without catastrophising? It probably makes sense — but old habits die hard. We often see only two alternatives — our problems are either serious, or there is nothing wrong at all (an example of black-and-white thinking).

There is a better way: learn to think in *moderate* terms. That means avoiding extremes (either positive or negative) that are out of proportion to what is going on and that hurt unnecessarily. Don't minimise your difficulties, though. Avoid so-called 'positive thinking'. What we are talking about here is *realistic* thinking — seeing things as they really are.

Take awfulising. In real life, very little is ever 100 per cent bad or 100 per cent good. The trouble with awfulising is that it often implies something is as bad as it could be. But how often is this the case?

Someone once asked me, 'What could be worse than taking a whole hour to die in agony?' Well, the answer to that is taking two hours to die in agony — or three, or four, or a whole day or more. You can undercut awfulising by viewing what is going on in relation to other, possibly worse, events.

I am not suggesting you deny reality by telling yourself that 'it could be worse'; rather, that you view things that are unpleasant, uncomfortable and inconvenient as just that and no more — not as the end of the world. Then you will avoid adding unnecessary emotional pain to the real problems you have. In other words, keep things in perspective.

Can't-stand-it-itis is just as irrational. To say that you 'can't stand' something is really implying that you will die if you are exposed to it. But is this true? Obviously not! Clearly you have stood many unpleasant events and circumstances, otherwise you wouldn't be here to tell the tale. They may have been uncomfortable, disagreeable or undesirable, but, in spite of this, you stood them.

If you see yourself as able to tolerate unpleasant happenings, you will avoid adding to the pain.

Mountains back to molehills

Read the list of typical catastrophising thoughts below. Alongside each is a more realistic alternative.

Catastrophising	*Realistic thinking*
It's awful and intolerable to experience physical or emotional pain and discomfort.	If I tell myself that pain and discomfort are awful, I'll only set myself up to feel anxious when I think they're coming.
It's terrible to be treated like this.	It's unpleasant and uncomfortable to be treated like this.
I can't stand it when people don't act as they should.	I don't like it, but I can survive it — and I survive better when I don't lose my cool.
This is an absolute disaster.	This is serious. But it's not the end of the world.

Catastrophising	Realistic thinking
This situation is simply unbearable.	This situation is unpleasant and uncomfortable, and I don't like it, but I am — obviously — standing it.
I couldn't imagine anything worse.	This is bad — but, in reality, it's better than some of the alternatives.

Helping yourself

Here are some strategies to help you change from catastrophising to realistic thinking:

- *Learn to catch yourself catastrophising.* Know the cues to watch for: words such as *awful, terrible, disastrous*; thoughts such as, 'I can't stand it'; and feelings such as anxiety and hopelessness.
- *Challenge exaggerated thoughts.* Resist going to extremes and get things into perspective. When worrying about forthcoming 'disasters', ask yourself, 'What is the worst that is really *likely* to happen?'
- *Remind yourself that you are standing it,* even though it may be uncomfortable and you don't like it. On the other hand, don't minimise your problems. The aim is *realistic* thinking.
- *Most important, be aware of any tendency to see physical or emotional discomfort as 'awful' or 'unbearable'.* If you learn to tolerate frustration and bad feelings, they will trouble you less in the first place.

In other words, get those mountains back to the molehills they really are.

7 People-rating: are you living down to your label?

What do you think you are? A bastard, beauty, whiner or witch? Do you see yourself as considerate, honest, lazy or crazy? Or believe you're a hopeless case, worrier, martyr, monster, bad person, good-for-nothing, neurotic or nerd? Ever call anyone a bad boy, good girl, bitch, bad egg, slob, gossip, hypocrite or slut?

You have probably used these — and worse — to describe yourself and others. Most of us do it; but it is illogical and troublesome. Why? Because we may end up believing the labels we use, then act in compliance with them.

When Tim was a child, his father used to tell him he was stupid, a no-hoper who would never amount to anything. He took his resulting lack of confidence with him to school. When he didn't try to achieve up to his potential, some of his teachers also applied the no-hoper label.

Leaving school early, Tim left home and went to another city in the hope of finding work. Unsuccessful, he began to drift with a group of unemployed youths who likewise lacked confidence and self-respect. Soon he was being picked up for theft and possession of marijuana, and then came a conviction for selling drugs. In his view, there was no point in trying. He had been told all his life he was a no-hoper — now the judge was saying the same thing. Tim decided that his father must have been right all along.

What is people-rating?

People-rating is like judging a book by its cover. Let's say the rating is directed at yourself. You start by evaluating one of your personal traits — how you look, what you are like at sports or study, how you do as a worker or parent — or you focus on something you have done, a behaviour.

You then rate (or evaluate) the trait or behaviour concerned. You decide whether it is worthwhile or has value. So far so good. If you stopped there, you would have no problem.

Like most people, however, you probably go a big step further and expand the rating of that one trait or behaviour into a rating of your *total self*. You end up saying things like:

'I did a bad thing, therefore *I'm a bad person*.'
'I said something bitchy — this makes me *a bitch*.'
'Because I can't handle her arguments, *I'm dumb*.'
'I lost my temper with the kids today — this shows *I'm hopeless* as a parent.'

It is as though, in some magical way, one *part* of a person becomes the *whole* person. This doesn't make sense. People are mixtures of positive and negative traits, but a single rating of your total self seemingly applies to *all* your many traits and behaviours. Not only is this an overgeneralisation, but you can never know every single one of a given person's characteristics and actions anyway. People-rating, too, implies that someone has always been that way and always will be, while in reality people are always changing.

People-rating also implies that there is a universally accepted guideline for judging the worth of people. To rate yourself as, say, a 'good' or 'bad' person suggests that you have some kind of standard of what is good or bad against which you can compare yourself. Yet there is no such standard with which everyone would agree. The standards which do exist for judging people and their characteristics vary over time and between social groups. People who behave aggressively, for instance, may be defined as 'courageous' in wartime but as 'violent' in periods of peace.

Note, too, that people-rating is based on the irrational process of demanding discussed in chapter 5. According to this, if you compare yourself with some kind of standard, you believe you *should* live up to that standard. In other words, you operate according to some kind of 'Universal Law of Human Behaviour'. But where does this universal law come from? Your own head.

Unfortunately, most of us engage in self-rating to some extent. You are probably doing it when:

- You forever strive — no matter what the cost — to achieve and succeed: at work, as parent and homemaker, with your possessions, or even in your recreation.
- You feel guilt or shame when you don't live up to what you expect.
- You get anxious about trying anything that may involve a risk of failure.
- You compare yourself with other people.
- You worry overmuch about how others see you.
- You get defensive and hostile, and feel hurt, when you think someone is criticising you.
- You go out of your way to seek approval from others, conforming to what they expect and putting their views before your own.
- You often check your opinions with others because you don't value your own judgements.
- You put up a false front by using grandiose talk or attention-seeking behaviour, or by trying to be one-up on others.
- You underrate and neglect your talents, thinking you aren't good enough to enjoy pleasurable things, and reject compliments by saying you don't deserve them.

Where does it come from?

Given that people-rating is so bad for us, why do we do it? For the same reasons we engage in the other types of irrational thinking: lazy brains, early learning, and the subconscious gains we receive.

People-rating seems to come naturally. Our brains find it hard to evaluate more than one item at a time, hence we often take the easy way and use simplistic, total ratings of ourselves and others. It's easier to say, 'I'm a bastard', than to say more precisely, 'I tend to voice my

People-rating: are you living down your label?

opinions without considering how other people might feel'; or 'She's useless', rather than 'She finds it hard to carry out tasks without someone telling her what to do.'

This innate tendency to one-dimensional rating is enhanced by conditioning. It is not hard to see where we get the idea from — parents, the mass media, educational institutions, the legal system, to name but a few. It is all around us. How many of us have been brought up on 'You're a naughty boy/girl' rather than 'That was a naughty thing to do'?

There are many reasons why people-rating is so pervasive. For a start, criticism (and praise) of another person is often used to shape or control their behaviour. As a client once summed it up: 'The only time my husband says anything good about me is when I fit in with what he wants. The rest of the time, especially when I want to do something for myself, I'm just "selfish" or a "bitch".'

Rating others may also be a way of justifying how we treat them. A graphic example is the mass murder of millions of people in concentration camps during the Second World War. It seems incredible that men and women treated other human beings in such a way until we see how systematically the victims were labelled as 'subhuman'.

We also see this dehumanising process in the way rapists view their victims. At a rape trial in Auckland it was shown that the gang members involved had referred to the victim, a young woman they had abducted, as a 'block' and described her in terms such as 'stupid bitch' and 'slut', which implied that she had asked for what had happened or had deserved to be raped and beaten. Just as significant were the labels they gave each other: by regarding themselves as 'animals' they could excuse, or at least explain, their behaviour.

People-rating can also help us avoid trying to understand those who differ from us in viewpoint, colour or culture. All we have to do is define them as 'wrong-thinking people', 'fascists', 'communists', 'religious fanatics', 'unbelievers', 'ignorant' and the like.

This is neatly illustrated by a 1946 quote from the *Saturday Evening Post*. A visitor declared that New Zealanders were 'so much alike that it is hard to remember the names of people you meet casually', and that they 'are a biologically standardised product', which makes for 'cultural uniformity'. I wonder how helpful this gentleman found it to explain away his poor memory for people's names by telling himself they were all the same anyway?

There is another reason — possibly the main one — why self-rating is so pervasive: we often unwittingly reinforce it when trying to feel better about ourselves. The notion of 'self-esteem' is a popular one, and to develop self-esteem we try to see ourselves as having 'value' or 'worth'. We are encouraged to add up our good points and see for ourselves that we are of value. We also hear that human beings are naturally 'worthwhile'. Quite how we happen to have such intrinsic worth is never spelt out — it just seems to 'be there'.

This conventional approach simply reinforces the tendency to self-rate. It creates the demanding belief that to be happy we *must* be 'worthy'. This may work for us if we have many talents, few flaws and the ability always to think positively; but how many of us are so endowed?

A better way: self-acceptance

Here is a better solution: dispense with the idea of self-esteem altogether. Forget about having a 'self-image'. Give up the notion of liking or disliking your 'self'. You don't need to worry about whether you are worthwhile, because 'worth' and 'value' are concepts that do not apply to human beings.

Sounds a bit radical? Let's take a closer look. What I am saying is: *don't rate yourself at all* — even in a positive direction. Instead, *accept yourself*. Self-acceptance is the opposite of self-rating. It is unconditional. You accept your entire self (flaws and all) as you are now, even if there are aspects you would like to change.

To accept yourself is to acknowledge three things:

1. You exist.
2. There is no reason why you should be any different from how you are.
3. You are neither worthy nor unworthy.

Like it or not, you exist as you are — with all your present traits, both good and bad. You know, too, that you have acted in certain ways in the past. To acknowledge these facts is to recognise reality, as opposed to demanding that reality be different.

There is no 'Law of the Universe' that says you *should* be different from how you are. You may not like some of your present traits and tendencies. You might not feel comfortable with some things you have done in the past. You might want to do something to change the way you are now, and perhaps plan to. Acceptance simply means you avoid *demanding* that the current you not exist — and that your past actions didn't happen.

Rate your behaviour rather than yourself

'Sounds great,' you say. 'But if I accept rather than rate myself, won't this stop me ever doing anything to improve?' Not at all. Rather than rating your *total* self, you can rate your various traits, behaviours and potentials. In other words, instead of wasting precious time and energy brooding over how 'worthwhile' you are, get on with deciding which *parts* of yourself you could usefully change or upgrade.

Maybe you would like to improve your physical health to achieve the goal of living longer. Great idea — but you don't have to label yourself as 'unfit' or 'weak'. You can develop your vocabulary without calling yourself 'a useless communicator'. You can admit your marriage is failing without thinking this makes you 'a failure'. You can acknowledge that although you sometimes do bastardly things, this doesn't make you 'a bastard'.

Value your existence

If you are prepared to rate specific tendencies and actions, you will be able to see whether they help you achieve an existence which is worthwhile or valuable to you. In the end, is it not the quality of your *existence* that matters?

Value your existence, then, rather than your 'self'. You can recognise you exist without putting any rating at all on yourself. You are neither good nor bad, worthy nor unworthy, useful nor useless. *You just exist.* Put your energy into maximising the *quality* of that existence. This will aid your total happiness much more than debating whether you have 'value' or 'worth' as a person.

People-rating or behaviour-rating?

Making the switch means changing what you think about yourself and others. Compare the lists below.

People-rating	*Behaviour-rating*
I'm a loser.	I lost out on this occasion.
You're a naughty child.	You did a naughty thing.
I'm a hopeless parent.	I could learn more about handling children.
I'm a poor conversationalist.	I want to improve my conversational skills.
She's a depressive.	She feels depressed at present.
I'm a failure.	I failed at this task.
I'm a bitch.	I did a bitchy thing.
I'm a useless cook.	My cooking skills are underdeveloped.
I'm stupid.	I sometimes do stupid things.
I'm a lousy lover.	I could learn more about sex.
I'm unfit.	I'd be in better shape if I exercised more.
I'm neurotic.	I'd like to learn to adopt more rational attitudes.

Notice that the people-rating statements include 'I *am*', 'you *are*', 'he/she *is*'. These expressions indicate that you are rating the entire person (be it yourself or someone else). They imply, too, that the person always has been, and always will be, what the label says they are. Rating behaviour, on the other hand, implies a belief that a person can, if they choose, change in specific ways to improve their existence.

Making the change

Let's summarise what self-acceptance involves:

1. You *acknowledge*, simply, that you *exist* — without making any judgement in respect of your 'worthiness' or any demand that you be different from how you are.
2. You *rate specific traits and behaviours* in a practical and nonmoralistic way.
3. You *concentrate on rating and valuing your existence* rather than your 'self'.

Unfortunately, self-acceptance is easier to describe than to practise. Self-rating is a habit for most of us. We also live in a world where people-rating is the norm, so others are unlikely to help us change. But it is not impossible. Here are some strategies which will help:

- *Be aware when you are rating yourself or others.* Watch for cues such as 'I am', 'you are', 'she/he is'. Change any self-rating to a behaviour-rating. Be *specific* about any changes you would like to make: instead of 'I must become a better person' say 'I'd like to learn how to type/start an exercise programme/get up earlier in the morning.'
- *Accept justified criticism from others of specific behaviours*, but reject ratings of your entire self. Note that disapproval from other people proves nothing about you. Remember, too, that when you do something to less than the standard you prefer, your performance may be flawed but you can still accept yourself.
- Whenever possible, *treat yourself to things you enjoy* — food, clothes, outings, time to yourself, etc. — but not because you 'deserve' them, rather because you *want* them. Remember that 'deserving' — like its opposite, 'undeserving' — is a subtle example of self-rating.
- *Be gratified when you succeed or receive approval from others*, but don't rely on such occasions to feel good. Remember that real self-acceptance is independent of your performance and the views of other people.

- *Keep in mind that none of us will ever reach perfection.* Total self-acceptance is an ideal few people are likely to achieve in their lifetime, but even 50 per cent acceptance is worth striving for.

If you still find the idea of living without self-rating radical, you are not alone. Most people probably subscribe to the idea that to be happy one has to see oneself as 'worthwhile'. For a moment, though, put aside conventional thinking. Look closely at those high-sounding words, *human worth* and *value*. They are, in reality, nothing more than that: words — ideas that exist in our heads. Whether or not we apply these ideas to ourselves or other human beings is a matter of choice.

8 Rational Self-Analysis

Knowing what causes your problems is a start. The next step is to move from insight to action. In this chapter you will learn how to *identify* the beliefs involved in your unwanted reactions, *dispute and replace* the unhelpful ones, and back this up by *acting* in new, more functional ways.

Introducing Rational Self-Analysis

The aim is to analyse specific situations in which you react in ways you dislike. This will help you achieve two purposes: to feel better at the time, and, by chipping away at the core beliefs that underlie your reactions, to change how you behave and effect a permanent improvement in how you feel.

As we saw in chapter 3, you can uncover your core beliefs by first looking for your *interpretations* of what is happening. Then ask yourself how you are *evaluating* these interpretations. Finally, work out the *core beliefs* on which your evaluations are based.

It is best to do this in writing, especially in the early stages. *Rational Self-Analysis* can help you here. This is an extended version of the *ABC* method described in chapter 1. To review: *A* is the *Activating event* — the event or circumstance that starts things off; *B* is *Beliefs* — the thoughts and beliefs you have about *A*; and *C* is the *Consequence* — the emotions and behaviours which result from those beliefs.

With Rational Self-Analysis you add *E, D* and *F. E* is the new *Effect* — how you would prefer to feel and/or behave differently in the future. *D* is *Disputation* — you question and dispute your beliefs, decide which are true and which are false, and replace the latter with more rational alternatives. *F* is *Further action* — what you plan to do to reduce the chances of thinking, feeling and behaving dysfunctionally in future.

To see how this works, let's revisit Alan, whom we met in chapter 1. Alan became depressed after his new friend passed him in the street without acknowledging him. Here is that event checked out with Rational Self-Analysis:

A **What started things off**
Friend passed me in the street without speaking to me.

B **Beliefs about A**
1. He's ignoring me. He doesn't like me. (*interpretation*)
2. I could end up without friends for ever. (*interpretation*) That would be unbearable. (*evaluation*)
3. I'm unacceptable as a friend (*interpretation*), so I must be worthless as a person. (*evaluation*)
4. For me to be happy and feel worthwhile, people must like me and approve of me — and I couldn't stand it to be otherwise. (*core belief*)

C **Reaction**
Feelings: worthless, depressed.
Behaviour: avoiding people generally.

E **How I would prefer to feel**
Disappointed that he may have ignored me, but more optimistic about the future than I do now.

D **New, rational beliefs about A**
1. How do I know he ignored me on purpose? He may not have seen me. Even if he did ignore me, this doesn't prove he dislikes me. He may have been in a hurry, or perhaps even upset or worried about something.
2. Even if it is true that he dislikes me, this doesn't prove I'll never have friends again. (Even if it did, this would be unpleasant rather than 'terrible' — I could survive.)
3. There's no proof I'm not acceptable as a friend. But even if I were, this proves nothing about the total me, or my 'worthwhileness'.
4. I'd prefer to have other people like and approve of me, but it's exaggerating to say I'd be totally unhappy if they didn't. I could survive, and even develop other ways to feel happy.

F **What I'll do to avoid repeating the same irrational thoughts and reactions**
1. Do some rereading on catastrophising and self-rating.
2. Go and see my friend to check out how things really are.

At first, Alan wasn't aware of his core belief (belief number 4). To uncover it, he asked himself, 'If I'm thinking that "it would be terrible to be without friends" and "I must be worthless", what rule am I operating by?' He saw that the evaluations in beliefs 2 and 3 are simply versions of the general rule in belief 4 applied to a specific event. Once you have worked out how you are evaluating something, the underlying core belief usually becomes evident.

How can you tell that Alan's beliefs are irrational? Because they contain *distortions of reality* ('I could end up without friends for ever'), *catastrophising* ('That would be terrible'), *demanding* ('For me to be happy . . . people must like me') and *self-rating* ('I must be worthless as a person').

Carrying out just one analysis, of course, won't permanently change any of Alan's deep-seated core beliefs. He will need to dispute them many times, chipping away bit by bit; but he has made a start.

Carrying out your own Rational Self-Analysis

To complete a Rational Self-Analysis of your own, take a good-sized sheet of paper, then follow this sequence:

Record what started things off

At *A* describe the *Activating event* — the event or circumstance that sparked things off. Be brief — summarise only the essential facts. Don't include any guesses about what happened.

Let's say, for example, your boss criticised you. Simply write what actually happened, e.g. 'The boss told me my work output was too low.' Don't include guesses about what this means, such as 'He thinks I'm useless' or 'He wants me to resign.' Save these *interpretations* for the beliefs section (*B*).

Note that *A* can be either an event or circumstance you have just witnessed or experienced, or merely a thought about such an event from your past. You may, for example, write down, 'I was thinking about what the boss said to me today/when my husband deserted me/how things have been for the past five years/etc.'

Usually you will be aware of what *A* was; however, when you are not sure, your imagination can assist. Spend five minutes or so in a quiet place and concentrate on your unwanted feelings. Be aware of the physical sensations involved. As you do this, clear your mind and allow it to relax. Be aware of any images that float into your conscious mind. These images will most probably reflect *A*.

Using your imagination in this way works because events, thoughts and feelings are not totally separate but remain closely linked in the brain.

Record your reactions
Next, at *C*, describe the *Consequence* — the *emotions* you felt (or still feel) and how you *behaved* or acted. Continuing with the example of the boss who criticised you, your feelings might be 'hurt' or 'angry', while your behaviour might be 'sat and moped all evening'.

Why complete *C* before *B*? Usually you will be aware of both what started things off and your reaction to it before you recognise the thoughts involved. Looking at your reaction will give you some clues as to what those thoughts may be. (As we shall see in Part II, specific feelings and behaviours tend to be associated with certain types of thinking.)

Some people find it hard to identify and name their emotions. Again, your imagination can assist. Imagine, as vividly as you can, the circumstance or event that triggered things. Hold the image till you feel the emotions involved. Move your attention back and forth between the image of the event and your feelings until you become more aware of what they are. Write them down while they are still with you.

If you are not used to putting names to your emotions, this list of 'feeling' words might prompt you:

Pleasant feelings

affectionate	amazed	amused	appreciative	calm
carefree	comfortable	confident	contented	cool
curious	delighted	eager	elated	encouraged
enjoying	enthusiastic	excited	fascinated	friendly
grateful	happy	hopeful	interested	joyful

loving	optimistic	peaceful	pleasant	relieved
satisfied	secure	stimulated	surprised	tender
thankful	touched	trusting	warm	

Unpleasant feelings

afraid	angry	anxious	bitter	bored
brokenhearted	confused	cross	depressed	disappointed
discouraged	disgusted	dismayed	distressed	frightened
frustrated	guilty	hateful	horrified	hostile
hurt	impatient	insecure	irritated	jealous
lonely	miserable	resentful	sad	sorry
terrified	uncomfortable	uneasy	unhappy	worried

Record your thoughts

Now return to *B — Beliefs —* and write down your thoughts. Start by asking, 'What was I telling myself to end up reacting the way I did to that event?' Remember, you are looking for three levels of thinking:

1. *Your interpretations.* At *A* you wrote, 'The boss told me my work output was too low.' This is your *description* of what happened. Your *interpretations* might be as follows:

    'He thinks I'm useless.'
    'He wants me to resign.'

    To identify your interpretations, ask yourself questions such as 'What am I assuming is happening here?' or 'What part of this am I reacting to the most?' Remember: irrational interpretations are usually *distortions of reality* (black-and-white thinking, filtering, overgeneralising, mind-reading, emotional reasoning, fortune-telling and personalising).

2. *Your evaluations.* These reflect what the event *means* to you. Continuing with the same example, your evaluation might be:

    'This shows that *I'm useless.*'

    To identify your evaluations, ask yourself, 'If my interpretation were true, what would this mean to me?' More specific questions to consider are 'What "should" or "must" am I holding here?', 'Am I viewing something as awful or unbearable?' and

'Am I rating my or another person's entire "self"?' Remember: irrational evaluations consist of demanding, catastrophising and people-rating.
3. *Your core beliefs.* These are the general *rules* according to which you operate. Your evaluations will point you to them. The evaluation above suggests a core belief like:

> 'To feel OK about myself I need approval from others and must avoid disapproval at all costs.'

Ask yourself, 'Given how I am interpreting and evaluating this situation/event/circumstance, what kind of underlying, general core belief might I be operating on?' Remember: most irrational core beliefs will be personalised versions of the 12 irrational beliefs listed on page 33. Use that list as a prompt if you find it hard to identify your core beliefs.

General guidelines for identifying and recording your beliefs

1. *Start with the obvious, then probe deeper.* Begin by noting the thoughts of which you are immediately conscious. These will usually be *interpretations*, e.g. 'He thinks I'm useless.' Then look for how you are *evaluating* these interpretations by asking, 'If this is true, what does it mean to me?' or 'How do I evaluate this?'

   At first you may come up with another interpretation — sometimes a chain of them, e.g. 'He's trying to hurt me . . . He doesn't like me . . . He'll say bad things about me . . . This will put others off me . . .' Finally you will get to the evaluation, e.g. 'This would be awful and prove I'm no good.'

   You will know you have arrived at an evaluation when you recognise demanding, catastrophising or people-rating. Refer again to chapter 3 if you are still unsure of the difference between interpretations and evaluations.

2. *Be honest about your irrational thoughts.* Most people find it hard to write down thoughts they realise are absurd. You may want to cheat and write down more rational versions. For example, 'I must never make a mistake' may get watered down to

'I hope I can avoid too many mistakes'; or 'He's a sod for treating me this way' could become 'I wish he wouldn't do that.'

One thing people often avoid is their self-rating. Most of us don't want to admit to the nasty labels we apply to ourselves — but they won't change until we confront them.

3. *Write beliefs down as direct statements, not as questions.* You cannot dispute vague questions such as 'Why is this happening to me?'; but you can challenge 'This shouldn't be happening to me.' Asking questions is often a way of masking statements and avoiding admitting to uncomfortable thoughts. Here are some examples:

Question	Real thought behind the question
Will I ever get better?	I'll never get better.
Why is she so late home?	She's had an accident ...
Where will I find the money?	I won't be able to find the money.

4. *Be specific when writing down your thoughts.* 'I can't stand the whole situation' is too general. What exactly is it about the situation you can't stand? Compare:

Vague statement	Specific statement
I'm inferior.	I'm not as good as Mike.
The world is no good.	People are always on my back.
I'm afraid of lifts.	If I get into a lift, it may crash, I'll be trapped, I'll go berserk.

The more specific you are, the easier you will find it to uncover your irrational beliefs and dispute them effectively.

5. *Make sure you don't confuse feelings with thoughts.* Many people use expressions such as 'I *feel* you're wrong' when they mean 'I *think* you're wrong'; or they say 'I *feel* I may not be able to cope with this' instead of 'I *won't* be able to cope with this.'

A feeling is an emotion. The two words mean the same thing. Confusion arises when people use the word *feeling* to refer to a *thought*. Dressing thoughts up as feelings can be a way to avoid making direct statements. Perhaps you lack confidence in your opinions, or don't want others to disagree. The problem, though, is you can't dispute feelings — so keep feelings at C and thoughts at B.

6. *Remember: work out how you are evaluating things*. This has already been said, but it is important: don't leave B until you are satisfied you have been honest with yourself and recorded what the event or circumstance *means* to you. This involves admitting to those demands, catastrophisings and ratings of yourself or others.

Specific techniques for identifying your beliefs

1. *If you have trouble identifying your thoughts, try using the power of your imagination*. Develop a vivid picture of what started things off (A) and recall the emotions and behaviours that made up your reaction (C). As you imagine A and C, ask yourself, 'What was I/am I thinking to have ended up responding this way to that event?'

2. *Observe your reactions*. As stated earlier, certain reactions are usually related to certain types of thinking. Ask yourself, 'What would I have been telling myself about A to end up reacting like I did at C?' In the case of hostile anger, for example, look for demands directed at the person with whom you are angry. In the case of guilt look for demands directed at yourself, and also self-rating.

   Continue to educate yourself about irrational thinking. The chapters in Part II describe the types of thinking which usually cause specific emotions and behaviours. Knowledge of these will show you what to look for when carrying out an analysis.

3. *Get into the real-life setting that sparked off your reaction*. If you panicked about going into the supermarket, for example, go back there. Stand outside or sit in the car. Get in touch again with your thoughts and fears, e.g. about fainting, other people

thinking you are crazy, how that would be terrible.
4. *Observe irrational thinking around you.* Watch for it in newspapers, especially in letters to the editor and statements by pressure groups and politicians. See it in TV dramas, hear it in pop songs and notice it in other people (although without getting sanctimonious or superior). This will give you practice in recognising troublesome ideas.
5. *Memorise the 12 irrational beliefs* on page 33. They will serve as a check list when you are looking for the core beliefs involved in your reactions.

Finally, here is a check list of questions to ask yourself to uncover the thinking that causes your unwanted reaction:

- What do I really think/fear is going on?
- What conclusions am I jumping to?
- In what ways might I be trying to read the minds of others?
- Am I blaming myself for something?
- Am I personalising?
- Am I predicting some bad consequence? If so, what do I fear might/will happen?
- What 'should' or 'must' am I applying to the situation?
- Am I viewing something as 'awful', 'horrible' or 'terrible'?
- Am I thinking that I 'can't stand it'?
- Am I rating either my entire 'self' or other people?

Decide how you would prefer to react

Now go to *E* — the new *Effect* you want to achieve. Decide in what way you would prefer to feel and/or behave differently from how you are currently feeling and/or behaving. An important tip: don't set impossible goals. It is tempting to say you would like to feel 'relaxed' rather than 'terrified', 'happy' rather than 'depressed', 'affectionate' rather than 'angry' — but such changes are too drastic. If you aim for the unachievable, you will become disillusioned and therefore probably give up.

The aim of Rational Self-Analysis is to achieve realistic change, e.g. to replace an intense negative feeling with a moderate negative feeling — 'terrified' with 'concerned', 'depressed' with 'sad', 'angry' with 'annoyed'. This will still be uncomfortable, but not disabling.

Dispute and replace your irrational beliefs

Now return to *D — Disputation*. This is where you question your beliefs, decide which are erroneous and substitute rational alternatives.

The three questions

The most effective way to dispute a belief is to ask three key questions about it:

1. *Does this belief help or harm?* Does it help me feel OK, act effectively and achieve my goals? This question is especially important: if you can see that a particular way of thinking is dysfunctional for you, you will be motivated to change it. Ask this about any type of belief.
2. *What does the evidence say?* Does it support this belief or does it suggest some other conclusion? This question is especially relevant to interpretations.
3. *Is it logical?* 'Because (I want something/it's unpleasant/I made a mistake/etc.), does it follow logically that (I must get what I want/it's awful/I'm a total failure/etc.)?' This question is particularly helpful for assessing evaluations.

Questioning interpretations

When checking out an interpretation, start by querying how helpful it is, then look for evidence of its validity:

- How do I know it is true?
- What evidence is there?
- Is it the best way to explain the facts I have observed, or are there other possible explanations?
- Is there any evidence that it may be faulty?
- In what ways might I be distorting reality? (Check for black-and-white thinking, negative filtering, overgeneralising, mind-reading, emotional reasoning, fortune-telling and personalising.)

Another good way to assess an interpretation is *hypothesis testing*. Write down what you think is going on or what you fear will happen, then develop assignments for actively checking this out. If you think someone is upset with you, ask them. If you fear people will reject you if you act assertively, develop an action plan for asserting yourself in a graduated fashion, beginning with low-risk activities and situations and working towards higher-risk ones. Observe the results and see how they match your assumptions.

Questioning evaluations

When questioning an evaluation and the core belief it reflects, first query its helpfulness, then ask:

- What grounds do I have for believing that I, other people or things generally should, must or have to be the way I expect?
- Does it follow that because I want . . . it must be?
- What exactly do I mean by 'awful', 'terrible', 'disgusting', 'can't stand it', etc.?
- What makes it so?
- Is this really the worst that could happen, or the end of the world?
- Does it follow that because . . . is unpleasant it is unbearable?
- How is it that this event or circumstance turns me (or anyone else) into a total bastard/bitch/good-for-nothing/idiot/martyr/victim/etc.?
- Where is the proof that anyone is completely stupid/bad/immoral/selfish/unfair/etc.?

Additional disputing techniques

As well as the three key questions, there are some additional techniques for checking out evaluative thinking. For instance, a good way to dispute demanding is the *double-standard* approach. Ask yourself, 'Would I encourage my (child/partner/best friend/etc.) to hold this belief?' If the answer is a resounding 'No!', you will realise it is time to give up the belief in question. Consider what you would say to the other person to dissuade them from holding it — then note your arguments so you can recall them to use when that way of thinking tries to reassert itself.

Tackle catastrophising with the *catastrophe scale*. On a sheet of paper draw a line down one side, write '100%' at the top and '0%' at the bottom, and add 10% intervals in between. Decide where on the scale you would place whatever it is you consider 'awful', and make a note in that position. Then, at each interval on the scale, write down something you think could legitimately be rated at that level. For example, at 0% you might write 'Having a quiet cup of coffee at home', at 20% 'Having to mow the lawns when the rugby's on television', at 70% 'Being burgled', at 90% 'Being diagnosed with cancer', and at 100% 'Being burned alive'. As you write each item, check how its position relates to the rating for your original item. You will find that you progressively get that item into perspective and alter its position on the scale, usually downwards.

To deal with self-rating, use the double-standard technique described above. Consider: would you encourage a loved one to use the self-downing term you are applying to yourself? If they did use it, what would you say to dissuade them from using it? Another approach is *reframing* — viewing yourself in a different way. For example, instead of saying 'I'm a stupid person', try 'I did a stupid thing.'

Is it so important to uncover and dispute irrational beliefs before you attempt to replace them? Yes — because if you don't, they will remain untouched and continue to bother you. Resist the temptation to rush ahead and tell yourself 'positive' thoughts until you have confronted the irrational ones.

Consider getting back into the situation to which you reacted so you can dispute the irrational thoughts 'on the spot'. This is especially useful when you are afraid of something you know is not really dangerous.

Developing replacement beliefs

The final step before you leave *D* is to develop and write down replacements for your irrational beliefs. The following alternatives to the seven types of inferential thinking can help you do this:

Black-and-white thinking	See things as falling along a continuum rather than at extremes.
Filtering	See life as consisting of both negatives and positives.
Overgeneralising	Keep negative experiences in perspective.
Mind-reading	Look at alternative explanations for the behaviour of other people.
Fortune-telling	Treat all beliefs about the future as predictions and nothing more.
Emotional reasoning	Know that emotions are caused by your own thinking about situations, not situations themselves.
Personalising	Remember that the universe doesn't revolve around one person, and that events may have many explanations.

Each of the four types of evaluative thinking also has a rational substitute:

Demandingness	View wanted events and circumstances as *preferable* or *desirable* rather than as absolutely *necessary*.
Catastrophising	See negative experiences and situations as *bad* or *unpleasant* rather than *terrifying* or *horrific*.
Can't-stand-it-itis	View discomfort and frustration as *unpleasant* but *bearable*.
Self-rating	Accept *yourself* even though you rate your *actions*.

Ensure your new beliefs are realistic, not just 'positive thinking'. Telling yourself, for example, that losing a valued friendship is 'good for my personal growth' may sound nice and affirming, but it won't hold up for long, because a bad experience is bad. It would be more realistic to view such a loss as 'sad' or 'disappointing'. Similarly, don't switch from 'I'm useless' to 'I can do anything.' Better to think, 'I'm not good at some things, but I am at others'. And don't try to replace 'I must pass this exam' with 'It doesn't matter if I pass or fail.' Instead, try something like 'I very much desire to pass, but there's no reason why I "must".'

Re-educating yourself will help your disputing. To develop effective and lasting rational beliefs, gradually expand your understanding of rational thinking. Most chapters in this book describe new ways of looking at life. If, for example, you are disputing one of the four types of irrational thinking, reread the chapter that describes that type. Seek out other literature, too, for more ideas. You don't have to agree with everything you read — just accept what suits. Note that there is a summary of rational principles in chapter 20, which you can use as a handy reference.

Get into action

Identifying and disputing irrational beliefs will get you part of the way. Putting the new rational alternatives into *practice* will take you the rest of the way. This is often referred to as 'homework'. Section *F* — *Further action* — is where you write down what you plan to do to reduce the likelihood of thinking and reacting in the old irrational ways in future. Actions can include any or all of the following.

Self-education

- *Reading* can improve your understanding of irrational thinking, specific problem areas and different ways of coping with things you dislike. Reread the sections of this book that refer to the problem area you are working on. Hunt out other literature. Don't read such material once and then discard it. Study it, highlighting passages that seem relevant to you.
- The *Internet* is a growing source of potentially helpful information, although it is important to be wary — there is also a lot of potentially dangerous misinformation online. For a list of Internet sites that have a good reputation for providing accurate and helpful material, start with the 'links' page of the website for the New Zealand Centre for Rational Emotive Behaviour Therapy (www.rational.org.nz).
- *Audiotapes*. You can listen to tape-recordings on rational topics while doing housework, driving, gardening, walking or undertaking other physical activities. You can also make your own with passages from books or pamphlets you find helpful.

At the back of the book is a list of places that supply reputable audiotapes.
- *Essays*. Research and write about a particular problem area, covering questions such as: What is known about the problem? What are the possible causes? What can be done about it? What blocks might get in the way of dealing with it? How can I overcome these? Processing the information you locate can provide an effective educative experience.

Rethinking techniques

- *Rational cards*. The rational card is an elegantly simple yet surprisingly useful aid for routine reinforcement of a new belief. On a small card, write the old belief at the top and the new belief below, then carry the card around with you for two or three weeks, reading it eight to 10 times a day. Here's an example:

> **Old belief**
> To feel OK and function in my life, I need approval from others.
>
> **New belief**
> Approval is good to have, but making it an absolute need puts my happiness and functioning at risk when other people don't cooperate to meet it. Better to see approval as desirable rather than necessary.

Reading the card will take only 10 seconds or so, but the repetition can be a great help in establishing a new rational belief. Ensure the old belief is on the card as well as the new one. If you simply repeat the new belief, the old one will be left untouched, but every time you read both together, the new one will challenge the old. Note that a new thought requires daily practice for several weeks to become a habit.

- *The 'Why change?' card*. This is a variation of the rational card. It can help if you are having trouble overcoming unhealthy habits or dysfunctional behaviours. List in detail the disadvan-

tages of these behaviours, then list the advantages of new behaviours. Summarise both lists on a card, then read the card eight to 10 times a day for two weeks.
- *Disputation essays.* If a self-defeating belief is of particular significance or is especially resistant to change, you could dispute it in detail by writing an essay that considers both sides of the issue.
- *Audiotapes.* Either simply record new beliefs in the form of forceful rational statements, or record a disputation sequence in which you argue from both the self-defeating and the rational points of view, delivering the rational view more forcefully. Listen to the tape while going about your daily activities.

Practising new behaviours

Probably the most important type of action is putting new behaviours into practice. Rethinking is important, but you need to take the final step and *act* in accordance with your new ways of thinking. This is the second part of the 'cognitive-behavioural' approach on which this book is based. Here are the main types of behavioural self-help activity:

- *Contradictory behaviour.* Practise acting in ways that are the opposite of your usual, unwanted reactions. If, for example, you think you are 'useless' or 'unworthy' and don't deserve anything nice to happen to you, indulge in some luxuries, e.g. take a long soak in the bath, meet some friends for coffee, get a novel from the library. If you strive for perfection, deliberately do some tasks to a standard below that which you usually expect of yourself. If you tend to rush around, take some long breaks in which you do nothing but relax.
- *Exposure.* Challenge irrational beliefs by acting against them. If you think you cannot stand disapproval, do something to attract it. Discover that while you don't like it, you won't die. If you believe you must vacuum the house every day, leave it for a week and observe that the house doesn't fall down. Deal with the idea that you can't stand to be in lifts by riding in one.

Be sensible, though, regarding situations in which people have power over you, such as your employer, teachers and police officers. There are plenty of less hazardous ones to practise on. Chapter 10 has some useful tips for confronting situations you fear, and exposure is described in depth in my book on anxiety-management, *FearLess*[1].

- *Stimulus control.* Behaviours often become conditioned to particular triggers or stimuli. For example, if you have trouble sleeping, your mind can develop a connection between being in bed and lying awake. The purpose of stimulus control is to lengthen the time between a stimulus and the response to it and thus weaken the connection. Continuing with the same example, if you are unable to sleep for 20 minutes or more, get up and remain up for 30–60 minutes until you feel tired. This will gradually break the connection in your mind that bed is a place in which to be awake.
- *Activity scheduling.* If you are depressed or stressed, you may find you function less effectively. Unfortunately, this can become a vicious circle: as functioning decreases, so does confidence, leading to even lower performance. A w*eekly activity plan* will help you get moving again. Draw up a table like the one below, but with a cell for each hour of the day you are usually awake. Plan and record activities for each segment of time. Then carry out each activity.

Weekly Activity Plan for week beginning: ....

	Mon	Tues	Wed	Thurs	Fri	Sat	Sun
8–9							
9–10							
10–11							
11–12							
12–1							

Plan for one day at a time. Ensure you include some pleasurable activities among the tasks and, as far as possible, select activities you find absorbing. As you carry out each task, focus on it exclusively, putting future tasks out of your mind. Change the plan as necessary to accommodate unexpected developments.

Note that for behavioural work to have a significant and lasting effect, it needs to be done repetitively over a period of time. Carry out contradictory behaviour, exposure or stimulus control on a daily basis if possible; and keep it going for weeks or months, as required, until the old ways of thinking and behaving weaken and become replaced by more functional ones.

Practical problem solving
You might decide to try changing whatever it is that bothers you in the first place — the *A*. This might involve asking another person to change the way they treat you, looking for a new job or ending an unhappy relationship. To learn more about dealing with the *A*s in your life, see the useful step-by-step problem-solving formula in chapter 18.

What else can you do?
Finally, employ any other methods your imagination can devise. Be creative. What about disputing irrational ideas using your home computer or video recorder, or putting rational ideas to music? Use anything that works for *you*.

Putting it all together

You have now been introduced to Rational Self-Analysis. Once you have been through the process a few times, you will find that it is easier than it looks at first. In the next chapter there are some simple exercises that will help you get used to the process. In the meantime, here is the example we have been using set out in the complete *A–F* format:

A What started things off
The boss told me my work output was too low.

C My reaction
Feelings: hurt.
Behaviours: avoided interacting with my colleagues for the rest of the day, then sat and moped all evening.

B Beliefs about A that caused my reaction at C
1. He thinks I'm useless. He wants me to resign. (*interpretations*)
2. I'm useless. (*evaluation*)
3. To feel OK about myself I need approval from others and must avoid disapproval at all costs. (*core belief*)

E How I would prefer to feel and behave
1. Concerned rather than upset and self-downing.
2. Keep active and make myself mix with other people at work.

D New, rational beliefs about A
1. How do I know he thinks I'm useless? It's more likely he was just trying to get me to work faster.
2. I'm not 'useless' — I just need to do better in some areas.
3. It's good to receive approval and encouragement, but how other people act toward me proves nothing about my total self.

F What I'll do to avoid repeating the same irrational thoughts and reactions
1. Have a talk with the boss. See what can be done to improve my speed — or at least see if he can accept the way I am. If we can't work it out, maybe I can do a deal to stay on until I find another job.
2. Reread material on approval-seeking and self-rating.
3. Keep a diary, for the next month, of the times I overreact to any criticism, then do analyses on selected entries.

When to do an analysis

If you analyse an unwanted reaction *while* it is happening, you can interrupt it. You can also analyse a reaction *after* it has happened, to deal with the irrational beliefs involved and thus reduce the likelihood of a repeat.

You may choose to analyse something from the more distant past.

Often we carry around bad feelings about things that happened as far back as childhood. Self-analysis, using your adult intellect, can help you deal with these.

You can also analyse an event *in advance*. This can prepare you to cope with things you are anxious about. Imagine yourself in the situation you fear, see yourself behaving as you expect to, and experience the feelings that come up. Then work out what you are telling yourself and dispute your thoughts.

Troubleshooting

Sometimes self-analysis doesn't seem to work. There are two main reasons: you are not applying the method we have covered, or you are using it ineffectively.

Are you using it?
Some people read about self-analysis but don't use it. Here are the most common reasons:

- *'It's easier to work it out in my mind.'* Writing your thoughts down may seem like a chore, so it will be tempting to try to work out your analysis in your head. If this does the trick, fine — but this is unlikely until you have had a lot of practice. It is worth making the effort to write everything down — it forces you to clarify your thoughts.
- *'It doesn't feel natural.'* Most people are not used to writing down their thoughts, so it seems strange and artificial. But this is true of many skills people learn in adulthood — typing, driving, cooking and so on. Self-analysis won't feel natural until you have been doing it for some time.
- *'It's hard to do an analysis when you're upset.'* When you are in the middle of a severe bout of, say, anger or panic, your brain isn't working too well. The solution is to calm yourself using some type of action method (see chapters 10 and 13 for examples), then to analyse what happened. Some people find they can achieve this simply by telling themselves, 'Hang on, I'm

just doing this to myself with what I'm thinking. I don't need to react this way.'
- *'It isn't possible to do an analysis while you're still in the situation.'* Often our unwanted reactions occur when it is difficult to take the time or find the necessary privacy to complete a self-analysis. As pointed out above, however, you can do an analysis after the event. The evening, for example, may be a good time to go over the events of the day and analyse any you still feel bad about.
- *'It only makes me feel worse to go over something that's happened.'* In the short term, looking closely at whatever triggered your bad feelings may make them worse. It will be tempting to drift along, especially as time eases the pain anyway. But if you want to prevent it happening again, learn to tolerate short-term increases in emotional discomfort for the sake of long-term gain.
- *'I'm afraid of what I'll find if I look at myself too closely.'* Many people fear that self-analysis will bring up things they would rather not think about. Again, however, avoiding temporary discomfort now means losing out in the long term. As a sign I once saw above a fitness centre put it: 'No Gain Without Pain.'

Is it helping?
Some people try self-analysis but it doesn't seem to do any good. If your analyses aren't helping, here are the likely reasons:

- *You are missing the real cause of the problem.* You may not be uncovering your evaluations and the core beliefs on which they are based. To understand the difference between surface interpretations and deeper thinking requires a bit of work. Re-reading chapter 3 will help you with this.
- *You dispute your irrational beliefs in a superficial fashion.* If you tell yourself, for instance, that you don't care what other people think of you, you are unlikely to be convinced. This is a variation of the positive-thinking trap — writing down positive thoughts, some of them unrealistic in themselves, without

confronting the irrational ones. These will still be there to do their worst, so make sure you believe what you are writing down.
- *You do your rethinking correctly but fail to put it into action.* Don't just change your thoughts: as part of your analysis write down what you are going to *do*. Then do it.
- *You get discouraged because the problem keeps recurring.* Do you feel better after doing an analysis, then get discouraged later when you find yourself feeling or behaving in the same old way? Remember: one analysis, or just a few, won't achieve permanent change. You will need to attack old thinking habits many times.
- *You don't understand what you are doing.* You may be rushing ahead to try self-analysis before you have gained an adequate grasp of the various steps. To get the most out of this book you will need to reread some sections.

Here is a tip. When doing your first half-dozen or so analyses, keep this chapter alongside. Before you begin each part of the analysis (*A*, *C*, *B*, *E*, *D* and *F*), reread the section of this chapter that refers to it. Skipping back and forth between the chapter and your analysis may seem laborious at first, but it will help you grasp the process faster than if you jump straight in. When you think you are getting the idea, move on to using the short check list below.

In addition, work through the training exercises in chapter 9. These will help you in a step-by-step manner. If you are having trouble motivating yourself, you may also find it helpful to read chapter 21.

Self-analysis check list

To conclude, here is a summary of the steps involved in completing a self-analysis:

Complete A and C first (start with either)
1. At *A*, record the *triggering event* or circumstance ('What started things off?').

2. At *C*, record your *reactions* ('What unwanted feelings did I experience?' 'What did I do that was unhelpful?').

At B, record your thoughts

1. Your *interpretations* ('What do I think has happened, is happening or may happen?'). Look for any *distortions of reality* (black-and-white thinking, filtering, overgeneralising, mind-reading, emotional reasoning, fortune-telling, personalising).
2. Your *evaluations* ('What does it mean to me?' 'How do I rate it?'). Look especially for:

   Demanding: 'What do I think should/shouldn't, must/mustn't happen?'
   Catastrophising: 'What do I think is awful or unbearable?'
   People-rating: 'What labels am I applying to myself or others?'

3. The *core beliefs* on which your evaluations are based (use the list of 12 irrational beliefs on pages 33–34 as a prompt).

   Remember: be honest with yourself.
   Do not write questions — make direct statements only.
   Be specific.
   Record thoughts, not feelings.
   Don't move on to the next step until you have identified your evaluations.

At E, record how you would prefer to feel/behave

When you come to D

1. Start by *questioning/disputing* your beliefs:

   Interpretations: 'What evidence is there to support (or disprove) my interpretations?' 'Are there any other possible explanations?'
   Evaluations: 'Why should/must things be the way I expect?' 'What's the worst that's likely to happen?' 'Where is the proof that I am hopeless/stupid/bad/etc.?'

2. Then write down *rational alternatives* to replace any irrational beliefs:
    Replace distortions with realistic thoughts.
    Replace demands with preferences.
    Replace catastrophising with moderate/in-perspective thinking.
    Replace people-rating with behaviour-rating.

At F, write down what you are going to do to reduce the chance of reacting the same way in future
    Reading
    Writing
    Behaving
    Practical problem-solving
    Any other creative actions you can devise

References
1. Froggatt, W., (2003). *FearLess: Your guide to overcoming anxiety.* Auckland: HarperCollins.

9 Learning self-analysis: practice exercises

The exercises in this chapter will help you learn self-analysis in a step-by-step fashion. Work through them in sequence, starting with number one. Restrict yourself to one section at a time and absorb each lesson thoroughly. Before you move on to the next exercise, check your answers with those at the end of the chapter. As you proceed, keep referring to the relevant sections of the previous chapter. This will help you connect each lesson with the part of the self-analysis process to which it applies.

Connecting events (As) and reactions (Cs)

The first step is to get used to linking your reactions (both feelings and behaviours) with the events or circumstances that start things off.

Exercise 1
Read each of the statements below and write down which part represents A and which C. The first has been completed as an example.

1. I feel lousy being picked up for drunk driving.
       A picked up for drunk driving   **C** feel lousy
2. I felt uncomfortable at the party.
3. When I saw Judy mistreated, I got angry.
4. I ran off when I saw them coming.
5. When she's not there, I'm so lonely.
6. I spent my whole week's pay at the hotel.
7. I felt guilty when I heard her name.
8. When John abused me, I just lashed out.

Exercise 2

Keep a diary of *A*s and *C*s for a week. It doesn't matter if the events you record are trivial: it is only for practice. Here is an example:

A *Circumstance/Event*	C *My reaction*
Daughter late home from date.	Worried. Rang boyfriend's parents.
Criticised at work.	Felt inferior. Avoided others at lunch time.

Identifying your beliefs (Bs)

Identifying your beliefs or thoughts is a little more difficult. One reason is that many beliefs are subconscious.

Separating beliefs from events and reactions

The next two exercises will help you get used to separating *B*s from *A*s and *C*s.

Exercise 3

Read each of the statements below. Write *A* next to those that describe events, *B* next to those that describe beliefs and *C* next to those that describe reactions (feelings and behaviours). The first three have been completed as example.

1. It's terrible to be treated like this. **B**
2. My daughter didn't come home until 2 a.m. **A**
3. I was upset and hurt. **C**
4. I was thinking about the way my father used to treat me.
5. She was trying to hurt me.
6. I stomped around the house.
7. I'm satisfied things have turned out for the best.
8. He should consider me more than he does.
9. It will be hard to find another job.
10. I felt sickened.
11. I saw an accident in which someone was killed.
12. It's not fair that he should be promoted ahead of me.

13. If I can't handle this, maybe I'm stupid.
14. I was made redundant eight months ago.
15. There are too many people bludging off the system.
16. I ran away.
17. They were planning to attack me.
18. I prefer to be punctual whenever I can.
19. I'm heading towards another breakdown.
20. Why shouldn't I be angry?
21. I'll never be happy again.
22. She's probably planning to leave me.
23. Without her love I'm nothing.
24. He looked angry.
25. I have no way of paying off these debts.

Exercise 4

Read each of the statements below and write down which part represents *A*, which *B* and which *C*. The first has been completed as an example.

1. I feel so angry. I shouldn't be treated like this — arrested just for having a few drinks.
   A arrested **B** I should not be treated like this **C** feel angry
2. I can't stand her rejecting me. Without her love I'm nothing. I took the pills because it's just hopeless.
3. Being made redundant is so depressing. I'll never get another job. I guess this proves how useless I am.
4. It makes me anxious to think about giving this talk. I've got to do it well, otherwise I'll be shown up as useless.
5. Anyone would be angry if they were treated as John treats me. He should know better.
6. When I see food I just have to eat it. I can't help myself.
7. I got angry when I saw it. It's not fair that this type of thing should happen.
8. I feel discouraged. I can't understand this therapy. Maybe this proves how inadequate I am.

Identifying interpretations and evaluations

As we saw in chapters 3 and 8, there are three levels of thinking to look for: (1) interpretations, (2) evaluations, (3) core beliefs. The next exercise will help you distinguish between the first two of these.

Exercise 5

Read the statements listed below. Write *I* next to those that are interpretations, and *E* next to those that are evaluations. The first two have been completed as examples. Note that not all of the beliefs expressed are irrational.

1. It's terrible to be treated like this. E
2. She was trying to hurt me. I
3. I'm satisfied things have turned out for the best.
4. He should consider me more than he does.
5. It will be hard to find another job.
6. It's not fair that he should be promoted ahead of me.
7. If I can't handle this, maybe I'm stupid.
8. There are too many people bludging off the system.
9. They were planning to attack me.
10. I prefer to be punctual whenever I can.
11. I'm heading towards another breakdown.
12. Why shouldn't I be angry?
13. I'll never be happy again.
14. She's probably planning to leave me.
15. Without her love I'm nothing.
16. He was angry.
17. I have no way of paying off these debts.

Exercise 6

This exercise will help you see how you tend to interpret and evaluate events and circumstances. For the next week or so, observe what happens around you, including what you see on television or read in the newspaper. Record in a diary some of the things you react to, then for each one write down (1) your interpretation, and (2) your evaluation. Here are some examples:

Event	*My interpretation*	*How I evaluate it*
News: interest rates going up.	Our mortgage will increase.	That's terrible.
Watched documentary about smoking and cancer.	They're exaggerating the link between smoking and cancer.	They shouldn't be allowed to upset people by showing things like this.

Learning self-analysis: practice exercises

Event	My interpretation	How I evaluate it
Had fight with son over homework.	I was unreasonable.	I'd do better to learn how to handle my temper.

Exercise 7

This exercise will help you understand the difference between interpretations and evaluations by identifying the types of irrational thinking that are involved in each case. Remember: irrational interpretations are usually *distortions of reality*; irrational evaluations involve *demanding, catastrophising* and *people-rating*.

Below is a list of interpretations and evaluations. Alongside write *DR* for distorting reality, *C* for catastrophising, *D* for demanding and *PR* for people-rating. Some items don't contain any irrational thinking — write *R* for these. Note that some irrational thinking is stated indirectly.

1. It's terrible to be treated like this.
2. I must be a real neurotic to behave like that.
3. I'll never be able to love anyone again.
4. He should consider me more than he does.
5. I simply have to eat whenever I feel hungry.
6. Everything's going wrong.
7. If I can't handle this, maybe I'm stupid.
8. There are too many people bludging off the system.
9. I guess I'm just lazy.
10. I prefer to be punctual whenever I can.
11. She hurt me.
12. Without her love I'm nothing.
13. What a rat he is.
14. I can't stand to be put down in public.
15. I've simply got to have that new car.
16. Why shouldn't I be angry?
17. I'm satisfied things have turned out for the best.
18. It's not fair that he should be promoted ahead of me.
19. I can't stand it when people treat me like this.
20. I don't like being abused.

Identifying misinterpretations
The next exercise will help increase your understanding of the various ways in which it is possible to misinterpret an event or circumstance.

Exercise 8 (distortions of reality)
Each of the statements below is an interpretation. Some are rational, others are distortions (misinterpretations) of reality. Decide which statements are rational (write *R*) and which are not; and for the latter, which type of distortion is involved — black-and-white thinking (write *BW*), filtering (*F*), overgeneralising (*OG*), mind-reading (*MR*), fortune-telling (*FT*), emotional reasoning (*ER*) or personalising (*P*). See chapter 4 for a description of each type.

1. If I drink and then drive, I stand a good chance of losing my licence for a long time.
2. Things are never going to come right.
3. I guess that if she's gone off me, I must have done something wrong.
4. He's always messing things up.
5. She deliberately set out to hurt me — why else would I be angry?
6. I can't see anything good about the world today.
7. He said that because he wanted to get back at me.
8. It's either right or it's wrong — there's nothing in between.
9. Life is a mixture of good and bad.
10. I feel so anxious I just know something bad is going to happen.
11. She's only doing this to prove how superior she is.
12. I only passed that exam because of luck.
13. There's only one reason some people are poor — they're lazy.
14. If I can't handle this job, I'll never be any good at anything.
15. He's going to end up a permanent dead loss.
16. If I don't act on this reminder, they may sue me — then I'll end up with court costs as well.
17. There's very little in life you can be absolutely certain about.
18. I wouldn't be depressed if my situation wasn't hopeless.
19. You hate me, don't you?
20. If I stay home today, the boss will forget about that mistake I made at work yesterday.
21. Nothing's going right for me these days.
22. You can't care for someone and still be angry with them.

23. I'll never get on top of these bad feelings.
24. She must have had to take the day off sick because I criticised her.

Identifying irrational evaluations

The following three exercises will help you learn how to recognise the three types of irrational thinking that can be involved when you are evaluating something in terms of what it means to you. It is important to have a good understanding of demanding, catastrophising and people-rating as they are the main causes of most dysfunctional emotions and behaviours.

Exercise 9 (demanding)

As we saw in chapter 5, the rational alternative to a demand is a *preference*. The list below consists of a mixture of demands and preferences. Decide which type each item is (write *D* or *P*). Don't get confused because you may disagree with some of the statements.

1. I must not make a fool of myself on Saturday night.
2. I'd like to see you do better.
3. You've got to do the best you can.
4. Everyone needs to be loved by someone else.
5. I'd do better to change the way I deal with stress.
6. This just isn't good enough.
7. I want more than you're giving me.
8. I'd rather you stopped doing that.
9. We'd be better off if we separated.
10. I ought to be able to handle my children more calmly.
11. Why don't we try it this way?
12. I need to be accepted for what I am.
13. Children should show respect for their parents.
14. I have to find a better way.
15. I want to achieve the best result I can.
16. People should be able to handle their own problems.
17. I wish people would stop the way they're going on.
18. You'd better get your teeth attended to soon.
19. I must take the car in to be checked.
20. It's not fair when other people take without giving back.
21. People would be happier if they quit their sinful living.

Check your answers with those at the end of the chapter (p. 114). If you have got any wrong, reread chapter 5 and work out why. There are a few statements in the list designed to make you think particularly carefully. In some, for example, the demand is not stated explicitly, but they are still based on the idea that things should be a certain way. Other statements may read like demands at first but are in fact rational because they don't insist that people should or must act on them.

Exercise 10 (catastrophising)
Some of the statements below are rational, others are examples of catastrophising. Decide which are rational (write *R*) and for the rest, identify the different kinds of catastrophising — awfulising (*A*) and can't-stand-it-itis (*CSI*). See chapter 6 for a description of each kind.

1. I can't hack it when people are late.
2. It's uncomfortable to be criticised in public.
3. What a ghastly thing to happen.
4. I don't like it when things don't go as I expect.
5. Things are simply unbearable.
6. I couldn't imagine anything worse.
7. I find aggressive confrontations highly unpleasant.
8. I can't bear the thought of looking a fool in public.
9. This is terrible.
10. I feel uneasy in situations like this.

Exercise 11 (people-rating)
This exercise will help you recognise people-rating and compare it with the rational alternative of *behaviour-rating*. You may find it helpful to reread chapter 7 first; then read each statement below and decide whether it is an evaluation of a person (*PR*) or of a behaviour (*BR*).

1. I'm a failure.
2. That was a naughty thing to do.
3. I've gone and done it again! What type of idiot am I?
4. She's neurotic the way she goes on.
5. I've failed.
6. He's a really good guy giving up his time like that.

7. You don't really mean that, you hypocrite.
8. I must be stupid to have failed that exam.
9. I behaved badly.
10. My social skills are rather poor.
11. I feel good about myself.
12. I've really messed up here.
13. He's just lazy. That's why his homework isn't done.
14. I'm a dead loss.
15. Only a hardened criminal would do a thing like that.
16. You're a naughty child.
17. I'd better learn how to handle my emotional problems.
18. Compared with most people, I'm not a success.
19. I feel anxious most of the time.
20. That job will be no problem for me.
21. I'm not very good at handling my children.
22. Let me do it. I can handle it.
23. I keep repeating the same old neurotic behaviour.
24. I can usually manage to cope very well.
25. I'd hate others to see me as a failure.
26. If I fail, I'll end up feeling bad about myself.
27. I can handle it.

Identifying core beliefs

An evaluation usually reflects a core belief to which you subconsciously adhere. Take the evaluation 'I shouldn't have to put up with this.' It reflects an underlying rule such as 'The world should always treat me fairly.' Most irrational thinking is based on a small number of core beliefs. We saw a list of these, 12 in all, in chapter 3 — here it is again:

1. I need love and approval from those significant to me, and I must avoid disapproval from any source.
2. To be worthwhile as a person I must achieve, succeed at whatever I do, and make no mistakes.
3. People should always do the right thing. When they behave obnoxiously, unfairly or selfishly, they must be blamed and punished.
4. Things must be the way I want them to be, otherwise life will be intolerable.
5. My unhappiness is caused by things that are outside my control, so there's little I can do to feel any better.

6. I must worry about things that could be dangerous, unpleasant or frightening, otherwise they might happen.
7. I can be happier by avoiding life's difficulties, unpleasantnesses and responsibilities.
8. Everyone needs to depend on someone stronger than themselves.
9. Events in my past are the cause of my problems, and they continue to influence my feelings and behaviours now.
10. I should become upset when other people have problems and feel unhappy when they're sad.
11. I shouldn't have to feel discomfort and pain. I can't stand them and must avoid them at all costs.
12. Every problem should have an ideal solution, and it's intolerable when one can't be found.

Exercise 12

Decide which of the 12 irrational beliefs is reflected by each of the evaluative thoughts listed below. Write the number of the belief alongside each one. The first two have been completed as examples.

1. Because I was put down as a child, I can never have confidence in myself. *9*
2. He's a real bastard for doing that. He should be put away for good. *3*
3. I'm not getting the encouragement and support I need to even survive in my job, much less do it properly.
4. How can I be happy with a wife like I'm married to?
5. I've got a pain in the stomach from worrying whether my son will fail his final exams. But I can't afford to stop thinking about it.
6. This self-help stuff is just too hard. I must find an easier way. Why can't my doctor give me some pills?
7. I can't stand the way my girlfriend handles her money. Why won't she let me show her how to do it properly?
8. When he hurts, I have to hurt. That's what love's all about.
9. I can't see the point in doing all this self-analysis. All it does is make me feel worse, so why bother?
10. I'd end up feeling terrible about myself if I started this course and then failed. So I'll leave it.
11. We missed the house that was our first choice. I could never be happy here.
12. I'll never survive now Mike's left me. I'll have to find another guy.

Exercise 13
Go back to exercise 6. Work out, in each case, what rule you are operating by and write it down. Note there are no right or wrong answers: this is just to give you practice in detecting underlying rules.

Exercise 14
Keep a diary of *A*s, *C*s and *B*s for a week or so. This will give you practice in working out what you tell yourself when you feel and behave in unwanted ways. Record the event or circumstance (*A*), your reaction (feelings and behaviours — *C*) and your thoughts (*B*). Here is an example:

A	B	C
Circumstance/Event	*Thoughts*	*My reaction*
Daughter late home from date.	They've had an accident.	Worried. Rang boyfriend's parents.
Criticised at work.	I'm a failure. Everyone thinks I'm an idiot. I couldn't face them.	Felt inferior. Avoided others at lunchtime.

Disputing and replacing irrational beliefs

Now you are ready to learn how you can replace irrational beliefs with rational ideas. There are two important steps here: *disputing* and *substituting*.

Reread the section on disputing in chapter 8. This will remind you about the questions to ask when disputing both interpretations and evaluations. Then try the following exercises:

Exercise 15
Go back over the statements in exercise 12 and dispute each one (don't forget to use the three key disputing questions), then formulate and write down a new rational belief. Compare what you write with the example answers on page 115.

Exercise 16
Review the list of 12 irrational beliefs on page 33. For each, consider and write down what you think is a rational alternative. Compare your ideas with the list of 12 rational alternatives on page 41.

Exercise 17
Go back over your diary of *A*s, *C*s and *B*s (exercise 14). Try disputing the beliefs involved. Remember that checking out interpretations requires slightly different questions from checking out evaluations (see pages 82–83).

Designing action strategies

In section *F* of Rational Self-Analysis you decide what actions you will take to stop yourself thinking and reacting irrationally in future. A number of suggestions are given on pages 83–86, and there are more in Part II, where self-analysis is applied to specific problem areas. Here are a couple of exercises to help you get the idea:

Exercise 18
On the left below is a list of common problems. The right-hand list is of possible helpful action strategies. Match each problem with the most appropriate strategy. Note that there may be more than one 'correct' answer, as there can be more than one solution to a problem.

Problems	*Strategies*
1. You feel guilty about treating yourself to nice things.	a. Do an assertiveness training course.
2. You worry about not getting things done and falling behind.	b. Have a long soak in the bath every night for a week.
3. You get anxious in social situations.	c. Next time you buy a personal item, such as clothing, don't consult anyone else.

Problems

4. You often fit in with what other people want, then resent it.

5. You often find it hard to communicate with others in social situations.

6. You tend to lose your cool when others disagree with you.

7. You worry about other people disapproving of you.

8. You don't trust your own opinions.

9. You believe that other people generally see you in a negative light.

10. You often get defensive when someone criticises you.

11. You often have trouble making decisions about how to spend your time and money.

12. You often overdo things because you think everything has to be done to perfection.

Strategies

d. Practise trying to see other people's point of view.

e. Get a good book on time management.

f. Vacuum the house no more than once a week.

g. Make a list of your goals and aims in life. Update the list regularly.

h. Do or say something you think is right for you, but which you know someone know else will disagree with.

i. Do a training course in social skills.

j. Attend the next party you are invited to.

k. Ask other people to explain when they make comments about you.

l. Ask other people what they are really thinking.

Exercise 19

Go back over your diary entries in exercise 14. Design an action strategy for each irrational belief you subsequently disputed in exercise 17.

Using the whole analysis

Now it is time to start using the whole Rational Self-Analysis. To add *E*, simply record how you feel after disputing and replacing your irrational beliefs.

Reread chapter 8 and go to it. Here are some full-length examples:

A **What started things off**
   Woke up this morning feeling a bit down.

C **Reaction**

   Feelings: more down than ever, anxious
   Behaviour: stayed in bed all morning.

B **Beliefs about A that caused my reaction**
   1. Oh, no — I'm getting depressed again.
   2. I'm going to feel worse and worse as the day goes on.
   3. There's no point in getting up because I'll never be able to cope.
   4. I can't stand discomfort and pain, so I have to avoid them at all costs.

E **How I would prefer to feel/behave**
   Get up and start some useful activity that will lift my mood.

D **New, rational beliefs about A**
   1. I'm not depressed, just a bit down.
   2. How do I know I'm going to get worse? I might feel better if I get up and about and do something useful.
   3. There's no evidence I won't be able to cope. Even if I were depressed, I could still do most things (even if not as well as I might like).
   4. I don't like emotional pain, but I can stand it. After all, I've survived it before. If I get up and face the day when I feel like this, I can get active and get my mind off how bad I feel.

F **What I'll do to avoid repeating the same irrational thoughts and reactions**
   1. Reread the chapters on distorting reality and catastrophising.
   2. Use a rational card on the core belief (number 4).
   3. From now on, each morning I wake up feeling down, I'll get up straightaway to avoid lying in bed and mulling over it.

LEARNING SELF-ANALYSIS: PRACTICE EXERCISES

A What started things off
Son refused to do his homework.

C Reaction
Feelings: angry, upset.
Behaviour: yelled and screamed.

B Beliefs about A that caused my reaction
1. He must always do as he's told without arguing.
2. I shouldn't have to nag him about his homework.
3. He's a lazy little brat.
4. He'll fail totally at school, never get a job, and end up as a dole bludger and delinquent.
5. People should always do the best they can. When they don't, they need to be brought to task and punished.

E How I would prefer to feel/behave
I would prefer to feel concerned, and to stop and think about better ways of handling the problem of his disobedience.

D New, rational beliefs about A
1. I'd prefer him to obey me, but telling myself that he 'must' only makes me lose my cool.
2. I don't 'have' to nag — I choose to. I'll keep doing it, but remind myself that it's a choice.
3. He's not a lazy brat, he only behaves lazily at times. Evaluating him as a total person only makes me angrier than I need to be — and it may even encourage him to live down to the label I put on him!
4. I'm exaggerating here. There's no evidence all these bad things will happen.
5. It's a good thing for people to do their best, but there's no 'Law of the Universe' that says we have to perform to the maximum at all times.

F What I'll do to avoid repeating the same irrational thoughts and reactions
1. Do some work on anger control — starting with reading the chapter on anger management.
2. Sit down and have a proper talk with him. Calmly try and help him see that not working now may reduce his happiness later in life.
3. See his teacher, and devise some sensible penalties if homework is not in on time and up to scratch.

A What started things off
Laid off from my job.

C Reaction
Feelings: depressed, discouraged.
Behaviour: stayed around home, didn't do anything, avoided friends.

B Beliefs about A that caused my reaction
1. Being made redundant proves I'm a failure.
2. People will see me as an unemployed bum, and I couldn't stand that.
3. To be worthwhile as a person, I must achieve, succeed, make no significant mistakes, and have the approval of other people.

E How I would prefer to feel/behave
I would prefer to feel (1) disappointed about losing my job, and (2) concerned about the future; and to begin taking some small steps to do what I can about finding a new job.

D New, rational beliefs about A
1. Being selected for redundancy is a bad event, but proves nothing about me as a person.
2. Some people may like me less because I'm unemployed. But I can stand this, even though I may not like it.
3. Failing to succeed and not getting approval from others proves nothing about my total self. I'm still the same person I was before I received my redundancy notice.

F What I'll do to avoid repeating the same irrational thoughts and reactions
1. Reread the chapter on self-rating.
2. Use a rational card on belief number 3.
3. Start looking for a new job.
4. Get my family to challenge me whenever they see me self-rating over this.
5. Use the extra spare time I've got at the moment to do those jobs round the house I've been wanting to get round to.

Answers to exercises

Exercise 1

1. **A** picked up for drunk driving **C** feel lousy
2. **A** at the party **C** felt very uncomfortable
3. **A** saw Judy mistreated **C** got angry
4. **A** saw them coming **C** ran off
5. **A** when she's not there **C** I'm so lonely
6. **A** at the hotel **C** spent my whole week's pay
7. **A** when I heard her name **C** felt guilty
8. **A** John abused me **C** lashed out

Exercise 3

1. B	2. A	3. C	4. A	5. B
6. C	7. B	8. B	9. B	10. C
11. A	12. B	13. B	14. A	15. B
16. C	17. B	18. B	19. B	20. B
21. B	22. B	23. B	24. A	25. B

Exercise 4

1. **A** arrested **B** I should not be treated like this **C** feel angry
2. **A** rejected **B** I can't stand her rejecting me. Without her love I'm nothing. It's hopeless. **C** took pills
3. **A** made redundant **B** I'll never get another job. This proves how useless I am. **C** depressed
4. **A** thinking about giving the talk **B** I've got to do it well, otherwise I'll be shown up as useless. **C** anxious
5. **A** John's treatment of me **B** He should know better. **C** angry
6. **A** see food **B** I can't help myself. I just have to eat it. **C** eat the food
7. **A** saw it **B** It's not fair **C** got angry
8. **A** can't understanding this therapy **B** this proves how inadequate I am **C** feel discouraged

Exercise 5

1. E	2. I	3. E	4. E	5. I
6. E	7. E	8. E	9. I	10. E
11. I	12. E	13. I	14. I	15. E
16. I	17. I			

Exercise 7

1. C	2. PR	3. DR	4. D	5. D
6. DR	7. PR	8. D	9. PR	10. R
11. DR	12. PR	13. PR	14. C	15. D
16. D	17. R	18. D	19. C	20. R

Exercise 8

1. R	2. FT	3. P	4. OG	5. ER
6. F	7. MR	8. BW	9. R	10. ER
11. MR	12. F	13. BW	14. OG	15. FT
16. R	17. R	18. ER	19. MR	20. F
21. OG	22. BW	23. FT	24. P	

Exercise 9

1. D	2. P	3. D	4. D	5. P
6. D	7. P	8. P	9. P	10. D
11. P	12. D	13. D	14. D	15. P
16. D	17. P	18. P	19. D	20. D
21. P				

Exercise 10

1. CSI	2. R	3. A	4. R	5. CSI
6. A	7. R	8. CSI	9. A	10. R

Exercise 11

1. PR	2. BR	3. PR	4. PR	5. BR
6. PR	7. PR	8. PR	9. BR	10. BR
11. PR	12. BR	13. PR	14. PR	15. PR
16. PR	17. BR	18. PR	19. BR	20. BR
21. BR	22. BR	23. BR	24. BR	25. PR
26. PR	27. BR			

Exercise 12

1. 9	2. 3	3. 1	4. 5	5. 6
6. 11	7. 4	8. 10	9. 7	10. 2
11. 12	12. 8			

Exercise 15

These answers are only examples. There is usually more than one way to dispute a particular irrational belief.

1. I may have been put down as a child, but I'm an adult now — and I can use my adult brain to learn how to stop evaluating myself. What controls me is not my past, rather what I think in the present.
2. I don't like what he did, but that doesn't make him totally (and nothing but) a 'bastard'. It simply means he is a person who has done a bastardly thing.
3. It's good to get encouragement and support, but making them absolutely necessary for me to carry out my job properly is setting myself up for failure. Better I keep them as preferences and learn to get on without them when they're not available.
4. I don't like my wife's behaviour, but she doesn't cause my feelings — I do. I could learn to be happy, in spite of her actions, if I chose to.
5. I can be concerned about my son failing, but without worrying (which doesn't change anything anyway).
6. This self-help stuff is hard, but I can stand it. It's also worth the pain, because I'll be better off in the long run.
7. I wish she'd listen to me, but there's no reason why she has to. I don't like the way she handles her money, but I can stand it.
8. I don't like it when he hurts, but getting myself upset too isn't going to help him learn to handle his emotions.
9. It would be easier in the short term to stop looking at myself, but I'd be better off in the long run to stick with it and learn how to cope.
10. Failure wouldn't make me any less a person, but worrying about failure does stop me from trying. Better I accept that making mistakes is simply part of learning and not an indication of me as a total person.
11. Things aren't ideal, but this doesn't mean I can't get some enjoyment out of life. Anyway, there's no point in making it worse.
12. Even though it will be hard at first, I can learn to survive on my own. And if I was less dependent on other people, I could probably form more satisfying relationships.

Exercise 18

1. b
2. e
3. j
4. a
5. i
6. d
7. h
8. c
9. l
10. k
11. g
12. f

Part II

Applying self-analysis to life's common problems

Introduction

The skills you learned in Part I can help you with just about any unwanted emotion or behaviour. In Part II we will see how they can be applied to some of the more common of life's problems.

Most chapters follow a similar format. First, the problem is described. Then typical triggers and reactions that can be used to identify it are noted. Next, the types of thinking most likely to be involved are reviewed, and rational alternatives discussed. Finally, possible strategies for moving from rethinking to action are considered.

Here is a list of common problems and the chapter or chapters most relevant to each:

aggressive or violent behaviour	13, 15
anger	13
anxiety	10
avoidance	10
circumstances you dislike	18
criticism and disapproval from others	14
decision-making	17
depression	12
fear	10
guilt	11
jealousy	13
lack of goals or direction in life	17
low self-confidence	14
manipulation by others	11, 15
motivating yourself	12, 21
obsessive behaviour	16
panic	10
perfectionism	16
performance fears	10, 14, 16

Introduction

phobias	10
procrastination	17, 18, 21
problems you cannot solve	18
resentment	13
self-downing	11
shame	14
stress	19
tension	10
trapped feelings	17
unassertiveness	15
unrealistic expectations	16
worry	10

10 What are you really afraid of?

'Fears are educated into us, and can, if we wish, be educated out,' wrote Karl Menninger in *The Human Mind*.[1] And who better, I would add, to do the re-educating than we ourselves?

Fear is a way of thinking. To say that you are afraid means you believe that something bad is going to happen. Fear is usually associated with a number of symptoms known collectively as *anxiety*. The more common of these include feeling shaky, getting short of breath, sweating, a pounding heart, an increased pulse rate, headaches, an upset stomach, muscles tightening up (tension), poor concentration and restlessness.

Fear and anxiety are two sides of the same coin. Fear is the *thought*, anxiety is the *feeling* which results. Anxiety is like a warning bell. Unfortunately, it often goes off when there is no real danger. When this happens, we call the fear irrational.

You can learn how to handle your fears without the anxiety alarm taking over. Fear, as we have seen, is a way of thinking: if you analyse your thoughts when you feel anxious, you can uncover and change the beliefs that make you afraid.

Know when your fear is irrational

Not all fear is irrational. When it is in response to real danger and keeps you careful and alert, it can be functional. Suppose that someone is about to attack you: fear could help by preparing your muscles for defence or flight.

But fear can get out of hand. Too much fear could freeze your muscles: then you would be less able to protect yourself. Furthermore, our fears are often out of proportion to any real physical dangers. Many of the things people fear involve social situations — performing badly, being rejected by other people and so on.

What are you really afraid of?

Irrational fear often shows up as *worrying*. You are afraid of something in advance and keep mulling it over without doing anything constructive. You may have little evidence that it will ever actually occur. It could even be something you cannot do much about, but you still worry.

Irrational fear can also show up in a more extreme fashion: as dread directed toward a specific object or situation. In such cases the fear is well out of proportion to the actual danger, and is sometimes called a *phobia*. People can develop extreme fears toward all sorts of things: closed spaces, open spaces, high places, being alone, being in a crowd, animals, the dark, blood, contamination or germs, thunder or lightning, pain, fire — to name but a few. One out of every 10 people has suffered from a phobia at some time in their lives.[2]

Keep an *ABC* diary for a while. This will clue you in to the extent of your anxiety and help you become more aware of what tends to trigger it. To pick out your irrational fears, watch for reactions like the following:

- Your anxiety is significantly affecting your life.
- You experience symptoms of anxiety when there is little or no evidence of real physical danger.
- You start with a more-or-less reasonable concern but mull it over and over instead of doing something about it, and pile more and more worries on top of it.

Look for fear-inducing beliefs

It is not always easy to get rid of irrational fear, because often we don't realise what it is we are afraid of. We think, for instance, that we fear rejection, violence or losing a loved one. But this isn't quite correct. What we really fear is how we will *feel* if we are rejected, assaulted or bereaved. In other words, *we are often afraid of our own emotions*. There are many feelings we might want to avoid, but two in particular seem to account for all our fears: discomfort and self-devaluation.

The fear of discomfort

Discomfort anxiety occurs when we perceive some threat to our physical or emotional comfort (or even our existence). Many things can trigger this fear.

Some people worry about their children. Others feel uncomfortable at the thought of financial insecurity or the possibility of having plans and hopes frustrated. Many fear specific objects and situations. They expect to feel highly upset if faced with such things as heights, dogs, flying, earthquakes, water, fire, crowds, being alone or being trapped. Many people dislike physical pain, to the extent that the drugs used to control it are a multimillion-dollar business. Many are so afraid of the dentist they won't go until it is too late to avoid extractions or other extensive work. Poor health and growing old are events we often associate with discomfort. Perhaps the final fear is of death: some people are so bothered about dying they don't enjoy living.

What kinds of thoughts create the fear of discomfort? They arise from a mixture of demanding and catastrophising:

> 'Life must be secure, orderly and predictable.'
> 'I must get what I want.'
> 'I must have the things I think I need.'
> 'I must not get what I don't want.'
> 'I must not experience discomfort.'
> 'I need to avoid situations in which I feel uncomfortable.'
> 'I should be able to live my life as I want to.'
> 'I must prepare for anything that may possibly go wrong.'
> 'It's terrible when I don't perform well.'
> 'It's disastrous when I don't get what I need.'
> 'I can't stand it when things go wrong.'

Do not underrate the power of demands to create anxiety. If we kept our values and desires as preferences, we would be just disappointed or concerned when they were not met. Turning them into absolute needs is what makes frustration seem catastrophic. It also creates an interesting phenomenon: the fear of fear. Because anxiety and its symptoms can be unpleasant, we get anxious about becoming anxious! This kind of 'secondary disturbance' can upset us even when nothing is going wrong. It can also lead us to avoid situations in which there is even the slightest risk of anxiety being triggered.

The fear of self-devaluation

Self-devaluation anxiety occurs when we think that our view of ourselves or our personal 'worth' is in question. Events or circumstances that may trigger this fear include:

- Failing.
- Criticism or disapproval from others.
- Losing control (not being able to cope with everyday tasks, requiring help, the thought of becoming insane, behaving in ways that leave one feeling humiliated).
- Being unattractive or overweight, or showing signs of aging.
- Having a disability.
- Anything else that we think might lead to rejection or self-downing.

The fear of self-devaluation is based on the idea that we must meet certain expectations of ourselves in order to justify our existence. This may lead to thoughts like the following:

'To be happy, I have to see myself as a worthwhile human being.'
'To be worthwhile, I should do well at whatever I try and succeed with my life generally, and must get approval and recognition from other people.'
'Because love and approval are *needs*, it is awful when I am deprived of them.'
'If I don't perform well or if I fail at something important, I will be *a failure*.'
'Other people must not see me in a bad light.'
'I couldn't stand to fail at something important, have others disapprove of or reject me, or for any reason at all end up feeling that I was not worthwhile.'

You might find it hard to admit to beliefs like these. Because self-rating is so unpleasant, people often deny to themselves that they are doing it. Be brutally honest about those labels you are putting on yourself.

Watch out for another type of self-labelling, too. If you think of yourself as a '—phobic', 'worrier' or 'neurotic', you set yourself up to feel and behave accordingly. Don't say, 'I'm an agoraphobic' — this diverts attention from working on the problem itself (disruptive avoidance behaviour) to rating yourself. Instead say, 'I fear being in public places, doing something stupid and being put down by other people.' This will enable you to focus on specific *behaviours* that you can work at changing.

Understand the fear of your own feelings

Fear of discomfort and fear of self-devaluation often overlap. You may, for example, fear the discomfort involved in going to the dentist, but also worry about appearing a coward in front of others at the surgery and putting yourself down for this. In addition, as we have seen, both types of fear represent a fear of our own feelings. We are not afraid of such and such happening: what we are afraid of is how we will *feel* if it happens.

How do we become afraid of our own feelings? As we saw in chapter 7, self-rating seems to come naturally. Learning adds to it. For example, we soon pick up the fear of guilt — supposedly as a way of keeping ourselves under control.

Humans also have an innate desire to predict what goes on around them. We want to control our environment to get more of what we want and less of what we don't want. Social and technological advances fuel this tendency. We enjoy increasing standards of living, and medical science becomes progressively more able to help people avoid physical and emotional pain. As a result, we have come to expect to feel good all the time. Emotional comfort no longer seems just desirable: in our minds it has become a 'must'.

Specific episodes of irrational fear can be triggered by misinterpreting events and circumstances. *Distortions of reality* like the following are commonly involved in anxiety:

- 'Everything's going wrong', 'There's no hope.' (*overgeneralising*)
- 'I'll never be able to cope', 'Things are going to get worse', 'I'll faint, and people will think . . .' (*fortune-telling*)
- 'It scares me', 'She gets me upset when she stays out so late', 'If I'm worrying there must be a good reason.' (*emotional reasoning*)

One common distortion involved in irrational fear is the idea that worrying about something will stop it happening or, conversely, that not worrying will result in bad things creeping up. This belief is one of the reasons many people find worrying difficult to give up — the thought of doing so induces anxiety!

When you are in a state of fear, ask yourself, 'What am I imagining might happen?' Look for a chain of thoughts like, 'She's late home . . . She's had an accident . . . She could be dead or maimed for life . . . I could never cope with that . . . I'll be unhappy for the rest of my life . . .', and so on. Fearful ideas often run in sequences like this, with one thought leading to another (usually more extreme) thought. Be honest. Uncover these distortions — even though you are tempted to deny them when you realise how exaggerated they are.

Identify your fears

Sometimes you may be anxious but find it hard to identify what you are thinking. Here are some techniques to use:

- *Try getting into the situation you are afraid of.* This will help you become aware of the thoughts involved. You can sometimes get a similar effect by using your imagination: see yourself in your mind's eye, as vividly as possible, going to the place or event you fear or doing the thing you have been avoiding.
- *Look for the consequences.* Keep in mind that when you are afraid of an event, what you are really concerned about is what will happen and how you will feel if it occurs. A dread of heart attacks, for example, represents a fear of discomfort (pain, suffering, restricted lifestyle and possibly death). If you fear going

to the supermarket, the real alarm is probably that you will collapse and need help, and that other people will think you are a mental case.

Make a point, therefore, of asking yourself, 'What do I fear will result if such and such happens?' Look for the fear of discomfort and the fear of self-devaluation. Be as specific as possible, and don't forget, as we have seen, that worrying thoughts often run in chains.

- *Look for the meanings*. Remember: misinterpreting what is happening will not by itself make you anxious. It is the irrational *evaluations* that do the damage — those demands, catastrophisings and self-ratings — so make sure that you go beyond your surface interpretations (e.g. 'People will think I'm a mental case') to your underlying meanings ('I'll feel awful', 'It would prove I'm a hopeless case', 'This would be dreadful', 'It mustn't happen to me', 'I couldn't stand it', and the like).

From fear to rational concern

How do you overcome the fear of your own feelings — and, in turn, the fear of specific events and circumstances? Here are four self-treatment aims that will help you get there:

1. Learn to accept discomfort as unpleasant rather than awful and unbearable.
2. Learn to accept yourself regardless of your performance or how others view you or treat you.
3. Work on the things you fear by confronting rather than avoiding them.
4. Adopt the principle of *rational concern* in your approach to life and its hassles.

Increase your tolerance for discomfort

Fear and discomfort are a normal part of life. They are only irrational when they disable you, which is more likely to happen when you tell yourself you cannot stand them. Of course you don't *like* discomfort

— but thinking that you 'must' avoid it at all costs will itself make you uncomfortable.

Give up the idea that you should be able to feel good all the time. Learn to tolerate unpleasant feelings. Find out how to change them but without demanding you avoid them entirely. When you are confident you can handle bad feelings and know that you can stand them, they will bother you less in the first place.

Value security, for instance, but accept you can survive when the unexpected occurs. Try hard to get the things you want, but don't tell yourself that you 'need' and 'must have' them. Try to do well at whatever you set your hand to, but without demanding that you always succeed. See failure or disapproval as facts of life you can live with.

Ask, 'Why is such and such terrible, rather than unpleasant?', 'What makes this a disaster, rather than a disappointment?', 'Would it be so awful if . . . ?' Don't pretend that everything is wonderful. Acknowledge that some things are unpleasant, uncomfortable and inconvenient — just don't make them into anything more.

Confront specific fears

If you are afraid of specific things, such as giving talks, speaking to strangers, sitting exams or flying, try the *blow-up* technique. Exaggerate your fear out of all proportion, to the point where you cannot help being amused by it. Laughing at your fears is a good way to control them.

This worked for Rick. He worried about making a fool of himself in front of the selection panel for a job he wanted, so he imagined being late for the interview, rushing into the room, tripping and falling flat on his face, standing up to discover his belt had broken and his trousers fallen down, being arrested for indecent exposure, and having his name on the front page of every newspaper in the country. Going to the interview with this absurd scenario in his mind helped counter his anxiety.

Observe that while you dislike them, you can stand unpleasant events and feelings. Witness the fact that you are still alive to tell the tale. Note, too, that if you learn to live with something rather than try to avoid it, most often it will bother you less.

If you have suffered (or fear) a loss you think you cannot survive, *time projection* (see chapter 12) can help you get the future into perspective.

If there is something specific you are afraid of, *coping rehearsal* may be a useful technique. Do a full Rational Self-Analysis, then imagine yourself facing the thing you fear. Be aware of the feelings and irrational beliefs involved. See yourself replacing your beliefs with more rational thoughts, experiencing the more helpful emotions that follow, and acting more in the way you would like.

Audrey found this helpful. Her job as a consultant advising on business restructuring involved some public speaking, which she had always found hard. She did a self-analysis and devised some strong, rational alternatives to her main irrational belief (that she must never make mistakes and be seen as incompetent). She then imagined speaking to a large group of people, standing in front of them, thinking her fear-inducing thoughts, disputing these using her new rational thoughts, and handling her talk in a calm and competent manner. After practising this daily for several weeks, she became less fearful.

As you challenge exaggerated thinking, don't fall into the trap of so-called 'positive thinking'. Telling yourself that everything is all right won't work for long. In the real world bad things happen along with the good — so acknowledge unpleasant realities but keep them in perspective.

Accept yourself

Keep yourself in perspective, too. As long as you believe you have to be a 'worthwhile' person, you will be at risk of worrying about the chance of something happening that will lead you to think you aren't one. Unless you are an unusual human being who can somehow succeed at everything you try and constantly meet your own and others' expectations, sooner or later you will fail at something, or someone will disapprove of you.

What is the best way to deal with this fear of self-devaluation? Give up the idea that you have to be worthwhile. If you have already studied chapter 7, this won't sound such a strange idea. Remember, also, to dispute any self-rating that perpetuates your fearfulness: learn to see yourself not as 'a worrier', rather as a person who sometimes worries (and who is going to learn how to worry less in future).

Check out what you fear might happen

Although your interpretations won't be the main cause of your anxious episodes (your evaluations will be), it is still worth checking them out. Query your beliefs about what is happening. How much, in reality, is going wrong for you? What is the worst that could happen? What evidence is there for believing this? How likely is it? A good way to get things into perspective is to rate the chances on a scale of zero to 100 per cent.

The *'So what if'* technique can also be useful. Write down your worry as follows: '*What if* I make the wrong decision/am criticised/don't get a pay rise/etc.?' Then add '*So*' and answer the question.

Helen did this. At first she was relieved when her unhappy marriage of 24 years ended, but then she began to worry about coping: 'What if I can't handle a cheque book? What if I feel lonely at nights? What if men start wanting to get involved? What if the car needs repairing?' She then asked herself, 'So what if I can't handle a cheque book? The worst that could happen is that I face the inconvenience of paying cash, or maybe getting someone to show me how.'

Learn to keep worrying under control

It may be useful at times to remind yourself that worrying isn't worth it. If you are reluctant to give up your worry habit because you think that it somehow helps you, run through the disadvantages involved:

Fear will limit your lifestyle if you make a habit of avoiding anything that might lead to anxiety. Furthermore, if you worry about your own performance, you will increase the chance of failure. Anxiety can disrupt many activities: sex, examinations, effectiveness at work, to name but a few. A surprisingly high proportion of people restrict their lives out of fear of becoming a crime victim.[3]

Worrying about a problem will also block you from solving it. Instead of doing something, you will just keep stewing.

Fear may lead you to avoid important realities. Getting early medical or dental treatment can save you pain, whereas leaving it may cost you. It might be comfortable now to put off the pain of changing your diet and exercising, but it won't be comfortable in the long run.

Consider what anxiety and tension do to your body. They can cause stomach ulcers, heart problems, breathing difficulties, high blood pressure, loss of energy and other physical problems. Worrying can keep you awake at night — it drains emotional energy. Your fear won't do anything to make tomorrow better, but it may disable you today. This is one of the main drawbacks of worrying about the future: it disturbs us in the present, whether or not the things we fear ever come to pass!

Is it possible, though, to stop worrying without putting your head in the sand when it comes to life's realities? Yes: by developing the attitude of being *concerned* rather than afraid.

Ignoring real problems is not a wise idea, but neither is fretting over something while doing nothing about it. *Rational concern* gets around both situations. It means facing life's troubles directly, but without adding bad feelings. Instead of worrying about a problem, take some practical steps: check out how real the problem is, dispute any irrational evaluative beliefs about it, then choose a solution and get into action.

Let's be realistic: it is easy for people to say 'Stop worrying!' but it is, in fact, quite hard to get control of this pernicious habit — as I well know from personal experience. I have developed a structured approach, called the *six-step worry plan*, that can help break the habit, and have presented this in my book on anxiety, *FearLess: Your guide to overcoming anxiety*.[4] Lack of space precludes a full presentation here, but a summary follows:

1. *Catch yourself worrying and pause.* To combat worrying, you need to recognise when you are doing it.
2. *Identify the real issue.* Find out what it is you are really concerned about.
3. *Do a reality check.* Ask yourself, 'How likely is it that what I fear will happen?' and 'How bad would it be if it did?'
4. *Decide whether action is required.* Ask yourself, 'Do I need to do anything about this, or is it something that is unlikely to

happen, or something about which nothing can be done anyway?
5. *Take action* to *solve* the problem if the thing you fear *is* likely to happen.
6. *Let the worry go* if you decide it *isn't* really an issue, using psychological strategies.

Getting into action

This brings us to the final step. Here are some suggestions for combining rethinking with action, a powerful way to break the anxiety habit.

1. *If you can, do something about it.* Is there any way to reduce the chance of the thing you fear happening? If not, accept this reality and adjust to it. If there is, stop stewing and do it.

   If you have financial problems, for example, check you are spending your money sensibly. Get budgeting advice if you are unsure. Enrol in a pension plan to protect your financial position in future. After you have done what you can to prepare, get on with life now.

   If you are fearful for your children, teach them to recognise and avoid real dangers and foolish risks. But as they get older, don't overprotect them from life's important lessons, or try to restrict and control their lives to make yourself feel more secure. When they are adults, let them go out into the world to get on with their lives. Apart from being ready to help (should they ask you to), get on with your own life — whether or not they are making the most of theirs.

   Prepare for the future as far as you can. Take care of your body now to reduce the chance of disability later. Plan financially for retirement. Change any tendencies to get depressed or anxious that might worsen as you grow older. But remember that worrying won't stop you from growing old, so learn to live now. If you don't enjoy the present at your current stage of life, you are unlikely to learn how when you are older.

2. *Know how to deal with difficult problems.* If you are faced with a problem to which you cannot see any solution, use a step-by-step method like the one described in chapter 18.

    Another strategy is to take a break. If you leave a problem for a while, the subconscious mind will often work on it and come up with solutions. Sleep on it; or leave it for an hour, a day, or for as long as you find helpful.

    Consider using outside help. Talk things over with someone who can listen without always giving advice. Using another person as a sounding board can help you explore new ways of solving problems.

3. *Look after yourself physically.* Tiredness can make you scratchy, irritable and likely to misinterpret things that happen. Keep yourself physically fit to help maintain a good energy level. Get the sleep you need. Watch your diet: are you consuming a lot of foods and drinks that boost your energy level then leave you flat? Address any alcohol misuse or other substance abuse — which can, for some people, reduce anxiety in the short-term but at the cost of long-term problems (including increased anxiety![5]). See chapter 19 for further information on self-care.

4. *Learn to relax.* If tension is a problem, consider doing a training course in deep-muscle relaxation. Choose a method that will train you to relax in the actual situations where you tend to feel uptight, e.g. when the pressure is on at work or the children want your attention. This will be more useful than one that requires you to go and lie down for half an hour and listen to a tape every time you feel uptight. See chapter 19 for advice on obtaining a suitable relaxation-training programme.

    Identify the things you find most relaxing, such as going for a walk, reading a novel or watching TV. Do them regularly. Haven't got time to relax? Recheck your priorities: whether we do it consciously or not, we all allocate our time to the things we believe are important. Keep in mind that anxiety uses up a lot of time and emotional energy.

5. *Learn to manage your time.* Do you often find yourself overloaded with tasks? If so, learn how to set priorities and attend

to the most important items first. Those left over will be lower-priority ones, so you will be less likely to worry about them. Remember, too, that urgent things aren't always the most important. Consider getting a good book on time management, or doing a training course. See chapter 19 for further information on time management.

Confront the things you have been avoiding

One of the most effective ways to deal with fear is to get into the specific situations you are afraid of. If you fear being alone, for instance, organise a weekend by yourself. If you are worried about how you look in a bathing suit, buy one and wear it at the beach. If you are afraid of getting into lifts, go and stand in one and deal with the thoughts that come up. If you avoid talking to people at parties, go to more parties and talk to more people. To tackle the fear of failing, take on a new challenge. If you fear losing control in public, go into public places. If you feel used by someone but worry they might stop liking you if you say anything to them about how you feel, take a risk and assert yourself. Face the fear of rejection by approaching someone and asking for a date.

Do it now. Make that appointment with your doctor or dentist, sign up for that exercise programme, register for that night class — or whatever it is you have been putting off.

This direct approach is useful in many ways. It will help you to identify the irrational thoughts that make you anxious and to dispute them 'on the spot'. You will realise that the event is not as bad as you had feared and that you can face it and survive. You will learn techniques that will help you cope with anxiety in the future. Most importantly, you will discover that even if you cannot control circumstances themselves, you can control your reaction to them.

Start by making a list of feared situations. Rank them in order of the degree of anxiety you associate with each, then work on the lowest-ranked item first. (You can throw yourself in at the deep end and confront high-anxiety situations at the outset, but it is usually better to use a graduated approach.[6]) Be sensible about what you do — don't take foolish risks, but make sure that you aren't exaggerating risk as an excuse to continue avoiding it. Next, carry out a self-analysis. This will prepare you, by reducing your anxiety and giving you new, rational beliefs to use when you are in the situation. When writing down your beliefs, use 'What if' questions to identify the worst possible outcomes you can foresee and how you would deal with them; for example, 'What if I enter the situation? What will happen, what will I feel, and what will be the result?' When disputing your beliefs, estimate the chance that what you fear will happen. Get rid of any ideas that you must cope perfectly or avoid looking foolish or hide your anxiety.

Remind yourself, too, that you are not afraid of the situation itself, but of the anxiety you think will result. Note some facts about anxiety:

- It won't kill you — even though it may sometimes feel as if it will!
- It is uncomfortable rather than awful.
- You can stand it even though you dislike it.
- You will do better to accept anxiety than to fight it.

In addition, don't tell yourself that you *have* to do these things — demanding will only make you more anxious. Keep in mind, though, that people *can* do things they don't *feel* like doing.

Now get into the first, lowest-anxiety situation on your list. If possible, remain there until your anxiety diminishes. (The longer you stay, the more likely you are to change your irrational beliefs and reduce your fear.) Focus on what you have planned to do to cope rather than on what you feel. Recall the rational beliefs you worked out earlier in your self-analysis. If you wish, take someone along with you (although only to begin with).

Afterwards, do another self-analysis to deal with any new irrational beliefs you have uncovered while in the situation. Compare what you expected to feel with how it actually felt. Then plan your next assignment.

This approach, known as *graduated exposure*, is a key technique for overcoming dysfunctional anxiety. For more information on planning and carrying out an exposure programme, see my book on anxiety, *FearLess: Your guide to overcoming anxiety*.[7]

From worry to rational concern

Here is a collection of typical anxiety-causing beliefs and some rational alternatives:

Worry beliefs	Concern beliefs
If I worry about things that might be dangerous, unpleasant or frightening, I can stop them happening.	Worrying about things that might go wrong won't stop them happening, but it will upset me now. Better I do what I can about the future, then get on with living now.
There are certain things in life I just can't stand.	Certain things are uncomfortable or unpleasant, but it's wrong to say I 'can't stand' them. If that were true, I wouldn't be here to tell the tale.
I need love and approval from people significant to me, and I must avoid disapproval at all costs.	It's good to get love and approval, but I can survive without them. And although I don't like it, I can stand the discomfort of disapproval.
To feel worthwhile, I must do well at everything I try and avoid making mistakes.	It's unrealistic to demand unfailing success and competence. It will only make me run myself down, feel anxious and paralysed, and avoid doing anything. Better I just accept myself as a person and stop connecting 'self-worth' with performance.
My circumstances have to be right for life to be tolerable.	It's disappointing when things aren't the way I'd like them to be, but it's not awful – and I can stand less than the ideal.
I should worry when others have problems or feel unhappy.	I can't change other people's problems and bad feelings by getting myself upset.
Because I can't stand discomfort and pain, I must avoid them at all costs.	Total avoidance would mean a very restricted life. Though I don't like discomfort and pain, I can tolerate them.
Every problem has an ideal solution, and I should not relax until I find it.	Problems usually have many possible solutions. It's most functional to select the best available and get on with it.

Learn to live in the here and now

Worrying about the future can disable you in the present. Why not turn this tendency on its head? Rather than dwelling on what might or might not happen, practise being aware of what is around you. Savour the things that are pleasant to observe, touch, smell, listen to and taste.

There was a time when I would rush to work in the morning, thinking and worrying about the day ahead. Now I enjoy my walk through an old reserve. I make a point of seeing the beauty around me, observing the trees, the birds and the way sunlight strikes the bushes. This sets the tone for the whole day. Putting from my mind all thought of what is ahead helps me cope better with it.

I am not suggesting you ignore the future, or what has gone before. If you want to stay happy through the years ahead, it is important to prepare now. It is also wise to learn from the past. But, having done that, make sure you live in the present — today.

References

1. Menninger, K., (1946). *The Human Mind*. New York, N.Y.: Knopf.
2. Wells, J.E., et al. (1989). Christchurch psychiatric epidemiology study. *Australian and New Zealand Journal of Psychiatry*, 23, 315–26.
3. Richardson, I., et al. (1988). *New Zealand Today*. Report of the Royal Commission on Social Policy, vol. 1. Wellington: Royal Commission on Social Policy.
4. Froggatt, W., (2003). *FearLess: Your guide to overcoming anxiety*. Auckland: HarperCollins.
5. Bushnell, J., et al. (1998). *Guidelines for Assessing and Treating Anxiety Disorders*. Wellington: National Health Committee.
6. Froggatt (2003).
7. Froggatt (2003).

11 Give up guilt: you don't need it

Guilt is one of the most common emotions humans are likely to experience. It is generally believed that people need guilt to keep them on the straight and narrow, but, as we shall see, this is not the case. In fact, guilt often has a harmful effect on the way people feel and behave. You may be surprised to hear this, so let's take a closer look at this dubious emotion.

What is guilt?

Guilt is the unpleasant feeling you sometimes get when you think you have done something wrong. It involves a mix of demanding and self-rating. You start by telling yourself that you have done something you 'shouldn't' have. Then you *rate* yourself in some way — as a bad person, a failure, or the like.

This is what Lynette did. After moving to Wellington from a small South Island town on transfer with a government department, she began a relationship with her supervisor, Bob. Before long she discovered he was married. Because of her strong feelings, Lynette didn't break it off or tell Bob she knew until some time later. Soon she began to feel guilty. She told herself that sleeping with a married man meant she must be a bad person.

Lynette's experience shows how guilt differs from shame. You can feel guilt whether or not others know about what you have done. Shame, in contrast, is the upset you feel when you believe other people are thinking badly of you. Whereas Lynette felt guilty as soon as she realised her lover was married, Bob didn't worry about his infidelity until found out. Then he wouldn't face Lynette and was so afraid she would tell others in the office that he ended up applying for a transfer.

What is wrong with guilt?

Unfortunately, Lynette's guilt wasn't much help to her or anyone else. This doesn't mean that rules or guidelines are meaningless. Life would be chaotic without them, and it is wise to be concerned when we break one. But guilt goes beyond guiding behaviour. Its combination of demanding and self-rating can have some insidious effects.

Paradoxically, it often maintains the unwanted behaviour. This happens because guilt fixates on the badness of the *person* rather than on what the person *does*. If you fail at something, then call yourself a failure, you are likely to go on failing. After all, how do failures act? If you see yourself as a lazy person, how do lazy people act? Or mad people, bad people, nasty people, or whatever it is?

People who are prone to guilt may not want to admit to their failings, because to do so would lead to considerable discomfort and self-devaluation. As a result, they become defensive and unable to learn from their mistakes. Guilt encourages approval-seeking and unassertiveness. Feeling bad about yourself can make you seek reassurance from others by trying to please them. It leads also to anxiety. Because guilt is so uncomfortable, if you see it coming you will get uptight. This may hinder you doing things that carry the risk of guilt, such as asking for what you want or saying no. As an anonymous person once said: 'Conscience gets a lot of credit that belongs to cold feet.'

Sex is a common area of guilt. Many feel bad about enjoying sex or trying new activities with their partners. Guilt about masturbation leads to much needless agonising but doesn't stop people doing it. At the extreme, some avoid sex entirely but still feel guilty about their sexual thoughts.

The self-downing involved in guilt can create feelings of despair and hopelessness, which can lead to depression. Guilt also stops you living in the present. If you keep going over your past sins and your badness as a person, you won't enjoy what is happening now.

GIVE UP GUILT: YOU DON'T NEED IT

Where does guilt come from?

Why is guilt so persistent? Primarily, it is a method of social control. We use it to try and keep ourselves in line. Others see it as a way of getting us to conform.

Because young children lack the capacity to analyse what they are taught, we grow up with a set of beliefs obtained largely from others. Some are valid and helpful, others less so. In either case, these rules are so ingrained by the time we reach adulthood that we are not always aware of them.

When you feel guilty, it is because you are tapping into one of your underlying rules. You don't need anyone else to bring it on. Once you think you have broken a rule, you automatically make yourself feel guilty. Other people are only too glad to help you. They bring up mistakes from the past. They label you. They may even say nothing — just sulk, look hurt or play at not speaking. External guilt messages may come from many different sources.

Take the state. The justice system tends to rate people rather than their actions. Labels like 'offender', 'criminal', 'thug', 'bad person', 'violent' or 'hopeless' suggest that people somehow are what they do — and always will be that way. Punishing people rather than helping them change their behaviour is an indirect type of person-rating. That a high proportion keep reoffending shows how labelling encourages the very behaviours the system is trying to stamp out.

Then there are the mass media. Advertisers use guilt to persuade us to buy their products:

'Shouldn't you buy this for your grandchildren?'
'Doesn't your family deserve this?'
'People who care about others use . . .'

All push the view that you are at fault if you don't conform and 'do the right thing' by your family, friends and others.

Some religious bodies use guilt to control their members by promoting the idea that if you err, you have offended against God himself (rather than against the humans who made the rules).

Parent–child relations can be a major breeding ground for guilt. Parents try to induce it with statements such as:

'Don't worry, I'll do it myself!'
'What I say doesn't matter, I suppose.' (big sigh)
'We've done all this for you, so you should . . .'
'You must not disgrace/embarrass us in front of . . .'

Parents may try to control their adult offspring by using a real or imagined health problem to get them to visit more often, to discourage them from moving too far away, or generally to keep a hold on the apron strings.

Children are just as good at using guilt to manipulate. Many parents hold beliefs that provide weak spots for their children to target:

'I can't stand to see any child of mine unhappy.'
'I must not be different from other parents. John's mother lets him . . .'
'My children must always see me as a loving and kind parent.'

Couples, too, may use guilt to pressure each other to keep in line, using statements such as:

'You don't really care about me.'
'I wouldn't want you to feel bad about leaving me alone.'
'If you really loved me, you would . . .'
'I haven't forgotten how you treated me when we were first married.'
'I'll do myself in if you go.'

Partners may use the silent treatment, get in a rage, resort to name-calling, dredge up the past, suggest that 'real love' involves such and such, or fall back on any number of other strategies of this kind to get the other person to feel bad.

However, although others may try to control us with guilt, they can only succeed if we cooperate. Guilt is a product of our own minds. It doesn't result from what other people say or think, rather it comes from what we tell ourselves about their opinions. We don't even need outside prompting. Guilt-causing demands become an ingrained part of our belief system. By the time we are adults, guilt has become an automatic reaction.

We may be reluctant to give it up. We might see it as a natural part of ourselves that somehow keeps us on the right moral track. We might think that feeling bad for a time is a way to pay for our sins and earn absolution, or that guilt 'proves' what caring, sensitive people we are.

Rational Self-Analysis can help you deal with the demands and self-ratings that create guilt. Do an analysis whenever you feel bad about yourself. As well as helping yourself feel better, you will undercut the irrational life rules that make you prone to guilt in the first place.

Recognising guilt

When you are feeling bad about something that you have done, ask, 'Have I broken a rule of conduct that I believe in? Or am I mainly worried about what others will think of me if they find out? In other words, do I feel guilt or shame?' If it is guilt, then read on. If it is shame, you need a different approach — see chapter 14.

For a while, keep an *ABC* diary of occasions when you feel guilty. Record the event or circumstance that triggers it, your reaction and the thoughts involved. You will soon become aware of the things you tend to feel guilty about, and your typical negative self-talk.

Note, too, that the self-help skills in this chapter can be applied equally well to guilt about things in the distant past as guilt over more recent events. Are you feeling bad about something that happened many years ago? Don't keep holding on to it.

Finding the beliefs that cause your guilt

As we saw earlier, guilt results from a blend of *demanding* and *self-rating*; hence, there are two questions to ask if you are to identify the beliefs that cause your guilt.

First, what rule do you think you have broken? What have you done that you think you 'shouldn't have', or not done that you 'should have'?

Second, what are you calling yourself because of what you have done? Ask, 'Having [done whatever it was], what does this make me?' Be honest here. What nasty label are you putting on yourself: 'bad', 'evil', 'selfish', 'a failure', 'stupid'? Even though you know it is illogical, admit to your self-rating so you can dispute it properly.

You may also be misinterpreting what has happened and *catastrophising* about the results. Note, too, any *personalising*. People who are prone to guilt often take responsibility for things that happen (including how other people feel) without checking the evidence. Look for *emotional reasoning* — thinking that because you feel guilty you must have done something wrong. Guilt, like many irrational feelings, can be a vicious circle. Be aware, too, of any *overgeneralising*. Exaggerating the effects of anything you have done can make you feel worse and feed the vicious circle.

Note, though, that misinterpretations are not the real cause of your guilt — so make sure you uncover those demands and self-ratings.

From guilt to concern

Can human beings survive without guilt? After all, rules are important. They enable us to learn from the past and apply the lessons of experience to the future. How can we maintain helpful guidelines yet avoid self-blame?

There is a solution. It is a variation of the principle introduced in the previous chapter — that of *rational concern*. With regard to guilt, this means being concerned about your *actions* and their *results* without moralistically blaming your *self*. Blame concentrates on how bad *you* are for having done something. Rational concern, on the other hand, focuses on the *results* of your *actions*.

Start by checking out your interpretations. Ask, 'Am I responsible for what has happened? Did I *knowingly* and deliberately do it?' Don't assume that you caused something until you have checked the evidence. Are you blaming yourself for how another person is feeling or behaving? Challenge any idea that you control what other people feel and do. This is grandiose thinking — do you really have such power over others?

Whether or not you decide your interpretations are true, make sure you tackle the underlying evaluations that are the real cause of your guilt. Take the demands. Demanding makes problems out of otherwise helpful guidelines. If you hold them as rules that you must observe in every circumstance and for all time, it will keep you from reassessing whether the rules are still helpful.

Take Philip. His father deserted his family when Philip was still very young. To survive, his mother had to work long hours for low pay, so never had time or money for recreation. By the time Philip was 30 he had succeeded in business but still found it hard to relax and spend money on luxuries. Even on holiday he would feel guilty and keep thinking about getting back to work.

What was the solution for Philip? He didn't have to give up the value of hard work altogether. All he had to do was accept that while his ideas about long hours and little recreation may have aided his survival at one time, they were not relevant to his present-day circumstances.

What do you do when you decide that a guideline does continue to have some relevance? You can still avoid making it a problem by retaining it as a *preference* rather than a demand. This will keep you motivated to live up to its strictures without catastrophising when you fall short. In chapter 5 there is a check list to help you re-examine life rules — here is a condensed version:

1. Is this rule helpful or unhelpful?
2. Does it aid me in achieving my goals?
3. Does it create emotions I can handle, or leave me distressed and immobilised?
4. Does it promote my happiness and survival, and those of other people?
5. Is this rule a preference, or am I holding it as a demand?

What do you do when you have broken a valid rule? Be concerned. Learn what you can from the experience to reduce the chance of repeating it, but don't put yourself down. Make it a *practical* rather than a *moral* issue. Keep in mind, also, that one bad act, or even a few, does not make the whole person bad. To feel guilty implies that you can and should be perfect, which amounts to thinking that you are somehow godlike and omnipotent. But you are not a supernatural being. You are a human — and humans are imperfect, fallible and prone to making mistakes.

Rate your *behaviour*, then, rather than your *self*. Take responsibility for your errors. Work at changing personal tendencies you are unhappy with. This is what 'conscience' is all about — changing behaviour rather than wallowing in self-blame. On the subject of self-acceptance, you will find it helpful to reread chapter 7.

Here is a check list of questions to ask whenever you are feeling bad about something you have done:

1. Am I responsible for what has happened? Or am I jumping to conclusions without checking the facts?
2. If I am responsible, just how bad is what happened? Am I seeing it in perspective, or exaggerating the results?
3. Did I deliberately do it, fully realising what the results would be?
4. If not, am I demanding that I be flawless, never put a foot wrong, and always foresee every possible result of anything I do?
5. Have I broken a rule of conduct that I still believe in?
6. If I have, am I rationally viewing my *behaviour* as unhelpful (and learning from the experience), or am I, instead, moralising about it and rating my *self*?
7. Am I still feeling guilt, or have I changed it to concern?

Acting like a concerned person

As well as working on your irrational beliefs, get into *action* to reinforce your new ways of thinking and make it less likely that you will repeat the 'guilt trip'.

1. *Put things right*. If you have broken a valid rule, ask yourself, 'Is there anything I can do to put it right?' If there is, do it — and in a tangible form that will benefit the person or people concerned rather than just appease your guilt. If you cannot do anything useful, put the matter behind you and move on. What has happened has happened. You cannot turn the clock back, no matter how much you may wish to. Feeling bad about the past won't change it, and no one is going to benefit because you keep wallowing in self-blame.
2. *Do things you now believe are OK for you*. Is there something you would enjoy: buying an item for yourself, indulging in an activity you think you don't 'deserve', or taking some time off from chores? Do it today. Show yourself that you can survive emotionally, even if it feels strange at first. Do something each day until you have weakened the guilt habit.
3. *Learn how to assert yourself*. Find out how to speak up to people who try to make you feel guilty. This will show them they are wasting their time on you. For some help with this, see chapters 14 and 15.

Guilt or concern?

On the left is a list of beliefs that often create guilt. Compare them with the alternatives in the right-hand column.

Guilt beliefs	*Concern beliefs*
I am responsible for how other people feel and behave.	I am not God. I do not control what goes on inside other people, nor what they do.
I should be perfect in everything I do and never make mistakes.	Perfection is a supernatural quality, but, whether I like it or not, I am a human being — and, therefore, prone to making mistakes.
When I behave badly, it proves I'm evil or stupid.	When I behave badly, it proves I'm a person who sometimes behaves badly — nothing more.

Guilt beliefs	Concern beliefs
I should be able to predict the results of everything I do.	It is wise, before I act, to consider what might result. But it's impossible to foretell the future with absolute certainty.
I deserve to be condemned, punished and unhappy when I don't measure up.	'Deserve' isn't a fact — it's just a moralistic idea in my head. Punishing myself is self-defeating. And being unhappy does nothing to change my behaviour.
Guilt is necessary. Without it no one would have a conscience and humanity would fall into chaos.	Not only is guilt unnecessary, it often perpetuates the behaviour we feel guilty about. The idea of *concern* better meets the aims of conscience — that is, to monitor and change unwanted habits and actions.
If I don't feel guilty about the past, I might repeat my mistakes.	Mulling over past misdeeds will only stop me changing in the present. The past is past. Better I learn from it, change myself, then get on with life now.

Guilt is a well-ingrained habit for most people. Because it seems natural and automatic, breaking this habit will take time and hard work. Those self-damning thoughts will keep sneaking back for a long while. And you will never be perfect: there will always be occasions when you slip up. But you don't have to let this throw you. People who are concerned about the results of their actions, yet accept themselves unconditionally, never need to feel guilty.

12 Climbing out of the black hole: no more depression

Negative feelings are a part of real life. They are not always a bad thing — sometimes they can even help. Feeling unhappy about something can push you into changing it, or grieving can help you overcome a loss. But unhappiness can turn into misery and despair — extreme feelings that stick around. Far from motivating, they make it hard to cope with everyday life.

This was Robyn's experience. She reached a stage where she didn't even want to get up in the morning. She felt tired and lethargic all day. She went through the motions of looking after things at home, but her heart wasn't in it. She neglected her appearance and avoided her friends. She stopped doing most of the things she used to enjoy. Her polytechnic classes suffered. Though she had been keen to train in data processing, she now thought of giving it all up.

What is depression?

We are not talking about ordinary sadness here: Robyn's problem was more than just a passing downer. Unfortunately, something like it will affect many people at some time in their lives. Because depression is so widespread, it is called 'the common cold of psychiatry'. But what a cold:

- *You feel low* in spirit — sad, gloomy, pessimistic, dejected, discouraged, heavy.
- *You lose interest* in things you used to enjoy. You neglect your friends and avoid social activities.
- *It's hard to do things.* You are less able to concentrate than usual, so you find it harder to read, follow a TV programme or

conduct a conversation. Your thinking, speech and actions slow down. You lack vitality and feel tired all day.
- *Your appetite and sleeping patterns change.* You either go off your food and possibly lose weight, or you go the opposite way and overeat. You have trouble getting to sleep, or you wake early in the morning and can't get off to sleep again.
- *You feel bad about yourself.* You might feel *guilty*, seeing yourself as unworthy, useless and a burden to others, and blaming yourself for all sorts of things both past and present. Or you *pity yourself*, blaming the world for treating you badly and thinking that others dislike you and are friendly only out of pity.
- *You worry* about all sorts of things, often quite trivial. Perhaps you fret about your health, fearing that various things are wrong with you. Or you feel restless and apprehensive, sometimes without knowing what you are afraid of.
- *Things seem hopeless.* You wonder whether improvement is possible and feel negative about the future. You might think that life isn't worth living, and perhaps even consider ending it all.

One individual won't have all these symptoms at the same time, and the mix will vary from person to person. Whereas Robyn felt lethargic, guilty and self-blaming, Paul was restless and apprehensive. He woke in the early hours of the morning. His mind was so active he couldn't get back to sleep. He felt uptight, pitied himself and blamed the world for his problems.

Depression is the result of a vicious circle. It can be triggered by a major event — a bereavement, for instance — or by a series of minor events which add up. Biochemical changes can also be involved: insufficient sleep, poor diet, hormonal activity, lack of exercise, and chemicals such as alcohol and other drugs can lead to a drop in mood.

Whatever the initial trigger, you begin to feel a bit low. Because of this, you slow down and become less active. So far there's nothing abnormal, but if you interpret your reduced activity as meaning there is something very wrong with you, the vicious circle may begin. You expect less of yourself, so you do less. Then you expect less still. You come to believe that you aren't capable of much, so you try less and less, then give up altogether. Because you see no point in trying, the future seems hopeless.

You can help yourself

You can learn how to break the vicious circle. Rational Self-Analysis is ideal for disputing and changing the beliefs that cause and maintain depression. Do an analysis when you feel depressed and can't seem to throw it off. With a more advanced depression, you may feel bad most of the time and find it hard to pick out specific events you are reacting to. Once you start to examine your moods, though, you will find there are variations. Often these result from what you tell yourself about internal events — feeling low when you get up, feeling tired, lacking energy and the like.

At first, Paul found it hard to accept he was reacting to anything in particular, but he soon realised that waking in the early hours was an 'activating event'. He would immediately tell himself something like, 'Oh no, it's only 3 o'clock. I'm wide awake, I'll never get back to sleep, and I'll have an awful day.' By doing a self-analysis when he woke up, he was able to confront and reduce the awfulising that caused him to feel worse than he needed to.

Uncovering depressive thinking

The beliefs that cause depression typically have a very negative slant. You may direct this negativism in three ways: towards yourself, towards the world and towards the future.

Thoughts about yourself
Depressed people tend to ignore their achievements and positive points and inflate their failures (*filtering*). They often *personalise* — unduly blame themselves for things that have gone wrong. Are you jumping to the conclusion that someone is unhappy, sick or having problems because of you? Or that you could have kept certain things

from happening even though they were not under your control?

Underneath these misinterpretations will be *demands* directed at yourself — for example, 'I should be a better person than I am' or 'I should have been able to do things differently.' These ideas, which are responsible for feelings of guilt, reflect rules such as:

'To be happy, I must be able to see myself as a worthy human being.'
'To see myself as worthy, I must achieve at important things and be successful with my life.'

Does thinking you don't match up lead you to adopt labels such as 'worthless', 'failure', 'bad person' or 'inadequate'? Do you see yourself as incapable of handling everyday life, or of helping yourself get better? Do you think you got depressed in the first place because you are physically, mentally or morally lacking? Do you believe you are 'undeserving' and therefore not entitled to pleasurable things and experiences? Or you should atone for your acts or inadequacies by punishing yourself?

Thoughts about the world

Depressed people may also direct filtering outwards, ignoring positives and seeing only the negative things about their environment. Are you telling yourself that the world does nothing but block you from your goals and deprive you of what you want? Are you *mind-reading* — seeing other people as deliberately frustrating, punishing and rejecting you, and putting you down?

Underlying these misinterpretations will be demands directed at the world: 'People should treat me better than they do', 'I shouldn't have to put up with this' and so forth. Ideas like these will lead to self-pity. They imply rules such as:

'I need love and approval from other people.'
'The world should be a just and fair place.'
'I must always be happy and never have to experience bad feelings.'

'People should treat me right and never deprive me of what I need to be happy — love/recognition/emotional and physical comfort/etc.'

Misinterpretations will also trigger *catastrophising*: 'It's *terrible* when I can't get the things I need to be happy'; 'I *can't bear* the way things are/how the world treats me/being frustrated/feeling so unhappy/etc.'

Thoughts about the future

A feature of almost all depressions is *fortune-telling* — negative thinking about the future. You expect unpleasant events to happen and assume you can do little or nothing about them. You predict that your circumstances and your bad feelings will be like this for ever — in other words, that it is hopeless.

This belief in hopelessness is the key to understanding depression — no matter how bad you feel about yourself or the world, you are only likely to become really depressed if you see little or no hope that things will get better.[1]

To sum up

If you are depressed, you are most likely viewing yourself as a loser. You can express this negative bias in two ways. You might (like Robyn) blame your *self* and feel *guilt* — which results from self-rating and internally aimed demands. Alternatively, you might (as Paul did) aim your demands outward and blame the *world* — and then *pity yourself* for the way it treats you. Whether you emphasise guilt or self-pity, common to both is a view of the future as hopeless and of yourself as powerless to do anything about it.

When looking for the thoughts that are causing your depression, it is important to note the key role that evaluative thinking — especially demanding — plays. Viewing yourself as having negative tendencies or characteristics will not by itself make you depressed: this comes from believing that you 'should not' be as you are, and that you are a 'bad' or 'defective' person. In the same way, seeing the world and other people as treating you badly will only cause you significant harm if you also tell yourself that things 'should' be better than they are and that it is 'awful' when they aren't. Likewise, predicting negative happenings in the future will turn concern into depression if you also believe that bad things 'should not' or 'must not' happen and that you 'can't stand it' when they do.

Disputing depressive beliefs

How do you get yourself out of the black hole? By learning to view yourself, the world and the future in more realistic terms.

Get your life into perspective

Start by recognising that the world is a mixture of positives and negatives. Here is an exercise to do right now. Take 10 minutes to list the things that are going well for you. Don't overlook the small or obvious things, the ones you usually take for granted. You will soon discover there are positives — it's just that you have stopped seeing them.

Don't deny the negatives — they are a part of real life — but observe that everyone has obstacles to contend with. Some you can influence, some you cannot; but you can always choose the extent to which you dwell on them. Check whether you are inflating yours. Are other people really treating you as badly as you think? Are your failures actually as significant as you imagine? Are your achievements of no account at all?

Deal with hopelessness

Get the future into perspective, too. When depressed, people tend to think they can predict what is going to happen for the rest of their lives; but such fortune-telling amounts to magical thinking. Who knows what the future holds? It's important to acknowledge any real problems you have, but where is the evidence that you will *never* be able to do anything about them?

Time projection will help you combat fortune-telling. Use it when you are facing loss, sadness or some other current distress. Imagine yourself going forward in time. First a week, then a month, then six months, a year, two years, and so on. Consider how things will be for you at each of these points in time. Remind yourself that life will go on, even if you have to make some changes to be happy.

This worked for Geoff. His wife had recently left their three-year marriage. He imagined himself in a week's time, probably still feeling down. He saw himself a month later, still upset but beginning to accept his marriage was over, and in six months' time, still grieving but getting on with life. After a year, he would be into a new lifestyle; then, after two years, laughing at himself for ever thinking he would never be happy again.

Question the idea that you have no control. Depressed people often feel a lack of power. They tend to regard external events and circumstances, such as a loss, rejection or failure, as the cause of their bad feelings. But the theory that external events cause depression is incomplete. It doesn't explain why two people facing the same event can react in quite different ways. What to one is a crushing blow may be a temporary setback or even a challenge to another.

Events and circumstances are important insofar as they trigger thoughts. In the end, though, it is thoughts that cause depression. You can learn to control your thoughts, whether or not you are able to change what triggers them, so don't make a trap for yourself by thinking that external forces determine how you feel.

Come to terms with the world

So far we have looked at how you can deal with misinterpretations about your present and future circumstances, but these aren't the primary cause of depressed feelings. In any case, some of your thoughts about what is happening may turn out to be correct. It is important, therefore, to get beneath your interpretations and look at how you are *evaluating* things — that is, find out what they mean to you.

Let's start with those ever-present demands. You probably want the world to be a fair place. So do I. No doubt we would both like always to get the things we want, and hardly ever to get what we don't want.

What is the reality, though? In many respects, the world is an unfair place. We don't always get what we want, and sometimes we get what we don't want. This doesn't mean that our desires are irrational. It makes sense to organise our lives as far as we can to get what we want and avoid what we don't. And if we keep our wants as just that — wishes, desires or preferences — we will only be disappointed or sad when they don't happen. Unfortunately, though, we often go beyond wanting. We tell ourselves we 'must' have what we want, or the world 'should' be as we wish. As a result, disappointment becomes despondency and sadness turns into hopelessness. By demanding that reality not exist, we set ourselves up to be disillusioned by reality. And for nothing. Because while there are many things we might want, there are few things that we absolutely need. Success, love, recognition — our lives will be better if we have them, but we can survive without.

If you want to stop turning disappointment into depression, *learn to accept reality*. This doesn't mean that you have to agree with it. To accept something is to see it as it really is and acknowledge there is no 'Law of the Universe' that says it should be different. You can still dislike it, and you can seek to change it. Just avoid turning your want into a demand and then disabling yourself with self-pity or anger. You don't have to throw all your values away — just turn them from demands to preferences. You will find detailed guidance on how to do this in chapters 5 and 11.

Come to terms with yourself

What about your self-rating? It is helpful to view your abilities and strengths realistically, but make sure you see your positives as well as your drawbacks. Stop for a moment and think, 'What are three things about myself that are OK?' Don't give up because this seems hard to answer at first — people are more used to criticising than praising themselves.

More importantly, you can admit your failings while still accepting yourself as a person. Instead of rating your *self*, rate your *behaviour*. Often there is little wrong with how we would like ourselves to be. It only becomes a problem when we believe that because we *want* to be a certain way, we *must* be that way. This is grandiose thinking: 'Because it is possible to be (kind/loving/hard-working/achieving/

etc.), I *should* be.' It denies the reality that you are a fallible human being. Concede that there are *specific things* you would like to change, but accept your *total self*. If you are feeling bad because of things you have done or because of what you think you are, chapters 7 and 11 will have some helpful advice for you.

Work to accept all your feelings
Finally, accept that sadness is a normal part of life. Challenge the notion that you must avoid all negative feelings. To demand that you always be happy is, again, to deny reality. It makes bad feelings worse than they need be — another example of how demands can bring on the very problem you may be trying to avoid. Remind yourself that unhappiness is unpleasant, but not awful — and that you can therefore stand it. Sadness is a rational response to unwanted circumstances. Depression is not.

Getting into action

When you feel low, get moving. Mow the lawns, go for a walk, visit a friend. Getting active will benefit you in several ways. Physical activity will give your mood a boost. Carrying out tasks will help you see you are not helpless or hopeless. Mixing with other people will give you feedback to challenge the idea that you are not an acceptable member of the human race.

When you are depressed, of course, getting into action will seem hard. You probably won't *feel* like doing things. You may also see yourself as inadequate, incompetent and unable to achieve much. The solution? Start doing things *before* you feel like it. The biggest block you will need to overcome is the belief that you cannot do anything until you 'want' to. This is a fallacy. You can do something by deciding to — then putting one foot in front of the other and carrying it out.

The five-step plan
Let's see how you can put this into practice. The following is a step-by-step plan that will help you get under way when you just can't seem to motivate yourself:

1. *Schedule activities each day.* Each morning (or the night before) list things to be done that day. To avoid setting yourself up for failure, don't record more items than you can reasonably expect to complete. Include only easily achievable ones, and keep the list short.

   The first list Robyn made had too many items:

   (i) Go to supermarket.
   (ii) Make Sarah's new dress.
   (iii) Do polytech assignment.
   (iv) Clean car.
   (v) Write four letters.
   (vi) Arrange quotes for new drains.
   (vii) Prepare dining room for repainting.

   She realised she couldn't do all this in one day, and that expecting to only made her feel worse; so she deleted everything except going to the supermarket and starting her assignment.

2. *Divide larger tasks into smaller subtasks that are easier to manage.* 'Do the housework', for example, can be broken down into vacuuming one day, dusting the next, and so on. Look ahead only one step at a time — this will stop you feeling overwhelmed.

   Robyn split the task of starting her assignment into four small steps:

   (i) Ring tutor and ask for extra time.
   (ii) Read project summary.
   (iii) Get together reading matter.
   (iv) Divide it into portions to deal with over each of the next five days.

3. *Grade your subtasks according to order of difficulty.* Give each item a 'difficulty score' — 1 for the easiest, 10 for the hardest. 'Make a shopping list', for example, might score 3, while 'Go to the supermarket' might score 8. As far as possible, start with the easier ones.

   Robyn decided that reading the project summary would be easiest. Next would be getting together the reading material.

She thought that once she had done that, she would feel better about asking the tutor for extra time.
4. *Treat yourself to luxuries whenever possible.* Make sure your list includes things that could be enjoyable, even if you think you don't 'deserve' them. Eat something pleasant, read a book, go to the movies, take a walk or a jog, have a break from the kids, go to a restaurant for your lunch break. Remember: this applies whether or not your work is up to date. (How many people ever have things up to date anyway?)

   Robyn realised that telling herself she was unworthy made her more depressed. She decided to counter this by giving herself a treat. She added to her list 'Buy a novel', and noted on the next day's list 'Spend an hour reading.'
5. *Tick items as you complete them.* Depressed people tend to ignore their achievements. Ticking completed items will show you that things are happening (even if more slowly than you would like). Record also any other things you have done which give you pleasure or a sense of achievement.

Keep in mind that *what* you do isn't so important. Simply getting into gear, even with minor activities, will help give your mood a lift. Once you are under way, it will become easier to carry on.

Remember, too, that the idea is to get moving rather than 'succeed'. Watch for and dispute any notions that you 'should' be doing certain things, or that you have to do anything to a high standard. Don't worry about 'getting it right' — just do it.

Activity suggestions

Almost any activity will help lift depression. Here are some of the more useful ones:

- *Physical activities.* Any form of exercise — jogging, walking, cycling, tramping, gardening — will help lift your mood. Games such as tennis or golf, or any team activity, will give you a double benefit by also getting you involved with other people. Joining a sports club, a gym or an aerobics class are popular

ways of mixing getting fit and social contact. Outings with a tramping club or an organisation such as the New Zealand Forest and Bird Protection Society will get you into new surroundings and among new friends.
- *Mixing with other people.* Even if you don't feel like it, go to a social function, call a friend for a chat, arrange to meet someone, talk to a neighbour, spend coffee breaks with co-workers, or take any other chance to spend time around people. You may find it hard to communicate, but making yourself mix with others will help pull you out of your self-absorption. Why not make a list of all the people you have stopped seeing and start with them?
- *Mental stimulation.* Make yourself read the newspaper, even if you can't remember later what you have read — you will still be gradually getting your brain cells working again. Watch TV. Read a novel, even if only a few pages at a time.

Ensure that each daily list includes some things that would normally give you pleasure. You may doubt that you will enjoy them right now, but they will help challenge the belief that you are 'undeserving', and enjoyment will gradually return. Again, start by making a list of the things you used to do. Everyone has their own ideas about what gives pleasure — here are some of the more common:

reading	*taking a bath*	meeting people
playing music	*having sex*	being with friends
camping	*doing art work*	driving
going to the beach	*doing favours*	swimming
playing board games	*doing up the car*	exploring
partying	*going to church*	watching sport
having a barbeque	*boating*	listening to music
helping someone	*tramping*	going to the movies
tracing your genealogy	*hunting*	fishing
gardening	*dancing*	buying new clothes
do-it-yourself activities	*giving gifts*	writing letters
making things	*writing poetry*	cooking

going to a concert
sewing
buying a lottery ticket
visiting
going to the hairdresser
shopping
pottering around
eating out
travelling
doing voluntary work
knitting
doing outdoor work
craftwork
going to night school

Depression is a way of thinking

Compare the most common depression-causing irrational beliefs with their rational alternatives.

Depression-causing beliefs	*Realistic alternatives*
I need love and approval (and must avoid disapproval) before I can accept myself and be happy.	Love and approval are good to have, but they're not *necessities*. There'll always be times when they're not forthcoming, so I'd do best to learn how to accept myself independently of what others think.
To be worthwhile, I must achieve and succeed at whatever I do.	It's OK to strive for excellence, but it's not realistic to *demand* it. I'll only put myself down and avoid doing anything. Best I learn to accept myself irrespective of my 'performance'.
I should always act correctly, because when I don't it proves how useless and unworthy I am.	No human is perfect. By thinking I should never put a foot wrong, I'm trying to make out I'm a supernatural entity.
I deserve to be depressed because of the type of person I am.	Who says I 'deserve' to be punished with unhappiness? Better that I learn from my errors, without moralistic blaming, and then get on with life.
The world (and the people in it) must treat me correctly and justly. Otherwise life will be intolerable.	I'd *prefer* things to be the way I want, but there's no reason they *should* be. If I stopped demanding, I could be simply disappointed with reality instead of seeing it as something I can't stand.

Depression-causing beliefs	Realistic alternatives
I can't do things unless I want to or feel like doing them.	This is a fallacy. People do things they don't feel like doing all the time. If I got myself moving, the activity would give my mood a lift.
I'm unhappy because of things that are outside my control, so there's nothing I can do to help myself feel better.	It's true that many things are outside my control. But external events and circumstances don't cause my internal feelings, my thoughts do — and I can learn to control them.

Overcoming blocks

Getting free of depression is almost certainly within your power. The biggest hurdle will be lack of motivation. You are not going to *want* to do things until you are feeling better; but you are not going to feel better until you have started doing things. The answer to this paradox is very simple — so simple that people overlook it all the time. *Just do it anyway.* Doing something *before* you feel like it will slowly lift your mood. Soon you will begin to enjoy what you are doing, and your motivation will return.

You can help yourself get moving by using the five-step plan. You could also make a simple contract with someone else that you will carry out a task within a set time limit. If you need outside help, see chapter 22 for advice.

Prevent depression from coming back

Even when you are feeling better, the underlying beliefs that cause your depressions will still be there. Events or circumstances are likely to trigger them from time to time. When you feel better, therefore, don't stop working on yourself. Here are some preventive strategies:

- *Keep using Rational Self-Analysis.* Keep doing analyses whenever you find yourself overreacting with bad feelings. You might need to chip away for years at some self-defeating core beliefs, but as time goes on they will affect you less. The effort you make now will serve you well in the long-term future. When you are feeling better, it will be tempting to stop doing self-help work; so keep reminding yourself that dealing with problematic core beliefs is what will stop depression from returning.[2]

- *Re-educate yourself.* Other chapters in this book cover the problems that contribute to depression: 5 (demanding), 7 (self-rating), 11 (guilt), 14 (disapproval), 16 (perfectionism) and 21 (overcoming blocks) are especially worth studying.
- *Improve any personal characteristics or problems that can lead to depression.* If you find it hard to ask for what you want, learn to assert yourself. If you feel awkward in social situations, take a social-skills training course. Learn how to solve problems — read chapter 18, for example. Do you think you lack other basic skills, such as reading, running a household, time-management or driving? Consider going on a training course or teaching yourself with books. If you have trouble handling alcohol or drugs, get professional help. Seek advice on persisting physical health problems.
- *Do something about circumstances you dislike.* Is your marriage unhappy? Maybe it is time to look at making some changes. If your children's behaviour is a problem, learn some child-management strategies or join a parent's support group. Are you bored at work or feeling a lack of direction with your career? Set some goals for the future, then look at a change of job or training for the type of work you would prefer.

Some things you won't be able to influence, but you aren't going to know which until you have checked them out. Even when you cannot change something, you can still avoid unnecessary bad feelings over it. So don't just drift along with your problems. Once you are out of the black hole, make sure you fill it in.

References
1. Treatment Protocol Project (1997). *Management of Mental Disorders*, 2nd edn. Sydney: World Health Organisation.
2. France, R., & Robson, M., (1997). *Cognitive-Behavioural Therapy in Primary Care: A practical guide*. London: Jessica Kingsley.

13 Anger: who's in charge?

Anger is a troublesome emotion for many people. Some bottle it up and feel bad inside. Others let it out in ways that are destructive to themselves and those around them.

Humans also complicate anger by turning it into a moral issue. Like many, I grew up with the idea that because anger was evil you should never even feel it, let alone express it. Then I began meeting people pushing an opposite extreme. It is good to feel angry, they claimed, and you should always let it out.

These opposing points of view cannot both be correct. How can we decide what is right for us?

We could start by noting that it is often harmful to bottle up anger. Annette will vouch for this. She would feel angry inside, but if she expressed it, guilt would follow. As a result, she learned to hold her feelings in. But that created other problems. Because she didn't want anyone to see her as hostile, Annette behaved unassertively. Although she had a full-time job, her husband and two teenage children came and went as they pleased, leaving her to cook and clean up after them. She wouldn't say anything for fear of losing her cool. Sometimes, unknowingly, she got back at the others by 'forgetting' to wash their clothes, burning meals or losing their things — but again she would feel guilty. Her repressed emotions were so powerful she began to suffer stomach pains.

Does Annette's experience show that it is always better to let your anger out? Unfortunately, no. This can have its problems, too — as Dean found. 'I've had a temper since I was a little kid,' explained the heavily built mechanic. 'My father used to beat hell out of me whenever I lost my cool, but it's made no difference. I guess I'm just a guy with a strong idea of what's right and what's wrong. I'm OK when everyone's acting like they should, but if someone crosses me, watch out!'

People did watch out for Dean. His workmates were careful around him. People would often avoid him entirely. His wife moved out, taking their young son with her. When Dean came after them and attacked her, she obtained a court order to keep him away. Dean also ended up with a conviction for assault, a suspended sentence and a direction from the judge that he had better get professional help in managing his emotions.

Expressing anger, contrary to popular belief, tends to reinforce it: the angry person just gets angrier and behaves in even more hostile ways.

By now you may be asking, 'If it doesn't help to express anger, or to bottle it up, then what on earth can people do?' There is a third alternative. *Eliminate the excessive anger itself* — by modifying the cause. This suggestion may surprise you. Perhaps it sounds like another way of telling you to hold your anger in. After all, doesn't everyone know that once you are steamed up you have to let it out, otherwise it just gets suppressed? Not necessarily. Emotions don't have a life of their own. You create an emotion through what you tell yourself, and the thoughts that start it keep it alive. If you change the thoughts, the feeling changes.

Identifying anger

Shortly we will see how you can modify anger-producing thoughts. First, let's clarify what we're talking about. Anger is what you feel when one of your expectations isn't met — that is, when you don't get something you want, or someone breaks a rule you regard as important. You can feel angry not just about things that are happening in the present, but also about events in the distant past or even events you anticipate will take place in the future.

Anger comes in three different forms: passive, aggressive and constructive. The first two, examples of which we have already seen, are based on hostility. Annette felt hostile towards her family, but passively kept it inside. Dean also felt hostile, but aggressively expressed it outwards. Both types of hostile anger are problematic.

Passive hostility can lead to physical illness — disturbed sleep, tiredness, hypertension, heart problems, ulcers and other physical complications. It can make you unhappy. Getting preoccupied with past hurts or future revenge will stop you enjoying life in the present. If you turn your anger against yourself, the resulting guilt and self-downing can develop into depression. It can also stop you working on the problem. Fixating on the 'wrongness' of what has happened and the evil of the offender may get in the way of making changes.

Aggressive hostility, too, can create most of these problems, as well as a few more. It may lead to inconvenience. If you get mad because you cannot find something, this makes it hard to think through calmly where you left it. Damaging something because you cannot get it to work could be expensive.

Then there is the chance of physical danger. Distorted judgement can make you take risks you would normally avoid — for example, becoming aggressive with people larger than yourself or getting steamed up behind the wheel of a car. Hostility can get out of control and lead to violence against someone you are close to, or even people you don't know. If there is a weapon to hand, rage could lead to results you cannot undo.

Anger damages relationships, too. Overreacting, saying things you don't mean, raving on, demanding and getting violent can put a real strain on relations with other people. Domestic violence is, unfortunately, quite common. Almost a third of all assault cases dealt with by the justice system arise out of domestic disputes.

You may lose control to others. If other people realise you cannot control your emotions, they can use this to manipulate you. Children, in particular, are adept at pressing the right buttons to get a reaction — it gives them a feeling of power over their parents. Others may retaliate. The people on the receiving end of your tantrums can get back at you physically, withdraw or not cooperate, dismiss you from employment, or react in other ways you hadn't bargained for.

So much for passive and aggressive anger. What of the third type — constructive anger? This, as we shall soon see, is a very different story. It avoids the disadvantages of both kinds of hostile anger, and, rather than being directed against *people*, is concerned with *solving problems*.

Recognising your anger and its triggers

To manage anger, it is important to be able to recognise it at an early stage, so you can take action before your brain becomes clouded. Start by identifying the situations that trigger your anger (the *A*s), and the internal signs and outward behaviours (*C*s) that indicate you are getting uptight:

- *Identify the triggers.* Note the people, situations or personal states that tend to trigger your angry episodes. Do they usually involve children, other family members, friends or workmates? Do they occur most often when you are driving, when you are sorting out your finances, when someone disagrees with you, or when you think people are rejecting you? Are you more prone when you are tired, have been drinking, are tense or have something on your mind?
- *Note the physical cues.* Watch for the physical signs that suggest you are losing your cool, e.g. tightness round the chest, general muscular tension, a burning sensation in the stomach, a change in your breathing, shaking, your head feeling as though it's expanding.
- *Observe your behaviour.* Note how you behave when you are getting uptight. Passive hostility shows itself in sarcasm, ridiculing, going silent, withdrawing, impatience, being late, 'forgetting' to do things or denying your partner sex and other forms of physical affection. Aggressive hostility can be expressed through verbal attacks (yelling, screaming, abusing, ridiculing and threatening) and physical violence (hitting people or things, breaking objects, driving dangerously and so on). Be aware, too, when you stop thinking straight, overreact, take risks you would normally avoid, make demands, hold resentments or seek revenge.

To help recognise your anger at an early stage, try keeping a two-column diary for a while. In the first column, record the events you react to (e.g. 'Son got home two hours later than we'd agreed'). In the other column, write down your reactions — your emotions, physical sensations and behaviours (e.g. 'mad', 'tense', 'headache coming on', 'yelled at him'). Keeping the diary will help you become aware both of recurring situations or events you tend to react to and the internal signs of anger.

Uncovering the beliefs that cause hostility

What makes humans get angry? 'That's obvious,' Dean said. 'Other people! They get to me, and I lose my cool. If they didn't act like they do and make life hard for me, I wouldn't need to get uptight. I'm only angry because I'm frustrated. It's as simple as that.'

Dean made it sound as though there was a button on his nose that people pressed and off he went. After all, how else could an *external* event cause an *internal* reaction? He also missed an obvious point. How is it that some people can lose their cool in response to a circumstance that has no or little effect on others? Most of us feel frustrated when we don't get what we want, but not everyone who feels frustrated also becomes hostile. Some engage in self-pity, others put themselves down. Still others react with disappointment (a more rational response). Some even see it as a challenge.

Frustration by itself doesn't cause anger, but the way we *view* frustration can. Extreme anger results when things don't happen as we want *and* we believe:

1. That because we want things to be a certain way, they 'must' or 'should' be that way.
2. That it's 'awful' and 'unbearable' when they're not.
3. That we must therefore find someone to *blame* and *punish*.

In other words, people get hostile not because they have been frustrated, but because they believe they 'shouldn't' be frustrated. They impose fixed, absolute and indisputable rules on the world and the people in it, and see it as catastrophic and unbearable for these rules to be broken. They also believe that rule-breakers are not just people who do *bad things*, but are themselves *bad people* who need punishing and putting right.

How can anyone hold such unrealistic beliefs? They arise mainly from the two types of fear we reviewed in chapter 10. The first is fear of discomfort. This stems from the notion that you can only be happy when your world is secure, safe and predictable. The second is fear of self-devaluation. This results, partly, from believing that you can only feel good about yourself if other people recognise, accept and like you.

Beliefs like these will make you overreact when you think others are breaking the rules. Why? Because you perceive their behaviour as a threat either to your sense of security or to your self-image — or to both.

You feel your comfort is threatened

Hostile anger is, foremost, the result of a frustrated demand. One of your 'rules for living' has been broken. Something is happening other than how you think it should or must happen. Involved in anger that arises from discomfort anxiety are demands like the following:

> 'I should be able to have the things I want, and act and live my life as I want to.'
> 'Other people should not do anything to frustrate me or deprive me of the things I want or believe that I need.'
> 'They must not disrupt the orderliness and security of my life.'
> 'When other people behave badly, I must get angry and let them know how I feel — otherwise they'll keep doing it and things will get worse.'

Do any of these ring a bell for you? Because they are stated quite bluntly, you may be tempted to deny them. But be honest with yourself — without thoughts like these, you are unlikely to get hostile.

Demands of this kind are often linked with catastrophising. Dean, for instance, told himself that if a meal wasn't ready on time, this was the ultimate in inconsiderate behaviour and the end of the world because it meant the household was falling apart. In reality, things weren't anywhere near that bad. Often, what we react to are self-created illusions of disaster. Anger may be a bellow of outrage against an interruption of our ordered and predictable world. Underlying this 'low frustration-tolerance' are beliefs such as, 'Because life should always be predictable and safe, it's *awful* and I *can't stand it* when things go wrong.'

You feel your self-image is threatened
If you believe, as many do, that you have to see yourself as 'worthwhile', you will be oversensitive to any real or imagined slight from others. You will interpret their behaviour as belittling or discounting you. Annette, for instance, rated her family's inconsiderate behaviour as somehow meaning she was a 'nonentity'. This plugged into doubts she already had about herself. Such self-rating is usually combined with demands like the following:

> 'Other people should not criticise me, put me down or behave in any way that threatens my sense of self-worth.'
> 'They must always treat me fairly and justly and give me the love, approval and recognition that I need.'

Do you think that if people act unfairly towards you, this reflects on your worth as a person? What you are saying is that you cannot feel OK about yourself unless other people give you recognition, acceptance and love, and never reject you or behave badly toward you. When someone does something you dislike, you tell yourself, 'The way they're behaving shows they think I'm nothing. If that's true, it makes me nothing.' Your anger — which is a defence against feeling bad about yourself — results from the additional thought 'They shouldn't make me feel that way and they're swine for doing so.'

Other anger-producing thoughts
Rating another person can add to the problem. If you label him or her (or them) in a negative and absolute manner — 'hypocrite', 'bitch', 'lazy sods' — it will fuel your hostility by making you think you are somehow justified in being angry.

Misinterpretations (*distortions of reality*) can initiate the demand–hostility cycle. A common example is *mind-reading* — thinking you can fathom other people's motives for what they do. You are more likely to get angry with others if you tell yourself that their actions were deliberate and calculated. You can make this worse with *personalising* — thinking they are trying to get at you in particular.

Watch out for *fortune-telling* — predicting that if circumstances aren't as they 'should' be, bad things will happen. Your resulting discomfort will, in turn, feed the demand that people and things 'must' be a certain way if disaster and misery are to be avoided.

Filtering may lead you to see only negatives and view yourself as powerless to control what is going on. This will contribute to your anxiety, and you will get angry by blaming others for your feeling of weakness.

Emotional reasoning can fuel the blaming process. If you tell yourself that because you are angry it proves someone must have done something wrong, you justify the anger in your own mind. If you are inclined to moralise about anger, emotional reasoning can also contribute to a train of thought like, 'I'm angry, I shouldn't be angry, it's awful to be angry, and I must punish the people who made me angry.' In effect, you get angry about being angry. Human beings often observe their own feelings in this way and then develop additional feelings about the original ones.

To sum up

When looking for the thoughts involved in an angry episode, ask yourself these questions:

1. In what ways might I be misreading what is happening, or *distorting reality*, e.g. mind-reading, personalising, fortune-telling, filtering and emotionally reasoning?
2. What *demands* (shoulds and musts) am I making? Am I telling myself that other people must never do anything to frustrate my wants or disrupt my sense of order and security?
3. How am I *rating* the person or people with whom I'm angry?
4. In what way am I seeing things as a threat to my self-image? How might I be rating *myself*?
5. What am I telling myself I 'can't stand' because it is disrupting my life and frustrating me, or threatening my sense of self-worth?

Replacing your anger-producing thoughts

Is there a more rational way to respond to events and circumstances you dislike? Yes: respond to frustration with the third type of anger mentioned earlier — *constructive* anger.

Constructive anger involves moderate emotions, such as irritation, annoyance, dissatisfaction, displeasure and disappointment. Sure, these are still angry feelings — but they won't cause you to lose your head. Constructive anger also involves moving beyond feeling angry to acting on it — in other words, doing something about the events and circumstances you dislike.

See your anger as a practical issue

How do you make the change? Begin by giving up any moralising about your anger. Moralising is pointless, because anger is neither good nor bad — it is just an emotion. And it is more useful to assess emotions in terms of their effects than it is to sermonise about them.

It is quite reasonable to feel displeased about things you don't like. It makes no sense to feel good when you don't get what you desire, or things aren't as you want them to be. Anger can in fact be constructive when it energises you to change situations with which you are unhappy. It only becomes a problem when it turns into hostility, grows out of proportion to the event that prompts it and takes you over. So evaluate your own feelings of anger in a *practical* way. Is it helping? Is it motivating you to change whatever you are unhappy with?

Move from demanding to preferring

The next step is to tackle the demands that underlie your hostility and replace them with preferences. If you don't get what you 'need' or 'must have', or something doesn't happen as it 'should', you will be prone to going over the top. But when a *want*, *desire* or *preference* isn't met, you are more likely just to feel disappointed or annoyed.

To help yourself move from demanding to preferring, ask, 'Where is it written that people should behave in certain ways, that I must never suffer bad feelings, that I need love and respect and others should give them to me, and that things generally should be the way

I want?' Recognise that, in the real world, some of the time you get what you want, some of the time you don't.

When you have identified the underlying core beliefs that keep creating your anger, there are two questions you can ask of each one. First, 'Is this rule still valid, or is it now outdated or irrelevant?' For some help with this, see the check list in chapter 5 (p. 56). Second, 'What about the rules I feel *are* still valid?' Well, you can keep your ideals — you don't have to give up your values and forget about things that are important to you. All you do is turn them from *demands* to *preferences*.

Dean, for instance, used to get angry when he wanted sex but his wife didn't; so he learned to see it as disappointing to be sexually frustrated, rather than telling himself it was a major deprivation he shouldn't have to suffer. He didn't have to stop *wanting* regular sex. He just changed his 'need' into a desire.

As for Annette, she came to accept that family members are human and will, therefore, act in inappropriate ways at times. This reduced her disabling hostility, leaving her free to be assertive and ask for some changes.

If you expect human beings to act imperfectly and the world to be less than fair, you are simply staying in touch with reality. You don't have to agree with the way things are or stop trying to make changes. Just avoid any demands that past and present realities not exist when you know they already do — then you will avoid unnecessary emotional pain. Remember: your demands will most probably hurt you more than they will others.

Stop rating other people

You can also reduce your hostility by disputing the idea that people *are* what they *do*. How is it that someone who *behaves* stupidly, unfairly or in a bastardly way *becomes* stupid, unfair or a bastard? Condemning the total person because of one or a few actions is like saying a car is useless because the radio doesn't work.

Identify your fears

Deal with your own insecurity. Confront the idea that if someone behaves unfairly towards you it is a challenge to your worth as a person. This kind of thinking shows you are relying on other people always liking and accepting you in order to feel good about yourself. Deal with the underlying problem — the idea that you have to be a 'worthy' person. Learn how to accept yourself — anger and all (chapters 7 and 14 will help you with this). As we have seen, anger is not a moral issue. If you put yourself down for getting angry, and rate yourself as an 'angry person', you risk living down to your label.

Is the sky really going to fall in? You *can* stand it when things aren't as you want. After all, you are still here to tell the tale. Remind yourself that although it may be unpleasant, it is not the end of the world when things don't go right or when someone behaves badly.

Again, however, keep in touch with reality. Don't try to tell yourself negative events are quite all right. This won't work, because you know it isn't true. View adverse circumstances as uncomfortable, unpleasant, disappointing or annoying — but not as disastrous or intolerable. If worry contributes to your angry reactions — as it does for many people — see chapter 10.

Check out your interpretations

If you can, recheck your interpretations. Did the person you're angry with in fact do what you are blaming them for? If they did, how do you know what went on in their mind and what their real motivation was? How do you know they were trying to get at you? Try to think of alternative motives for their behaviour. Remember, though — don't just settle for questioning interpretations. Concentrate mainly on the *evaluations* that are the main cause of your hostile anger — the demanding, catastrophising and labelling of other people and yourself.

Acting against hostility

Techniques for interrupting hostile anger

Now it is time to put your new rational beliefs into practice. To begin with, you may want to know how to interrupt your anger once it is in full flow. Keeping a diary as described earlier is one way — it can help by making you stop and think. Here are some more action strategies to help you check angry episodes before they get out of hand:

- *Time out.* If aggressive hostility — especially violence — is a problem for you, this is an effective and well-proven way to quickly interrupt the anger cycle. Talk in advance to your partner or others with whom you would like to use it. Explain it to them and obtain their agreement to cooperate. It works like this:

    When you detect the early signs of hostile anger, tell the other person how you are feeling, then leave the room, and don't return until you have cooled down (about an hour seems right for most people). Do something physical, like going for a brisk walk or run. Don't drive or drink alcohol. When you are ready to come back, return and check in with the other person and offer to talk about what happened. Sometimes it will help to do a self-analysis before you reopen the discussion. You can get your thoughts sorted out and deal with any irrational beliefs likely to set you off again.

    Keep in mind that the purpose of time out is to stop an angry response from escalating, not to avoid discussing uncomfortable issues. You and the other person may agree to postpone discussing the problem until another day, but don't make a habit of leaving issues unresolved, otherwise they will only mount up.

- *Handle any personal states that trigger or aggravate aggressiveness.* If you are more likely to lose your cool when you are tense, worried or tired, do something about this tendency. If you are often tired, look for the causes. Are you unfit? Are you trying to achieve too much in a day? Are you drinking too much alcohol? Don't just drift along — do something about it.

    When your body is physically tense, you are more likely to fly off the handle. Relaxing can help reduce your arousal level. The trick is to 'let your body go' whenever you feel yourself becoming angry and tense. See chapter 19 for advice on how to relax.

- *Reward yourself for avoiding hostility.* Make a contract with yourself or the others you live with to take a reward if you have, say, a full day without behaving aggressively. The reward can be anything you find pleasurable.
- *Accept the consequences of aggressive hostility.* If you have behaved aggressively, do what you can to put it right. This may involve fixing things you break, comforting people upset over your behaviour, or apologising. As well as helping repair the damage, this will help you see that aggressiveness isn't worth it.
- *Analyse angry incidents.* The most effective long-term solution is to do a self-analysis as soon as possible after every angry episode. This will show you what thoughts tend to make you overreact, and before long you will be able to identify these at an earlier stage. Patience and consistent hard work will pay off. If your anger is the passive type, do an analysis while you are still inwardly stewing. This will help you feel better, and free you to do something about whatever it is you are stewing over.

Changing the things you dislike

As well as interrupting your hostile anger, take steps to deal with the triggering events and circumstances. Use your frustrations about whatever is bothering you as energy to change it. Here are some action strategies to help you move from people-condemning to problem-solving:

- *Do something about problems before they get out of hand.* Don't sit on resentments, concerns or disagreements. Address the little things as they occur — before they become big things. If you talk to other people at an early stage, there will be less to get hostile about in the first place.
- *Assert yourself in a level-headed manner.* Communicate assertively with the people involved. Share with them what you are concerned about and what you would like to see changed. Responsible assertiveness will increase your chances of getting what you want.

   Assertiveness is not aggression; rather, it involves saying

what you think, feel and want in an honest and direct fashion, while respecting other people and taking into account their feelings and interests. See chapter 15 for help with this.
- *Ask the other person for their point of view.* Part of assertively communicating with others is to find out what is going on for them. Check whether you are misreading their motives. If possible, ask them directly. Listen to what they say without arguing until they have fully explained their point of view. Even if you end up disagreeing, to understand the other's viewpoint can at least make it easier to 'live and let live'.
- *Negotiate a solution.* Assertiveness will help you work towards solutions to your concerns that everyone can live with. This may mean compromising, but it is often possible to reach a deal that is an improvement on how things have been until now. Keep in mind, though, that there will be some things you cannot change, so make sure you recognise and deal with any demands. Then, when you don't get what you want, you will at least be able to hack it without excessive pain.
- *Once again, analyse your irrational thinking.* While the above strategies can help you improve your circumstances, they won't deal with the underlying cause of your hostility. Deal with the irrational idea that you need to be 'worthy' and other people must never do anything to make you feel unworthy, and you should not have to endure the awfulness and discomfort of frustration. Analysing your angry episodes on a regular basis, using a procedure like Rational Self-Analysis, is the most effective way to achieve fundamental and lasting change.

Note, too, that self-analysis is as relevant to dealing with resentments from the past as it is to handling angry episodes in the present. If you are sitting on bad feelings about something that happened 10 years ago — or 20 or 40 — analyse them. Don't hurt yourself any longer over things that are gone.

From hostility to constructive anger

To keep anger under *your* control, change what you tell yourself. Compare the two lists on the following page:

Hostility-causing beliefs	Rational alternatives
I can't feel good about myself unless other people recognise, accept and love me.	Relying on the behaviour of other people to feel good is too risky. The only sure way is to learn to accept myself.
Others must never do anything to devalue me.	The actions of others can't 'devalue' me. I don't magically change because of what others say or do.
I can only be happy when life is secure, safe and predictable.	I can try to make my life safe up to a point, but total stability is unachievable. Best, then, I learn how to stand it when things unexpectedly go wrong.
I should be able to have the things I want and to live my life as I choose.	It's OK to want things my way, and to try to make them that way, but there isn't a 'Law of the Universe' that says they must be so. It's disappointing when things go wrong, but I can stand it — especially if I avoid demanding and catastrophising.
Other people should never behave in ways that frustrate or deprive me or upset the stability of my existence.	I'd prefer it if people didn't do things I dislike but, in real life, they sometimes do. Anyway, it's not their actions that frustrate me — it's my demanding thoughts.
If the world were a better place, I wouldn't need to get upset.	Unfortunately, the world isn't a better place, but I can avoid being upset about this fact by changing the way I view it.
If I didn't get mad, things would never change.	Getting mad disables me. I'm more likely to change things by keeping my head and being assertive rather than aggressive.
Anger helps me keep others in line.	Do I want others to cooperate with me only out of fear? What happens when they learn to stand up to me? I'd do better to negotiate their willing cooperation.

Hostility-causing beliefs	Rational alternatives
People should always behave in a correct and proper fashion.	In real life, people don't always behave correctly. No amount of demanding is going to make this reality go away. Anyway, who decides what's correct or proper?
People who behave badly are bad people, and they deserve blame and punishment.	People are not what they do. Behaving badly doesn't make someone a bad person, just a person who sometimes behaves badly.
People only do things to frustrate me.	Am I God, that I can see into the inner recesses of others' minds and discern their motivations?
I wouldn't be human if I didn't lose my cool.	Just because something is human doesn't make it desirable. Anyway, to be reasonable and understand someone else's viewpoint is also human.
Anger is evil and destructive.	Anger is neither good nor bad — it's just an emotion. I can choose whether I express this emotion constructively or destructively.

A quick summary: how to handle angry episodes

When anger is getting out of control, it can be hard to think rationally. Here is a check list of the steps to take:

1. Acknowledge your anger. Don't deny that you are feeling hostile.
2. Accept that the hostility is irrational.
3. Take responsibility for your anger. Recognise that you are creating it.
4. Don't moralise about the fact that you are angry.
5. If necessary, interrupt your anger by using time out, relaxation or any other means of distracting yourself until you calm down.

6. Talk over, in an assertive (rather than aggressive) way, whatever it is you are unhappy about: (a) explain what you are concerned about, (b) find out the other person's point of view, and (c) negotiate a solution.
7. At some stage, during or after the episode, fully analyse the irrational thoughts that created your anger in the first place. Look for shoulds and musts, awfulising and can't-stand-it-itis, ratings of the other person and any self-downing. Retain any realistic wishes, but dispute your demands and turn them into preferences.

One final note: do you have children? If so, don't pass your anger on to them. Young people are just as capable as adults of learning the strategies in this chapter. Teaching them to young children requires only a little imagination;[1] with adolescents the key thing is simply to communicate in their language.[2]

Overcoming the blocks to change

It isn't easy to get rid of hostility. One of the main reasons for this is that hostility is based on self-righteous demands. We are convinced that our way of looking at things is the right way, and few of us are keen to surrender our claim to rightness.

The answer, as already stated, is to analyse your thinking when you feel yourself burning up, or as soon as possible thereafter. The latter may seem like locking the stable door after the horse has bolted, but you will still be chipping away at the underlying rules that create your anger, and with time you will find yourself overreacting less and less.

Another block is the belief that you need to get worked up before you can change things. Sure, moderate anger can energise; but getting hostile stops you thinking clearly, so you are less able to act constructively. Furthermore, because of the moralising that underlies hostility ('People should not behave the way they do'), you can get stuck in the rut of rating people rather than solving problems.

Do you worry that you would be less human if you didn't fly off the handle every so often? Remind yourself that hostility is indeed human — along with depression, anxiety, alcoholism, cancer, war and unemployment. Being human doesn't make these things any more desirable.

Another block to giving up hostile anger is that you might be getting something out of it you are loath to do without. Are you, for instance, managing to control other people by getting in a rage? Stimulating guilt or fear is a common way of manipulating people. Or do you lose your cool to protect yourself against feeling bad? No one likes to think they are a failure, and blaming someone else when things go wrong is one way to feel better about yourself — and perhaps even superior to others.

Are you afraid to get close to others out of fear you will get hurt? Staying angry towards someone can give you an excuse to keep your distance without admitting to yourself that you feel insecure. Maintaining anger may also be a way to avoid the pain of change. Thinking that the world should treat you fairly can lead to self-pitying anger that protects you from looking at yourself.

As you become aware of the psychological 'gains' you get from being angry, tackle the problem areas concerned. Work on your self-downing, fear of intimacy and avoidance of change. For further help, check out chapters 5 (on demanding), 7 (on self-rating), 10 (worry), 11 (guilt), 15 (assertiveness) and 16 (perfectionism).

Keep anger in perspective

In this chapter we have considered mainly excessive anger, but don't forget that anger can be functional — as long as it is under your control and kept in perspective, and you do something constructive with it. I hope that working through these pages will help you feel more confident about being in charge.

As you work on your anger, then, keep in mind that it isn't a moral issue. It is a practical one. Anger can damage, but it can also help. Give up any idea that it is right or wrong; instead, learn to evaluate your anger according to its results.

References
1. Wilde, J., (2001). Interventions for children with anger problems. *Journal of Rational-Emotive & Cognitive-Behavior Therapy*, 19:3, 191–7.
2. Gibbs, J.C., Potter, G.B., & Goldstein, A.P., (1995). *The Equip Program: Teaching youth to think and act responsibly through a peer-helping approach.* Champaign, Ill.: Research Press.

14 You don't need approval

I like to be liked: you probably do, too. There's nothing wrong with that. It is fine to want approval. Unfortunately, though, people often go beyond wanting it. They make approval a *need* — an absolute must without which they think they cannot survive. When this happens, approval-seeking becomes a recipe for self-defeat.

It can be a source of anxiety that restricts your life. You avoid taking risks, trying new things at which you cannot guarantee 'success', or any situation in which you fear people might think badly of you. It makes you conform to what others expect rather than ask for what you want or pursue your own goals. You become oversensitive to criticism. Feeling hurt stops you using feedback from other people as a means of learning. Approval-seeking gets in the way of dealing with your underlying lack of confidence and self-acceptance. You keep striving for what is an impossible goal. You will never be able to get approval from everyone significant to you, and even if you could, would they all love you enough ever to satisfy you?

Other people may even end up liking you less. Do you like or respect people who hurt easily, don't say what they mean, always try to conform, say yes to things they don't want, avoid taking charge of their own lives, or are always seeking love and attention? The more you demand approval, the less you end up with.

Why, then, do we get obsessed with what others think of us? The learning starts early. As children, we discover that if someone disapproves — be it a caregiver, teacher or parent — they can make life difficult for us. We learn to connect disapproval with physical punishment and going without food, affection or other things that give us pleasure.

In adolescence, we become less dependent on our caregivers, but we transfer concern for approval to the peer group, conforming more to what our friends think than to what the adults in our lives might wish. Much in the way of teenage drug and alcohol abuse, dangerous driving and promiscuous sexual activity is the result of wanting approval from other young people.

The mass media — especially advertising — exploit this. They tell us we must avoid rejection at all costs. Others won't accept us unless we dress right, wear deodorants or drive late-model cars. We must not have smelly houses, send our children to school in shirts that aren't whiter than white, or deprive our grandchildren of expensive toys.

Unfortunately, the counselling profession sometimes adds to the problem. Much of the literature pushes the view that to be happy you need love and approval from others.

One thing seems sure — you cannot live among humans and avoid disapproval. So why not learn to be less affected by it? Rational Self-Analysis can help you tackle approval-seeking and even benefit from criticism.

Know when you are approval-seeking

Stop and reflect when you find yourself feeling or acting in ways that show you are inappropriately worried about what others think:

- Saying yes to something you don't want to do.
- Making a statement you don't believe in, agreeing with an opinion you oppose, or paying a compliment you don't mean.
- Reacting to a criticism by getting defensive or attacking back.
- Apologising when you have done nothing wrong.
- Seeking someone else's opinion on a matter of taste — for instance, on what to wear.
- Asking permission before you speak up, make a decision or buy something.
- Asking others to confirm what you say — 'Isn't that right?'
- Going out of your way to impress other people.

Identify the irrational beliefs involved

The next step is to uncover the irrational beliefs that lead to your overconcern with what others think of you. The fear of disapproval is often triggered by the various ways in which we *distort reality*:

- *Mind-reading*: you assume someone is unhappy with you but fail to check it out; or you jump to conclusions about a critic's motives by thinking their intentions are hostile — they're out to get you, hurt you, control you or make you lose your cool.
- *Personalising*: you imagine criticism is directed at you even when it isn't.
- *Black-and-white thinking*: you tell yourself that if people don't love you, they must hate you.
- *Overgeneralising*: you think disapproval from a few people means no one will ever like or respect you; or one criticism means you are being totally rejected as a person.
- *Fortune-telling*: you assume disapproval will lead to serious consequences for you.

Be honest about your fears — then you can check out how real they are — but note that while misinterpreting may trigger them, it will not be their underlying cause. The real problem is the *evaluations* or personal meanings you apply to disapproval — the demanding, self-rating and catastrophising that are your responses to it.

If you worry about how others see you, this shows that *you don't accept yourself*. You rely, instead, on other people to confirm you are OK. When you don't get the love and respect you think you 'need', this stirs up self-doubts that already exist in your mind. People who moralise and rate themselves ('I made a mistake, which proves I'm useless') tend to get defensive when criticised. Criticism most probably hurts because you treat it as somehow proving there is something wrong with you as a person: 'If she thinks I'm (rotten/stupid/no good/ etc.), I must be.'

Underlying this self-rating (or the fear of it) will be *demanding*. Don't pretend you just 'want' approval: if you are anxious, hurt or hostile, you are telling yourself you 'need' it. Watch for thinking such as 'For me to be happy and feel worthwhile, other people must love, accept and recognise me and hardly ever disapprove of me.'

Catastrophising will make disapproval or criticism seem worse. Are you telling yourself that if someone were to dislike or stop loving you it would be 'awful' and you 'couldn't stand it'?

To summarise: when you are worried about approval or disapproval, look for thoughts that are variations of the following:

'I can read what is in other people's minds.'
'Because _____ is upset with me, bad things are going to happen.'
'I'm only OK if others think I am.'
'Love, recognition, approval and respect are needs.'
'If someone thinks ill of me, it means there must be something wrong with me as a person.'
'I can't stand disapproval from people significant to me.'

Dispute the need for approval

Can human beings overcome the irrational fear of being disliked, unloved and rejected? Yes — by grasping the idea that *approval is not a need*.

This is not to say that approval is irrelevant to your life. It is good to receive love and acceptance from others. It contributes to satisfying and helpful relationships. It is useful when others have authority over you or control access to things you want, e.g. your parents, teachers, employer, bank manager or landlord. Approval becomes a problem, though, when you exaggerate your desire for it into a necessity. In other words, you tell yourself that you 'must' have it in order to feel good about yourself and be happy.

It is often said that human beings need love and attention to grow and develop. To some extent this is true of babies and young children, who are under the control of their caregivers and lack the mental powers to question what others say about them. But it is not true of adults. You and I are much less dependent on others to provide for our survival needs. We have the ability to change what we tell ourselves in a way we couldn't when younger. In other words, it is possible for adults to live happy, satisfying lives without constant love and approval from others.

What is the solution then? Seek approval wherever you can get it; do what you reasonably can to avoid disapproval from others; work on yourself and your relationships to increase the chance of receiving the love and affection you desire. But remind yourself all the time that while approval is important, you can survive without it. Then, when it isn't forthcoming, you will feel merely disappointed rather than anxious or depressed, and you will be less likely to give up your own wants in order to please others.

In fact, expect disapproval. In the real world, positive feedback from others won't always be forthcoming. Not everyone is going to like you. Because different people have different ideas about what they want you to be, pleasing others will work only some of the time. If you expect disapproval, you will be less likely to overreact when it comes your way. And when it does, keep it in perspective. Check out any fears you have about what may result from the experience. Are you going to be sacked because the boss has criticised you? Will you be without friends for ever because someone has rejected you? See chapter 10 for some tips on dealing with specific fears.

Remember, too, that it is human to be imperfect, so if you have been criticised because of something you have done, it is proof of your humanity. If the criticism is mistaken, it shows the critic is human. Either way, you don't have to feel bad because someone dislikes you.

To get a criticism into perspective, take another look at what you think your critic is up to. How do you know what their motives are? What evidence exists that they are out to get you or hurt you?

Let us say you are upset over something a co-worker has said. Are you sure they are referring to you, or do they talk about most people this way? Do they mean what they are saying, or are they just emotionally upset, physically unwell, tired, ill, or suffering from a stomach ache or the strain of a bad day? Is it possible they feel threatened or insecure, and their criticism of you is a way of defending themselves? Put yourself in your critic's shoes for a moment and ask, 'What's going on for them?' Stop simply mind-reading.

This approach will help you work out whether the criticism is worth listening to. Check out how valid the critic's opinion is. People often criticise when all that is at issue is a simple matter of personal taste or belief. Because they don't like something doesn't prove it is lacking.

Don't, however, reject the criticism out of hand. Stop to consider what you could gain from it. Don't miss the chance to learn something that may be in your interests.

While you are learning, accept your*self*. When a criticism is valid, it doesn't mean you are totally flawed. If you are able to rate behaviours without applying the rating to your total self (e.g. 'I'm not useless, just a person who sometimes makes mistakes'), you will find it easier to listen to and learn from criticism. Reread chapter 7 for a fuller discussion of self-rating versus self-acceptance.

Finally, note that disapproval or criticism is not unbearable. You have been criticised before and you are still alive. You don't like it, but it's uncomfortable rather than awful. If you remind yourself of this, you will make it less uncomfortable.

To summarise, here are some useful questions to ask yourself when analysing approval-seeking and overreactions to criticism:

1. How do I know what the other person is thinking? Could I be jumping to conclusions, and in what ways?
2. What evidence do I have for thinking that because someone is upset with me, bad things are going to happen?
3. How does someone else's view of me prove anything about me?
4. How is it that I become a totally bad person because one or a few aspects of my behaviour are subject to criticism?
5. What law says that I in particular should never have to face disapproval from others?
6. Why can't I stand disapproval? Haven't I stood it so far? Is it catastrophic — or just highly uncomfortable?
7. What evidence is there that I must have external approval? Why can't I survive without it? Wouldn't I do better to develop internal self-acceptance?

Getting into action

Now it's time to move from rethinking to action. We will look at two sets of techniques — one for dealing with the general fear of disapproval, the other for handling critics.

Acting against the fear of disapproval
Of the following strategies, the first few will help you get moving against approval-seeking right away. The rest are for longer-term use.

- *Practise handling disapproval.* Deliberately set out to attract disapproval from other people. The idea is to practise handling it under low-risk conditions of your own choice — to discover you can stand it and that the sky won't fall in. For example, express an opinion (and stick to it) to someone you know will disagree; buy some clothing you want but which your partner thinks doesn't suit you; or let your lawn grow longer than usual.

    Be sensible. Don't try this on people who have authority over you, or where your financial security or personal safety could be significantly endangered; but don't avoid it either.
- *Start tackling the things you have been avoiding.* Attend the meetings, social gatherings or other occasions you have been sidestepping for fear of what others may think. You probably won't feel ready, but go anyway. To help yourself cope, do a self-analysis in advance. Note what goes through your mind while you are there, then do another analysis afterwards. See chapter 10 for more detailed advice on confronting things you usually avoid.
- *Do more of the things you would like to.* Make a commitment to give yourself, each day, something you want or to do something you think you would enjoy. As time goes on, it will become more natural to act on your own desires without fear of what others will think. This is quite important. It demonstrates that you can reduce your demand for approval and get more enjoyment out of life by giving priority to your own wants instead of what other people may expect of you.

- *Resist the impulse to ask someone else's opinion.* When buying clothes or other items, when the choice involves nothing more than individual taste, act on your own. Seek advice from experts when it is appropriate — for instance, when buying a car or house — but when it comes to the final decision, it is your choice.
- *Don't always seek confirmation of what you say.* As well as getting in touch with your own wants, be more independent in expressing your opinions. Avoid, for example, the habit of finishing sentences with '. . . don't you think?', '. . . wouldn't you say?', '. . . isn't that right?', etc.
- *Don't apologise for things you aren't sorry about.* Constantly saying 'sorry' can become a bad habit, designed to avoid any chance that someone may think badly of you. It is especially inappropriate when you apologise to another person for something they have done. I'm intrigued when people say 'sorry' to me when I have interrupted or disturbed them: it is as though my action is somehow their fault, so they owe me an apology.
- *Check out your interpretations.* Sometimes it might be a good idea to ask other people just what they are thinking. Prepare yourself in advance, though. In the real world there will be times when other people will disapprove, so remind yourself that although you won't like it if they do, you can still stand it; and that while you'd prefer their approval, you don't absolutely need it.

Responding to critics

Learn to see criticism as a chance to learn rather than a horror to avoid at all costs. You will then be freer to speak back, get your point of view across and clear up misunderstandings. Here are some techniques to use when others openly express their disapproval to you:

- *Stop reacting in your usual automatic fashion.* Pause before you react — at least until new and more helpful habits replace the old defensive ones. You may not find this easy at first. For a while, do an analysis after you have overreacted to criticism

to help yourself understand the thoughts that caused your reaction. Soon you will be able to identify them at an earlier stage.
- *Leave the responsibility for what others think with them.* Their thoughts are their thoughts. Don't always react to a criticism by defending yourself. Instead, you can say something like 'You feel upset about my . . .?' or 'You don't like me doing . . .?'

    You can *acknowledge the critic*, but *ignore the criticism*. For instance, say 'OK', smile sweetly and drift away; or just nod to the critic to show you have heard but say nothing. This is useful when the criticism is so absurd there is no point in wasting time on it, or it isn't the right time or place to argue. Another strategy is simply to agree with the criticism: 'Yes, you're probably right!' or something similar. This will quickly deflate most critics.

Some people will choose not to see your point of view no matter what you do or say. When their disagreement doesn't greatly matter, you can choose to stick to your own beliefs and not waste time trying to convince them. Sometimes, though, you may want to handle the criticism more 'elegantly'. Perhaps the critic is someone important to you, or you want to check whether they have got something helpful to say. Use the following techniques in such cases:

- *Question the critic.* Request information. Ask them to say exactly what they are concerned about. Don't try to defend yourself. Just keep asking for more and more specific details until you are satisfied you have grasped their concern:

    Critic Look, you should know that some of us aren't happy about the way you've been acting since you joined the sales team.
    You What do I do that you dislike?
    Critic Everything!
    You What things in particular?
    Critic It's the way you shoot your mouth off in meetings.
    You What have I said you're unhappy with?
    Critic Well, yesterday you told the managing director it was time for a new approach to sales promotion.

You	What bothers you about that?
Critic	You seem to be suggesting that everything the rest of us have been doing up until now is wrong.
You	OK, you think that I presented you in a bad light yesterday. How would you prefer me to put my suggestions across?
Critic	Well, why not, say, talk to the rest of the team first — before raising it with the boss?
You	OK, that sounds reasonable. Are there any other things I might have done you're upset about?

Questioning can disarm a critic and reduce any tension, allowing you both to clarify any problems worth working on. From the example, you will see that this technique involves:

1. Asking for more information
2. Asking the critic to clarify unclear points
3. Asking for specific examples
4. Asking the critic to detail how they would like you to do things differently in future.

- *Acknowledge that you have heard your critic.* Even if you regard the criticism as mistaken, you can still tell the critic that you understand their concern, given the way they view things:

Critic	You're a bitch for what you said at the party.
You	I don't think I'm a bitch. But I'm sorry you feel so strongly.
Critic	You had no right to say what you did to Mike.
You	You're really annoyed with me because of this?
Critic	Yes. It was a stupid, thoughtless thing to do.
You	You think that I wasn't considering you?
Critic	Well, it seemed that way.
You	I'm sorry that it looked like that. What I was really trying to do was . . .

- *Thank your critic.* You can say something like 'Thanks for pointing that out to me. I'll give it some careful thought.' You are not saying you agree with the criticism, just that you will consider it. The thank-you technique (used honestly) can help you avoid being either too defensive or too apologetic. It can also help reduce any tension between you and your critic.

- *Explain your point of view.* Having disarmed your critic, you can explain how you see things and work out any real issues. If you think they are mistaken, you can say you have a different point of view that you would like to explain, but avoid condemning the other person for getting it wrong. After all, everyone makes mistakes, and even critics aren't perfect.

    You   I can see you're upset because we're not coming to your place for Christmas this year. It's not because we're selfish, or don't care about the family. You see, Judy and I have been married for three years now, and we haven't spent one Christmas with her family. What we've been thinking about is alternating . . .

- *If you are wrong, accept the criticism.* At least, accept those parts of it that are valid. This is the quickest way to get your critic's respect, especially if you are also prepared (when it is warranted) to apologise and put things right. Remember, though, that to agree with criticism of a *specific behaviour* doesn't mean you have to accept condemnation of your *total self.*

Approval-seeking versus self-acceptance

Is it time to change what you tell yourself about what other people think of you? Compare the two lists below:

Approval-seeking beliefs	*Self-accepting beliefs*
To feel worthwhile and be happy, I need love, approval, acceptance, recognition and respect from others.	These are all good things to seek and have, but they aren't needs — I can survive, albeit uncomfortably, when I don't get them. Better I learn to accept myself independently of what others think.
If someone doesn't like me, there must be something wrong with me.	Not necessarily — critics are right only some of the time.

Approval-seeking beliefs	Self-accepting beliefs
I can get people to like and respect me if I ignore my own wants and do things just to please them.	If I act like a doormat, I'm likely to be treated as such. People tend to have more respect for those who know what they want, are able to say no, and can accept criticism without putting themselves down.
Because I can't stand to have others think badly of me, I must avoid disapproval at all costs.	I don't like disapproval, but obviously I've stood it until now. It's uncomfortable — not the end of the world.
I shouldn't have to face criticism and disapproval.	Why should I, in particular, be exempt from criticism? It's part of everyday life, so it's best to expect disapproval and learn how to handle it.
It's shameful to make mistakes or behave badly.	There is no law against making mistakes. Not only is it human, it can aid learning. I can acknowledge the mistakes I make without moralising or feeling ashamed.
To agree with a criticism is to admit there is something wrong with you as a person.	To agree that you've erred is to admit that you're a person who sometimes errs — nothing more.
If you agree with a critic, you give them power over you.	To concede that you've made a mistake will most often earn you a critic's respect. Overreacting and getting defensive may leave you with less power.
Critics are always out to hurt you.	Critics may sometimes want to hurt you, but most people are concerned more about actions than about condemning a person.
The opinions of other people are more likely to be right than mine, so I'd better not trust myself.	I've got just as much chance of being right — or wrong — as anyone else. I'd better take note of others' opinions, but, in the end, decide for myself what's best for me.

Don't forget to keep re-educating yourself. For further advice on developing a more self-directed philosophy, see chapters 7 (on self-rating), 10 (on fear), 11 (guilt), 15 (assertiveness) and 21 (overcoming blocks to change).

There is one block you may want to get out of the way now — the fear that you will become less than human. Do you worry that if you stop 'needing' love, approval and acceptance from others you will become self-centred or somehow nonhuman? This is far from the truth. In reality, you will be freer to love and concern yourself about others when you don't expect them always to repay you in kind. Accepting yourself will make it easier to accept others, too.

Finally, keep things in perspective. While you don't need approval, it is of course still desirable to have some people like and accept you. Could a few changes be to your advantage? If there are things about you to which people react negatively — slovenly appearance, habitual lateness, losing your temper, aggressiveness or other tendencies — and you dislike the disapproval, consider making some positive changes.

There may be some things you cannot change — for example, the shape of your body or a disability that makes you less physically attractive. But you could still develop social or communication skills or other assets that will, to some extent, compensate for this and add to your appeal.

Remember, though, that you don't have to change. If the disapproval doesn't bother you, it isn't an issue. By all means make changes to gain more recognition from others, but bear in mind that it isn't essential to your survival. If you keep the approval of others as a preference rather than a need, you are more likely to stay in charge of your own life.

15 How to get more of what you want and less of what you don't

Do you ever feel like a doormat? Are you living your life to suit everyone else but yourself? Does it seem as though your time, energy and money are at the beck and call of others? Perhaps you passively put everyone else first; or you get angry because others take advantage of you, but bottle it up until the pressure explodes.

Quiet compliance and angry outbursts often have the same cause — beliefs such as 'Others should always come first' or 'You must never hurt someone else's feelings.' Rules like these are the reason so many people say yes when they would rather say no and avoid asking for what they want.

Would you like to balance your interests with those of others? The solution is to deal with the beliefs that keep you acting unassertively.

Know when you are acting unassertively

Whenever you find yourself acting unassertively, or as soon as possible afterwards, stop and think. How can you know when you're doing it? Look out for behaviours like the following:

- *You want something but are afraid to ask for it.* You buy an item that turns out to be faulty but doubt your own judgement, or worry what the salesperson will think if you return it. You would like to ask a visitor to refrain from smoking in your home but are afraid of hurting their feelings. Or you need help with a task but don't want your neighbour to think of you as imposing.
- *You do something you don't want to do.* You do something out of a sense of duty, or you comply to avoid making another

person feel bad. Either way, you end up fitting in with their wants rather than your own.
- *You find yourself totally ignoring the interests of others.* You go to the opposite extreme and say no to everyone and everything.
- *You feel resentful.* Because you feel forced to do something or deprived of what you want, you feel bitter.
- *You are afraid of what others might think.* You fit in because you are worried about how other people see you, believing that you 'need' them to like you.
- *You become hostile.* You get so fed up with acting like a doormat you hit back at others without respecting their concerns, wants or values. The aggression may not always be direct: ignoring people, sighing when they say something, being late or 'forgetting' to keep appointments, and overcooking meals are some of the many passive-hostile ways to get at others without making your resentment obvious.
- *You try to justify yourself.* If you do say no, you make excuses in the hope that the other person won't feel too bad toward you.
- *You feel guilty.* Guilt is an unpleasant and powerful emotion. People will go to great lengths to avoid it, even when it means denying their own interests.
- *You ask someone else's permission or advice before you say or do things.* You don't trust your own opinions and see other people's views as being worth more than yours.
- *You aren't yourself around certain people.* Because you are afraid of their opinions, you find yourself behaving dishonestly when you are with others. You agree with ideas you really oppose, dress to suit their preferences, or do other things to avoid their disapproval.

It is also helpful to know when other people are trying to manipulate you. Some methods are obvious, others are more subtle. Here are several of the more common:

- *The guilt trip.* People use all sorts of tactics to try to induce guilt. These include bringing on the tears, sulking, reminding you of your obligations, or implying you have broken some universal law of human behaviour.

Another variation is to get sick and blame you. People who complain of headaches, sore stomachs or other ailments in order to manipulate you may not be doing it consciously. Using illness to control others can be a long-standing habit learned in the past. It might be a result of parental role-modelling, or being rewarded by getting off school, escaping punishment or receiving attention. What is important is that you don't continue to reward this childlike behaviour.

- *Threats.* Some people might suggest they won't like you if you fail to comply. Others may try to frighten you into submission by becoming verbally aggressive — swearing, yelling or abusing. They could get physically violent, towards you or objects. People who use violence are often poor at communicating, or their belief in the violent approach has been reinforced in the past by others who have given in to their aggression.

   The ultimate threat may be suicide. No one wants to feel responsible for someone else's death, and some hard-playing manipulators will exploit this. A suicide threat may be made directly — for example, 'If you leave me, I'll have to end it all.' Or it might be more a hint, like 'Without you, life won't be worth living' or 'There won't be any point in carrying on.'

To help identify your unassertive responses and what tends to trigger them, keep a diary for a while. Use the *ABC* format: record the relevant events and the circumstances surrounding them (*A*), how you feel and act (*C*), and the thoughts that prompt your emotions and behaviour (*B*).

Identifying the beliefs that keep you down

Manipulation is only a problem when you play along with it. What makes you give in?

Distorting reality can be the start of unassertive behaviour. You may be *mind-reading* — assuming other people will dislike you if you don't please them, or you will lose their respect if you ask for what you want. Note any *fortune-telling* — expecting people to reject you, turn others against you, or in some other way make life difficult for you. You may also be *personalising* — thinking that when people are upset, you are the cause.

Your interpretations, though, won't be the main cause of your unassertiveness. The underlying cause is most likely to be one or more of the following: you feel guilty, you are afraid of disapproval, or you think your wants and opinions are less important than those of others. These all result from irrational evaluations.

For a start, if you feel pressured by another person, you are almost certainly putting pressure on yourself with *demands* like the following:

'It's selfish to put your own interests first, so you should always think of others before yourself.'
'You should never turn someone down without giving them a good reason.'
'I must always have other people think well of me.'
'You should never do or say anything that might make someone else feel upset or hurt.'
'You should always help out someone who has a problem.'

Underlying these demands will be *self-rating*. Do you believe that to be happy you must feel 'worthwhile' — which means being a caring, unselfish person on whom others can rely? The fear of feeling bad about yourself will pressure you to conform. If you think your worth as a person is suspect, your wants will seem less important than those of others. Or perhaps you see yourself as unintelligent so don't trust your own judgement and feel it is safer to go along with other people's ideas and priorities.

A lot of self-rating is subconscious, so you may not be aware of it; but many people give freely of their time, money, possessions and even their bodies because they feel bad about themselves. Look out, then, for those negative labels.

Watch out, too, for any *awfulising* or *can't-stand-it-itis* about disapproval or other possible consequences of standing up for yourself — thoughts like 'I couldn't live with myself if she thought I was selfish/he did anything stupid/they all turned against me.'

Disputing unassertive thinking

The next step towards self-directed living is to change the beliefs responsible for your unassertiveness. Start with the notion that approval is a 'need'. Sure, we all want other people to like us, and this is fine; but turning the desire for approval into a must makes it a problem: you are at risk of acting against your own interests in order to get it. It is good to have appreciation from others, but it isn't a necessity. If this sounds radical, see chapter 14.

It is as well that approval isn't a necessity, because no matter how hard you try, you can never get everyone to like you. You can please only some of the people some of the time. There will always be some displeasure you cannot avoid. Remember that people don't usually respect doormats anyway.

Standing up for yourself will actually make for better relationships. If you fit in with others when you decide to, and when they are clear about where you stand and what you want, you are more likely to relate to them in an open and satisfying way. They will benefit as well. When you are honest about what you want and how you see things, you are showing respect for the other people in your life. You are also giving the message that it's OK for them to do the same.

You don't have to feel guilty about saying no or asking for what you want. Guilt — or the fear of it — often makes people give in to others against their will. As we saw in chapter 11, however, guilt is unhealthy and unnecessary. It is based on two types of irrational thinking — demanding and self-rating. You think you have done something (or are about to) that you 'shouldn't', and believe that you are, therefore, bad, evil, selfish or unkind.

The solution to the guilt trap is to be *concerned* about your actions and their results, but without moralistic self-blame. Then you can act assertively without fear of putting yourself down if you later decide you made a mistake. (After all, no one is perfect.) Nor do you have to give up your values about what is right or wrong: just hold them as preferences rather than demands. This will free you up to question your rules and to identify the ones that lead to unassertive behaviour. See chapters 5 and 11 for extra help with demands and guilt.

What about this idea that you shouldn't be selfish? That's all selfishness is — an idea. It's just a way of describing behaviour. There is no universal agreement between people as to what is selfish and what is not. Why not eliminate this ill-defined word from your vocabulary? After all, you are just as important as anyone else. To think of acting in your own interests as selfish implies that you see yourself as less important than others. But what 'Law of the Universe' says other people are more important than you? What yardstick are you using? Intelligence, contribution to society, how much money a person has? Do you think most people would agree with you on what makes one human being more valuable than another?

One thing that arises from such deliberations is that helping someone is a choice. It is good for people to cooperate with each other, but it isn't helpful for them to be dependent. Ideally, while people may ask for help with a problem, they will use the experience to learn how to handle it themselves in future. Does the help you give to others encourage their independence? Cooperation with others is a two-way thing: you help them and they help you. That way, everyone benefits. If you are constantly giving but not taking in return, ask yourself why. Are you trying to prove how 'worthwhile' you are? Are you trying to be some kind of social worker or therapist, with your relatives and friends as your clients?

There is an interesting side effect of the 'therapist syndrome'. If you always help someone but don't ask in return, or listen to their problems without ever sharing your own, you create an unequal relationship that keeps that person in a subordinate position.

Grasp the fact that you are not responsible for other people's feelings. To many, the fear of making someone else feel bad is a real block to saying no or asking for some kind of change. Yet this notion is based on a fallacy — the idea that you can be responsible for how someone else feels. Why is this untrue? Because you cannot cause another person's feelings. The real cause is what they tell themselves about you and your actions.

This doesn't mean that what you do is completely irrelevant, of course. Let us suppose you tell your partner you are going to leave him. Using the *ABC* model, what you say to him is *A*, the trigger that starts things off. But it is *B* — what your partner tells himself about *A* — that causes his reaction, *C*. And what he thinks is his choice. He could, for example, rationally tell himself, 'This is sad and disappointing, I will miss her a lot.' He would then feel sad, concerned and disappointed — emotions that are in proportion to what is happening. His reaction in this case would be partly your responsibility but mainly his.

He may, though, choose to tell himself 'To be happy, I must always have a relationship and never have to suffer rejection' (*demanding*), 'This is terrible and I can't stand it' (*catastrophising*), 'This proves I'm an undesirable nothing' (*self-rating*), and 'She's a rotten bitch for doing this to me' (*other-rating*). He may then feel depressed, worthless, hopeless and hostile; and perhaps drink heavily, become violent or threaten suicide. Thoughts and reactions like this are out of proportion to what triggers them — and, therefore, hardly your responsibility.

The final cause of someone's emotions or actions is what they choose to tell themselves. What you do may trigger their thoughts, but whether those thoughts are rational or irrational is entirely up to them. You do not control what goes on inside other people.

Discover enlightened self-interest

To avoid behaving like a doormat, you don't have to go to the opposite extreme of being totally self-centred. There is a useful principle that will help you find a more balanced approach: it is called *enlightened self-interest.*

What is enlightened self-interest? In a nutshell, it means looking after your own interests while taking into account the interests of those around you. Let us see how this helped two people get things into perspective.

Pat had always put her family first. Unfortunately, this did not bring her the love she longed for. Others enjoyed the presents she so thoughtfully provided on their birthdays, but few remembered hers. Her brother kept coming round to ask for loans, which he never repaid. Her husband and children expected meals to be there but never offered to help out so Pat could find time for herself.

Unwittingly, Pat had trained those around her to take her for granted. What was the problem? Her belief that she should always put others' wants before her own. When Pat was able to see she was responsible for her own happiness and others for theirs, it became easier to say no. She still made herself available to friends and family, but only when it fitted with her priorities. She learned to put herself first, with others a close second. That way everyone got something.

Tony's starting point was very different from Pat's. He had always adopted the approach of looking after himself. Unfortunately, though, his self-interest wasn't very enlightened. Tony believed that as long as he could get what he wanted, it didn't matter about others. When his wife announced she had had enough and was thinking of leaving, he realised for the first time that his self-centred approach to life might not be so good for him. He came to see that putting time and energy into other people's happiness gave him a better chance of staying happy himself.

What are the lessons here? Act in your own self-interest, but keep it enlightened. Avoid getting totally absorbed in yourself. Recognise that your own interests are best served if you take into account the interests of others.

Responsible assertiveness

To put enlightened self-interest into practice, act in a *responsibly assertive* fashion.

To be assertive is to communicate with others in such a way that they are likely to hear you and understand your views. You can do this by:

- Choosing when to fit in with other people, but otherwise saying no.

- Asking other people for what you want, but without demanding they give.
- Saying what you believe and feel in an honest and direct fashion, while respecting other people's views and taking into account their wants, values and concerns.

To behave assertively does not, as some people think, mean being aggressive. It involves handling disagreements, saying no and expressing concerns, while also dealing with other people in positive ways — asking for what you want, giving and receiving compliments, sharing, and improving relationships. Even when you say no or confront someone, you can also try to understand and care about their reaction. The aim of being assertive is not to attack people, rather to solve problems.

For instance, honesty doesn't mean that you always have to say what is in your mind. There are times when you might decide not to give an opinion — for example, when someone has a new outfit they are proud of but you think is appalling. The trick is to decide what is important to you and save your energy for that.

Acting like a self-directed person

How does an assertive person act? We have already identified the techniques that don't work — giving in, getting aggressive, ignoring the interests of others. Here are some strategies that you will find more constructive:

- *Don't say yes until you are sure.* When you are under pressure to give an answer, allow yourself some breathing space. Say 'I'd like to think about it', 'I'll get back to you' or something similar. What if the other person maintains they must have an answer now? You can explain that if there isn't time to consider, your answer will simply be 'No.'
- *Keep saying no for as long as you need to.* Sometimes people keep insisting even after you have said no; or they push you to give a reason. The 'broken-record' technique can help you here.

Simply keep repeating your point, in a reasonable but firm manner, until the other person gives up:

Other We were wondering if you'd like to join our committee?
You Thank you, but I don't think so.
Other There's not a lot of work involved.
You I'd rather not, thanks.
Other Well, you know, we only meet once a month.
You Thank you, but I'll leave it.
Other It's a really worthy cause.
You I'm sure it is, but I'll give it a miss.
Other Without more committee members, we might have to fold up.
You I'm sorry to hear that, but I'd rather not.
Other Why not?
You Because I've decided not to.
Other But for what reason?
You I've decided not to.
Other Well, I'm very disappointed.
You Yes, I understand that. But I've decided not to.
Other Are you sure you won't reconsider?
You Thank you for asking, but no.

You can vary the wording slightly each time, or simply keep repeating the same words. Resist the temptation to be rude to persistent individuals. It is usually more effective to keep your cool and come across as polite but firm and in control of yourself.

- *Ask for what you want*. You will feel more like saying yes to other people's requests if you get more of what you want. Then everyone gains. Make your requests in a positive way. Don't apologise for asking: let's face it, that's all you are doing. Be clear and specific about what you want.

Sometimes you will face resistance from others. If you believe they are being unreasonable, the broken-record technique can help here too:

You I'm afraid the car is still using a lot of oil, even though your mechanic worked on it two weeks ago. I'd like to get it fixed properly while it's still under guarantee.
Other Well, how about giving it a bit longer to see whether the oil consumption settles down?

You It's been using oil since it was new, and the guarantee expires in six weeks, so I'd like to get it fixed now.
Other But labour is so expensive these days. It would be wasteful for me to put a mechanic onto it when it's probably something that will settle down in time.
You I just want to get it fixed before the guarantee runs out.
Other How would it be if I gave you a couple of these bulk oil packs to compensate you for the extra you use till the engine settles down?
You Thank you, but I just want to get the problem fixed now.
Other Well, OK. I'll get it booked in for you.

Take care, though, that you do not adopt the attitude that you *should* get what you want. This could have several side effects. If you come across as demanding, you are likely to put other people off, thereby reducing the chances of their cooperating. This applies especially when you are asking for a favour. Furthermore, telling yourself that you 'need' or 'must have' what you want will make it harder to cope when people turn you down. Be prepared to compromise. Settling for something all parties can live with is often better than continuing to push for exactly what you want.

- *You don't have to explain yourself.* If you don't comply with a request, people will sometimes pressure you to explain why. If you provide a reason, you invite them to debate your excuse. It is often best simply to say no and leave it at that.

  There will be times, though, when you think it is appropriate to explain. The other person may have the authority to require you to do certain things (your employer or bank manager, for instance); or they may be asking you for something to which they are entitled. What is important is that you consider each case on its merits, rather than automatically trying to justify yourself.

- *Know what your goals are.* Keep in touch with your goals and wants (and what you don't want), otherwise you are easy prey for people who are inclined to try to use you — neighbours after a babysitter, sex after dates, salespeople after your money, and so on. If you know what your general life goals are (see chapter 17 for advice on this), you will be better able to decide what you want to do in specific situations. Let us say, for example, your life goals include the following:

- Some time to yourself each day.
- To encourage your children to experience life widely.
- Saving sufficient to go overseas.

You can take these goals into consideration when making everyday decisions such as:

'Shall I join that committee?'
'Shall I agree to help out with this school trip?'
'Shall I buy that new kitchen the salesman thinks he can get me a discount on?'

- *Talk to the people who use you.* Your partner, friends, family or co-workers might not be aware how you feel. Most people, when you tell them, will consider treating you differently. Remember, though, that there will always be some who won't see there is a problem or will get defensive when confronted — so prepare yourself. Make sure you have dealt with any idea that you 'need' their approval. Don't expect to accomplish change without some hard work. Finally, accept that some people may never alter the way they relate to you, but remind yourself that this is their problem, not yours.

Unwilling conformity or self-directed living?

Identify and replace the irrational beliefs that block you from acting assertively.

Unassertive beliefs	*Self-directed beliefs*
I should never make others feel bad, which is likely to happen if I say no or insist on what I want.	Adult humans are responsible for their own thoughts, emotions and behaviours. While I can be considerate of other people's feelings, I can't always prevent them getting upset.

Unassertive beliefs	Self-directed beliefs
I should always give other people a good reason for whatever I think, do or say.	While it may sometimes be appropriate to do so, I don't have to offer other people reasons or excuses for saying no or asking for what I want.
I must always be consistent, stable, decisive and constant, so that other people can depend on me.	It's OK for me to reconsider and change my mind. I can take into account how any change might affect others without losing sight of my own interests.
I should always try to help anyone who has a problem.	I can choose to help, but I'm under no obligation to find solutions to other people's problems.
I should avoid being a burden to others by asking for what I want or sharing my problems with them.	It's good to help each other when that help is forthcoming out of choice. The other person is just as able as I am to say no if they don't wish to grant my request.
People should always act in a correct fashion, and it's embarrassing and shameful to make mistakes or blunders.	It's human to make mistakes. I can take responsibility for mine without rating my total self.
I must never reveal my stupidity to others by asking questions or failing to give an answer.	It's OK — and often helpful — to say 'I don't know', 'I don't understand' or 'I'd like to think about it.'
It's essential that other people always think well of me.	I'd prefer other people like me, but I can act assertively with them even when they don't.
It's selfish to put my own wants before those of others.	Time for myself is just as important as time for anyone else. Enlightened self-interest is a better idea for *all* concerned.
I can't turn people down when they want things from me.	It's for me to decide what I do with what's mine. I don't have to give of my property, body, time or energy when I don't wish to. And I don't have to feel guilty about saying no.

This chapter has introduced just a sample of assertiveness techniques. Why not develop your skills further? Consider, for example, doing a training course. You can rehearse procedures before using them in the real world, get feedback on how you come across, and see the effects of different approaches. Alternatively, obtain some of the many good books on assertiveness now available. (See the list on page 267.)

However you go about it, keep in mind that studying assertiveness techniques won't do much good by itself. I have met many people who have done training courses but not used what they learned. This is because they haven't uncovered and disputed the irrational beliefs that continue to block them from directing their own lives. So before you get into action, deal with those unassertive ideas.

Use assertiveness wisely and appropriately

A final note, and one of caution, on using assertiveness techniques. It is rarely helpful to get pushy. Some people constantly use aggressive strategies to get their own way. Research shows that such people tend to have lower salaries, experience higher levels of tension in the workplace, enjoy less job satisfaction and suffer more personal stress than people who use lower-key approaches such as friendliness, bargaining and reasoning.[1] Unfortunately, people learning assertiveness often come across as aggressive before they have grasped some of the finer points. It is hard to avoid this: after all, you are learning new and unfamiliar skills that are at odds with old habits. You can speed up the learning process by analysing inappropriate reactions. Recognise where you went wrong, and note a more useful response for next time. Don't despair or put yourself down because you don't get it right the first (or tenth) time.

Always keep in mind the principle of enlightened self-interest. Don't misuse assertiveness — for example, don't refuse to cooperate when your car is blocking an entrance, or use the broken-record technique when you are asking someone for a favour. In addition, don't practise on people who have authority over you: start with safer areas of your life. When you are comfortable with the finer points of diplomacy and know how to pick the right issues, you can move on to asserting yourself in more tricky situations. Remember, too, that people won't be used to you standing up for yourself. You may face resistance at first. Talk to those who are significant to you about the changes you are making.

When asserting yourself, be sensitive to any cultural differences between yourself and the other people involved. In New Zealand, for example, Maori and European may view some situations differently — Pacific Islanders even more so — and what is assertive to one may be seen as aggressive or insulting by the other. This doesn't mean patronising members of other cultural groups. To reach the cultural understanding that peoples worldwide are striving for we need to be honest and to treat one another as equals rather than assume the other needs 'protecting'. If we do this assertively rather than aggressively, we will make progress.

Don't wait until you 'feel ready' to direct your own life — just get on with it. As with any other area of personal change, you won't feel like being assertive until you have practised it for a while. By working at it, you can live a self-directed life. It is worth the effort, too. In the words of Thomas Aquinas: 'The highest manifestation of life consists in this: that a being governs its own actions.'

References
1. Schmidt, S.M., & Kipnis, D. (1987). The perils of persistence. *Psychology Today* (Nov.), 32–4.

16 Are you trying to be perfect?

To be human is to be imperfect. Yet many people try to be more than human. Some strive for the ultimate in everything they do, no matter what the cost. Others go to all lengths to avoid ever making a mistake, even to the point of restricting their lives.

David, a draughtsman, believed that only the best was good enough. His output was low, but his work was excellent. Clients who wanted top-rate drafting were prepared to pay his prices.

Lorraine had a similar approach to life. She prided herself on the way she presented her home, herself and her family. She could spend hours choosing the right clothes to wear. She vacuumed the house every day. She chased the children to keep clean and worried about the chance of them picking up stray germs.

What's wrong with seeking perfection?

People like David and Lorraine often find it hard to admit to their perfectionism. To them it seems normal. David used to think that expecting the best was how it should be. People who settled for less were sloppy and lazy and they would never get anywhere in life. Lorraine believed that protecting her children from unexpected harm was her duty as a mother and would avoid misery in the future.

Both were convinced that perfectionism was in their interests — but it wasn't. Things began to go wrong for David. As recession started to bite, new building work declined, so there was less demand for his services. Clients sought draughtsmen who could work faster at lower cost. David's response was to charge less and work more, but soon the tension from which he had always suffered caught up with him. A heart attack was the result.

Lorraine's family life was also in trouble. Her husband spent more and more time away from home to avoid her demands and fussiness.

The children, growing older, began to complain about the things she wouldn't let them do because of her overconcern for their cleanliness and safety.

As Lorraine's and David's experiences show, perfectionism is not as good as it sounds. It can bring about a variety of problems.[1]

For a start, it creates dissatisfaction. If you demand unrealistic standards of yourself, you will rarely do as well as you think you ought to. Then you will end up feeling bad about yourself because you have fallen short. Striving to be perfect usually increases the risk of failing. Thinking that you have to achieve a perfect result will make you anxious, which in turn will make it harder for you to cope with many activities. Odd, isn't it? The people with the highest standards set themselves up to fail.

Perfectionism is a block to productivity.[2] You can spend so much time polishing up one task that you get little else done. Or you may give up too easily. Do you sometimes try something, make one slip, then give the whole thing away? This is a consequence of telling yourself that you must either do things perfectly or not at all. Perhaps you bypass challenges completely. If you think you must avoid any risk of failure, you will find it easier to stay in the same old boring job, avoid learning new skills or trying different activities, and restrict yourself to what seems safe.

Your health can suffer, too. The anxiety and tension that perfectionism causes can lead to physical problems such as hypertension, heart disease, headaches and stomach ulcers.

Relationships also come under stress. Others get irritated with your striving and fussiness. If you demand that they too behave perfectly, you create a recipe for resentment, anger and conflict. Perfectionism can also get in the way of starting new relationships. Other people find it off-putting, and if you are waiting for the perfect partner you could be waiting a long time.

Finally, you miss chances to learn. Are you afraid to admit to yourself or anyone else that you are less than perfect? If so, you will tend to get defensive when criticised rather than welcome it as a learning experience. Furthermore, by avoiding things when there is any risk of getting them wrong, you can miss out on learning from your mistakes.

Why do we do it?

If it is so harmful, why do we engage in perfectionist behaviour? The cause seems to be a combination of biological make-up and conditioning.

To start with, the human brain prefers to keep things simple. This means we have a natural tendency to see things in black and white — good versus bad, perfect versus useless, success versus failure, and so forth. Early learning builds on this tendency. Children take perfectionist parents as role models. Parents may express anxiety or disappointment at low performance, or indicate to children that they won't love or accept them unless they do well.

The wider culture contributes also. We are constantly surrounded by messages urging us to perform to the maximum — at school, in sporting activities, in our social lives, even at sex. Advertisers push the idea that to be worthwhile you have to be perfect — own the supreme car, have a flawless body or maintain the ideal home.

Perfectionism may provide a dubious gain — an excuse for avoidance. If you believe that things must be done perfectly or not at all, you give yourself a permanent let-out for dodging difficult or uncomfortable tasks, including changing yourself.

Striving for perfection often provides a defence against the two principal fears described in chapter 10 — self-devaluation and discomfort. The fear of feeling bad about yourself is a powerful motivating force. Constantly seeking to do the best you can and avoid mistakes may be a way to ward off criticism from others or avoid putting yourself down for not doing well. You may also dread that your world will collapse if you lower your standards. The thought of becoming disorganised, careless, dirty, incapable and unwanted is highly uncomfortable. Though your striving creates anxiety, it seems less threatening than the prospect of chaos and disintegration.

Rational Self-Analysis can help you interrupt the perfection cycle and change the underlying beliefs that keep it going.

Catch yourself trying to be perfect

Stop and think whenever you recognise signs like the following:

- You worry about your performance.
- You put things off.
- You continually redo things.
- You repeatedly check locks, windows, taps, switches, sleeping children, etc.
- You are excessively tidy.
- Conversely, you are excessively sloppy or untidy, because you believe nothing should be done unless it can be done perfectly, so in fact you do very little.
- You worry about cleanliness — wash your hands more than you need to, vacuum the carpets every day, forbid your children to play in the dirt, or avoid activities such as camping, picnics or even sex because you are afraid of mess or contamination.
- You engage in compulsive behaviours — you feel as though you are compelled to do things like read books or magazines right through no matter how boring, eat everything in front of you whether you like it or not, or repeatedly wash your hands or tidy your desk if things get even a little out of place.
- You worry that others will disapprove or you will put yourself down if you don't 'measure up'.

For a week or so, keep an *ABC* diary of the times you find yourself overdoing something. Record where you were and what was happening (*A*), your perfectionist feelings and behaviours (*C*), and the thoughts involved (*B*). This will help clue you in to the extent to which you behave in this way and the typical triggers.

Look for your perfectionist thinking

Several kinds of misinterpretation are often involved with perfectionism. *Black-and-white* thinking is common: you view things in extremes, such as total success versus total failure, superb versus lousy, right versus wrong, perfect versus useless. One blemish means the whole thing is no good and needs to be discarded or completely redone. One flaw proves someone or something is hopeless. Anything that you cannot do perfectly isn't worth doing at all. One failure means you may as well give up entirely. *Overgeneralising* can lead you to think that because high standards are possible, perfection is too; or that one or a few mistakes mean you are 'always making mistakes'.

Such *distortions of reality*, though, will not by themselves cause you to strive for unrealistic goals. The real problem is *demanding* — jumping from the belief that perfection is possible to the conclusion that therefore you 'should' or 'must' achieve it — coupled with the idea that if you don't achieve it, this reflects on your self-worth (*self-rating*) or will lead to dire consequences and unbearable discomfort (*catastrophising*).

Self-devaluation fears

Look out for any thoughts related to the idea that if you don't do well or if you make a mistake, this will reflect on you as a person. They may be variations of the following:

> 'Whatever I do should be to the highest possible standard if I am to justify my existence or see myself as a worthwhile person.'
> 'I must minimise any risk of making a mistake or turning out a shoddy result, because this would prove me to be useless, lazy or careless.'
> 'To feel all right about myself, I need to have other people see me as careful, concerned, hard-working and successful.'
> 'It would be terrible if other people saw me as less than competent.'
> 'I couldn't stand to think I had failed or not done my best.'

Discomfort fears

Also involved may be thoughts about your life becoming disorganised and chaotic, the consequences of which would be disaster, discomfort and misery:

'Every problem has the ideal solution, and I can't rest until I find it.'
'To avoid disaster, I must keep my life predictable and have everything under control.'
'It would be dreadful and frightening if my life and circumstances were to get out of control because I stopped striving.'
'At all costs, I must avoid the emotional discomfort I'd feel if I failed to maintain my standards.'

From perfectionism to excellence

How can you break out of the perfection trap? Start by getting the idea itself into perspective.

To aim for high standards isn't a bad thing. It is satisfying to do well. It also helps ensure some degree of quality in human endeavours. High standards only become a problem when they become demands — in other words, when you believe you always have to achieve to a high level.

Is it possible, though, to settle for less than the ultimate and still maintain high standards? Yes — there is a solution. It is called *realistic excellence*. This means going for the best you can but taking into account some realities:

1. Your personal abilities and limitations.
2. The resources (time, energy, money, etc.) you have available.
3. The range of activities you want to put those resources into.
4. Which activities are most important to you.
5. Any limiting features of your circumstances over which you have no control.

Resources such as time, energy and money are limited. Your finances could be tight, or perhaps your job obliges you to get through a certain amount of work in a given time. You cannot do everything to the same level of excellence. Circumstances outside your control may restrict what you can achieve: you may, for instance, have a disability that limits what you can physically do; or you might simply lack the knowledge to carry a task beyond a certain point.

Aim to spread your resources round the various things you want to do so each gets the time and energy you think it deserves. You may elect to put only a little time and energy into one activity in order to conserve them for another. Let us say, for instance, you would like to mow your lawn once a week. You may decide to settle for every fortnight instead, because you want to spend more time on a hobby.

You will be freer to make rational choices when you get rid of the irrational thinking that creates perfectionism. Start by giving up the idea that perfection is possible. Perfection exists only as an idea in the mind. No matter how high the quality of something, it can always be higher still. There is nothing that cannot be improved. Personal attractiveness, architecture, music — everything has the potential to be just that little bit better. Don't believe this doesn't apply to nature either — beautiful gardens usually have weeds. So give up the idea it is possible for anything ever to reach a point of finalised perfection.

Check this out for a day or so. Keep asking yourself, 'Is this chair entirely comfortable, entirely uncomfortable, or something in between? Is that person completely attractive, completely repulsive, or, again, something in between?' You will soon realise it is too black-and-white to see anything as totally good or totally bad.

The same applies to people's behaviour. Making mistakes is something humans do. You are a human being, so surely you would expect to make mistakes. Why, then, do you think you should never get anything wrong? This is like elevating yourself to the status of a supernatural being.

Mistakes are necessary for growth and development. When you stop making them, you stop learning. Remember, too, that one mistake is no reason for totally giving up on something. If you eat an item on your diet's forbidden list, you don't have to abandon the whole diet. Learn what you can from the mistake, then carry on. Bear in mind, also, that you can accept yourself no matter what your performance. Question the myth that to be 'worthy' you have to match up to some universal standard. What standard are you using? Who set it? Anyway, why do you have to be 'worthy', as opposed to accepting yourself regardless of your performance or achievements?

I'm not suggesting you reject any idea of improving yourself — far from it — but you can set out to improve *specific* aspects — for example, your appearance, parenting skills or fitness — while still accepting the total you. Furthermore, self-acceptance doesn't depend on how others see you. Most people won't think badly of you for making a mistake, but even if they did, you are still the same person as you were before. Their views don't magically change you into something else.

If you need more help with self-acceptance, see chapter 7 for in-depth coverage. Chapter 14 will give you some tips on dealing with the fear of disapproval.

As we saw earlier, people with perfectionist tendencies often fear that if they let up they will become mediocre or their lives will become disorganised and chaotic. But this is just an illusion. For such people to become disorganised, they would have to deliberately try. If you unbend a little, the most that is likely to happen is that you will approach things somewhat more realistically.

In any case, note that perfectionism leads to inefficiency. There is a time-management principle known as the 80/20 rule that illustrates this. You achieve 80 per cent of the value of a task in the first 20 per cent of the time you spend on it. The other 20 per cent of value takes up the remaining 80 per cent of the time. If you are smart, you will settle for doing five tasks to an 80 per cent level of value (a total gain of 400 per cent) rather than only one task to a 100 per cent level. This illustrates the common paradox of demanding: thinking that you 'should' or 'must' achieve perfection will often reduce your performance.

To summarise, here is a list of questions to ask when disputing perfectionist beliefs:

1. Is perfection really possible?
2. What are the advantages of striving for the ultimate?
3. If there are any, are they worth the hassle?
4. Does it actually help me achieve more, or does it in fact lead to inefficiency?
5. Am I enjoying what I'm doing, or am I only concerned with the outcome?
6. What evidence is there that life will fall apart if I lower my

standards? Would it be any worse than it is now, or would it be a little better?
7. How does behaving less than perfectly make me 'unworthy' or a 'failure'?

Action approaches to realistic living

Undercut your perfectionist habits by combining rethinking with action. Here are some strategies to get you moving:

- *Reduce the performance level you expect of yourself.* Right now, plan to do some things to a lesser standard than before — then do them. Observe the results. Does it lead to disaster? You will probably feel uncomfortable, but you will stand it.

  Setting lower goals will increase your motivation. If, for instance, you cannot seem to get moving at weekends because you have too much to do, here is a useful time-management technique. Make a list of tasks. Assign a priority to each item and reorder the list accordingly. Then delete or postpone the bottom 50 per cent of tasks.

  Do you think physical exercise is 'too hard'? If so, resolve to do it for, say, five minutes instead of making your usual attempt at 20. You can always build up the time once you have firmly established the exercise habit.

  Remember: to increase your success rate, reduce your expectations.

- *Deliberately check things once only.* Do you tend to check locks, switches, tasks you have completed and so forth more than you need to? Force yourself to do one adequate check — then walk away. At first you will get anxious: you will feel a compulsion to go back and check again. If you know it isn't necessary, resist the temptation: every time you give in to it and feel better temporarily, you reinforce the habit.

  Learn to tolerate anxiety rather than avoid it — you can survive the discomfort. Doing a self-analysis at the time can ease it.

- *Set yourself time limits.* Stop forever polishing up tasks. Set

yourself time limits and stick to them. When time is up, leave the task you are on, even though you know you can improve it. This will free you to move on to the next one. It will also stop you putting things off because you think they will take too long.
- *Don't deny your slips and shortcomings.* There will always be times when you don't know something, or you cannot cope with a task or perhaps some major area of your life. Why not own up — at least to those people you regard as important? Most people will feel better about you for showing you are human. Furthermore, each time you make such an admission, you will undercut your perfectionist tendencies a little more and reduce the fear of disapproval.
- *Make sure you see the positives.* Paradoxically, people who strive for the ultimate often get little pleasure from their achievements: they tend to focus instead on the ways in which they fall short. For a couple of weeks, therefore, note in a diary the things you do to an acceptable (not perfect) level. It won't come easily at first, but you just might surprise yourself.
- *Enjoy the doing rather than worrying about the outcome.* Finally, note that giving up perfectionism will increase the enjoyment you get out of life. Recreation is more relaxing if you are less concerned about high performance. Tasks are more satisfying if you set achievable standards. So what if the end result isn't ideal? If you have enjoyed the doing, you have got something worthwhile from it.

From perfectionism to realistic living

Perfectionism is a way of thinking. Here is a list of the most common beliefs that underlie it, along with rational alternatives:

Perfectionist beliefs	*Realistic beliefs*
It is possible for some things to reach a stage of perfection if we work hard enough at them.	In reality, nothing can ever be perfect. I could work at something for ever and there would still be room for improvement.

Perfectionist beliefs	Realistic beliefs
If I don't set high standards, I'll end up a failure.	Perfectionism sets me up to fail. My achievements have been in spite of my perfectionism, not because of it. I could achieve more if I set realistic standards.
I can get the recognition and approval I need from others by trying to be good at everything I do and never making mistakes.	Approval is not a need. Anyway, trying to be perfect isn't going to make other people like me.
To be worthwhile as a person, I must be successful at whatever I do.	This demand will only lead me to put myself down. I'd do better to accept myself as a person irrespective of my performance.
If I tried hard enough, I could do well at everything I put my hand to.	It's impossible to achieve to a high level at everything. Expecting to do so will only lead to frustration, disappointment and self-downing.
If I can't do something to a high standard, there's no point in doing it at all.	An acceptable standard is all that's needed. Anyway, some things you can enjoy simply for the doing, no matter what the outcome.
Making mistakes is evidence of personal inadequacy.	Making mistakes is evidence that I'm a human being.
I'm a failure.	I'm not a failure. I'm a person who has failed at some things.
Every problem has the ideal solution, and it's intolerable when I can't find it.	Problems usually have many possible solutions. It's more useful to select the best available and get on with it than wait for ever for the perfect one. I can live with less than the ideal.
I couldn't stand the discomfort of knowing I had failed and that others also knew.	I don't like discomfort, but I can stand it. My life would be very restricted if I never did anything that involved some difficulty and pain — like making mistakes.

You don't need to be perfect: nor is it in your interests to be so. Take risks. Try new things. If you succeed, fine: if you don't, you will have learnt something. Either way, you cannot lose.

References
1. Flett, G.L., Madorsky, D., Hewitt, P.L., & Heisel, M.J., (2002). Perfectionism cognitions, rumination, and psychological distress. *Journal of Rational-Emotive & Cognitive-Behavior Therapy*, 20:1, 33–48.
2. Burns, D., (1980). The perfectionist's script for self-defeat. *Psychology Today* (Nov.), 34–52.

17 What do you really want out of life?

Life is full of decisions: we make hundreds of them every day. Some are conscious, most are automatic. They range from minor, everyday choices like what to have for lunch, to major concerns such as choosing a marriage partner.

Not being able to make a decision can be more than a minor nuisance. Time may run out. Others get in ahead for that new job, the special offer on an overseas trip expires, or a medical condition goes beyond the point at which it can be treated. Indecision can lead to anxiety. You can feel helpless, which may become a vicious circle. The longer you remain undecided, the harder it is to see any hope of a solution. You then feel less motivated to keep looking for one.

Most decisions, including those you are likely to have trouble with, fall into one of four main categories:

1. *Commonplace practical decisions*: for example, what to wear, what to buy for someone's present, which tasks to do first, where to go for the holidays, priorities for spending money, or what travel arrangements to make.
2. *Major practical decisions*: such as changing jobs, buying a house or getting married.
3. *Conduct/ethical decisions*: such as whether to confront someone over an issue, what to do about an unwanted pregnancy, how much freedom to allow an adolescent, whether to hand in a wallet you have found.
4. *Decisions about general goals*: these concern what you want to do with your life in a general sense — to be secure, have excitement, achieve career success, make money, and so on.

These four categories are not totally discrete. For instance, the values that lie behind ethical decisions influence practical decisions, and the first three are influenced by a person's general goals.

It is possible to get stuck in any of the four areas. I am prone to uncertainty in ice-cream parlours and clothing shops (my family refuse to come shopping with me). Some have trouble with major decisions involving finances. Others find the area of conduct/ethical decisions difficult — Karen, for instance. She is a young mother with two pre-school children who would like to have some space apart from them, but thinks that wanting time away from her children is somehow 'not right' for a mother. This belief limits her ability to look at possible solutions.

What causes indecision?

Do you often find yourself frozen with doubt over issues large and small? If so, the way you make decisions is most likely to be the problem, rather than the issues themselves. If you want to avoid getting stuck, the first step is to understand why it happens. There are three common blocks to watch for:

1. Irrational beliefs.
2. Confusion about your values.
3. Using only half your decision-making capacity.

Irrational beliefs

Let's start with irrational thinking. The main culprits are shoulds (which conflict with wants), the demand for the perfect solution, and fear of the wrong decision.

Much indecision results from a conflict between what people *want* to do and what they think they *should* do. For instance, Karen's desire to have personal space (a want) conflicts with her belief that she should always be there for her children (a demand). The demand stops her reaching a compromise. It is hard to give equal regard to two values when you see one as a must, the other as 'just a want'. The problem is, a want doesn't go away just because there is a should blocking its fulfilment.

Do you believe that 'for every problem there is a perfect solution' or 'every decision must be the right one'? This kind of demanding, common to people with perfectionist tendencies, is based on *black-and-white thinking* — the idea that decisions are either fully right or fully wrong. This sets you up not to decide at all, because, in real life, the choice is often between options that are all less than ideal.

Many people find it hard to make decisions because they fear the consequences of making a wrong choice. The two types of fear examined in chapter 10 can be involved here: fear of discomfort and fear of self-devaluation.

- *The fear of discomfort* occurs when you perceive some threat to your physical or emotional comfort. There is often internal conflict involved in weighing up one thing against another, and it might seem easier to avoid this discomfort by putting off a decision. To decide on a course of action is also to commit yourself to carrying it out and taking responsibility for the consequences. There are risks involved. You might, for instance, start something you cannot finish, or things could turn out badly. In addition, to decide in favour of one option is to let go of the others. Indecision may be a way of trying to hold on to all of them. The desire to find a more exciting job may compete with an unwillingness to forego security; or the desire for companionship may conflict with a resistance to giving up personal freedom.
- *The fear of self-devaluation* is based on self-rating. You connect your 'self-worth' with making the right decision, and expect to feel bad about yourself if you make the wrong one. Putting yourself down is very unpleasant, and most people will go to great lengths to avoid it. By not making a decision you avoid taking the risk. Worrying that other people will disapprove of your choices can add to your fear of self-downing.

Incidentally, putting off decisions can lead to another variation of self-rating: you end up rating yourself as a person who lacks judgement and cannot make good decisions. This creates a vicious circle in which you live down to the label you have given yourself and put off decisions or look to others to tell you what to do, which in turn reinforces your self-labelling.

Confusion about your values

The second problem area with making decisions is that of values. Values are the rules by which we live. Whether or not we are aware of them, they guide our day-to-day choices. They involve matters of taste — for example, 'I look better in jeans than in a suit' or 'I prefer jazz to Beethoven.' They also involve ideas about what is appropriate behaviour for humans in general — such as 'Punctuality is a good thing' or 'It's wrong to murder.'

Most of the time you won't know what value you are operating according to because the process is subconscious. But values are essential to an ordered existence: without them you wouldn't know where you were going. There are two value problems most likely to block decision-making:

1. *Your value system hasn't matured.* Children take on the values taught or promulgated by their parents, teachers and friends, and by the books and television programmes to which they are exposed. Ideally, they later rethink these externally imposed beliefs and shift to an internal value system they have thought out for themselves. Unfortunately, some people close off the maturing process and retain their childhood values.

    An illustration of this is the story of an elderly woman living in an occupied country during the Second World War. Several members of the Resistance were hiding in her village. When the security forces asked if she knew where they were, she owned up. As a result, her countrymen were arrested and shot. She explained later that she had been brought up since childhood always to tell the truth and was thus 'unable' to tell a lie, no matter what the consequences.

    The decisions an adult faces require more than a child's value system.

2. *You indiscriminately give many values the same weight.* Do you find it hard to see that some values are more relevant to a

specific issue than others? If so, you will have trouble choosing between conflicting values.

Let us say, for example, you are running late for an important job interview but you have always believed it a sin to leave the house with dirty dishes in the sink. It could be a quick and simple decision to act according to the more important value; instead, the choice becomes an agonising dilemma that threatens to jeopardise your goal of new employment.

Are you leaving out half the process?

Finally, many people use only half their decision-making capacity. To choose between alternative courses of action, two things are important. The first is that you know what you want to do. This means being in touch with your intuition, your 'gut reactions'. The second is that you have the ability to analyse what the outcome of different choices might be. This involves being able to think things through in a logical way.

Sometimes people undervalue one or other of these two things. Some follow their emotions without considering the outcome: others are too logical and out of touch with their wants. The trick is to use both intuition and logical thinking. We will return to this matter soon.

Overcoming the blocks

You will find it easier to make decisions when you get rid of the self-defeating thinking that gets in the way.

Dispute your irrational beliefs

The best place to start is with the irrational thinking that makes it hard to identify options and choose between them:

- *Get rid of those demands.* As we have seen, holding values as demands makes it hard to take wants into account. You don't, though, have to give up your values — just change them into preferences. Karen retained her belief that it was important to

be available for her children, but kept it as a preference rather than an absolute must, so was able to weigh it against her desire for some space and reach a compromise.
- *Give up the notion that to every problem there is only one 'right' solution.* By all means go for the best solution, but remember that 'better' doesn't mean 'right'. It just means some outcomes will be more to your liking than others. So reject any black-and-white distinctions between 'right' and 'wrong', 'correct' and 'incorrect'. Stop seeking the perfect solution and get on with working out which option is likely to be the most useful.

This will also help dispel any idea that you are trapped. Feeling helpless is a real block to solving problems. Remember: there is always a choice, even when none of the options is ideal.

Neil's story illustrates this. After his wife died, leaving him with two young children, he remarried. He discovered too late that his new spouse had a severe alcohol problem. Unfortunately, she wouldn't agree to accept help, and because Neil had always believed that divorce was wrong, he could see no solution. Yet choices were available:

1. Stay and put up with things as they are.
2. Stay and develop a separate life for himself and the children.
3. Stay and commit his wife to a treatment clinic against her will.
4. Leave, and accept he would be acting at odds with a strongly held value.

None of the options was ideal or easy to put into practice, but once Neil could see he had a choice, he felt less trapped. This enabled him to develop a plan. First, he would try to help his wife by committing her for treatment. If this didn't work, he would accept he had done his best and leave, living with the ethical discomfort involved.
- *Combat the fear of making a mistake.* The fear of feeling bad if you make a 'wrong' decision can be a major block to deciding,

but you don't have to feel terrible if you discover you didn't choose the best option. You can hack it by reminding yourself that mistakes are usually no more than inconvenient or uncomfortable, not catastrophic, and that by making a mistake you don't become a lesser person than you were before. We all make mistakes: in fact, if you are not making mistakes, you have stopped learning.

If you know you can handle your emotions when something goes wrong, you will be more prepared to take risks. The self-analysis skills you have been learning throughout this book are the key.

- *View problems as a normal part of life.* There is no 'Law of the Universe' that says you shouldn't have to cope with problems. If you keep this in mind, you can avoid the disabling effect of telling yourself how unfair it is and forever asking, 'Why is this happening to me?'
- Finally, remind yourself that you are not an *indecisive person*. You are a *person who sometimes behaves indecisively* — and who is going to learn some effective problem-solving skills.

Develop your intuition and logic

I have heard it said that you cannot improve intuition, that you either have it or you don't. It is also claimed that intuition is entirely a female trait, and that men are inherently more logical than women.

Both ideas are wrong. For a start, there is nothing magical about intuition. It is simply a kind of short cut the brain uses to put together various bits of information and reach a conclusion. You may not know how you arrived intuitively at a particular conclusion, but this merely shows the process is subconscious.

Intuition is a type of thinking. Like any other, it can be accurate or misleading. Take Don's experience. His intuition told him his business associate was about to drop out of their partnership. How did he work this out? Max had begun calling in sick every few days, neglecting his sales contracts, and seemed to have an excuse every time Don wanted to talk to him. Don relied mostly on his gut reactions. He didn't stop to consider any other explanations — and got it wrong.

Max finally confessed he had been having tests for leukaemia, which his doctor thought might be the cause of his lack of energy. He had been avoiding Don so as not to worry him until it was confirmed one way or the other.

If you don't collect the right information, or you misinterpret some of it, your intuitive conclusion will probably be wrong. But don't give up on your intuition because it sometimes makes mistakes — you can train it to be more accurate. Learn to *stop and think* before you act. Try writing things down — this makes the brain sharper. The more you *consciously* use logic and teach yourself to think clearly, the more this will 'rub off' on your intuition.

What if you are out of touch with your intuition? Practise using it more. Develop the habit of asking yourself 'What do I really want?', 'What do I really think is going on?', etc. Listen to what your feelings tell you. Collect as much information about a problem as you can, then sleep on it. Your subconscious will get to work and you will most probably see things in a clearer light the next day.

Incidentally, any variance between the sexes in the application of logic or intuition is more likely to be a result of how we are brought up rather than of any inherent physical difference — and we can learn to rise above our childhood conditioning.

Know what your values and goals are

What are the principles that guide your existence? How would you like the world to be? What do you want to do with your life? If you can answer these *general* questions, you will make better *everyday* decisions.

Values are the things you *prefer*. They range from minor preferences ('I like chocolate ice cream') to major life rules ('Honesty is the best policy'). Goals are the things you want to *do* or *achieve*. They arise mostly from your values. Deidre, for instance, values having a cosmopolitan outlook on life, so a goal for her is to travel overseas. Ian values family life: his goal, therefore, is to get another job that doesn't mean being away from home during the week.

Here are some tips to help you become more aware of your values and goals:

1. *Be specific.* 'Be a better person' is too vague. 'Be able to assert myself with others' is more useful. The more specific and clearly stated your goals are, the better able you will be to judge whether particular courses of action will help you achieve your overall aims.
2. *Write them down.* Writing down your values and goals will help you be more specific. It will also fix them in your mind and make it easier to review them from time to time.
3. *Look ahead.* Keep in mind that the past is gone. Focus on sorting out what you want to do with your life from now on.
4. *Be honest.* What do *you* want? Don't worry that other people might think some of your goals are silly or improper. The list is not for them.
5. *Observe your everyday actions and emotions.* Some values and goals may be subconscious, but there are several things you can do to bring them to awareness. One is to take note of the things you find yourself feeling and doing, then 'read between the lines' to deduce why. Ask yourself 'What value is guiding me? What goal am I aiming for?' Ian, for instance, noted that lately he had been spending more time with his children and didn't want to go back on the road when the weekend was over. He realised that his family had become a priority for him.

    In addition, take note of the outcomes of any self-analyses you complete. If you take the trouble to uncover your underlying rules (not all of which will be irrational), over time you will become more aware of what is important to you.
6. *Check specific situations against your goals.* When you are having trouble deciding what to do, write down the issues involved and check them against your life goals. Nicci did this when her boyfriend, Pete, suggested he move in with her. She was uncertain, and asked herself why. She listed all the things she wanted to get out of an intimate relationship: long-term commitment, financial security, good and safe sex, companionship, sharing of interests, and consideration. Then she checked Pete against her wish-list. She found that he did well in some areas: he was considerate, reliable with money, and they had a lot of

interests in common. He measured up less well elsewhere, however: he was unlikely to offer much companionship because of his career aspirations; for the same reason he wouldn't make a long-term commitment; and Nicci doubted that sex would be very safe because he had had many partners. On balance, she decided to turn him down.

A final note: make sure you hold your values as preferences, not demands. Then they will be useful guidelines, not millstones around your neck.

Getting into action

It is of little use to make a decision if you don't put it into practice. The next chapter describes a step-by-step method that will help you get into action to change circumstances with which you are unhappy. Some further reading may also be helpful. Information relevant to overcoming decision-making blocks can be found in chapters 5 (on demanding), 10 (on fear and anxiety), 11 (guilt), 14 (disapproval), 15 (assertiveness) and 16 (perfectionism).

Indecision: it depends on what you tell yourself

Making up your mind and solving problems will be easier when you get rid of any irrational thinking. Compare the two lists below:

Decision-blocking beliefs	*Rational alternatives*
Facing life's problems is hard. It's easier just to avoid some decisions.	It is hard to face life's problems, but it's only easier in the short term to avoid difficult decisions. Putting things off can make them worse in the long run (and give me more time to worry).
I must worry about making a wrong decision in case there are unpleasant results.	Worrying about bad things won't stop them happening. It will just get in the way of calmly thinking up sensible solutions.

Decision-blocking beliefs	*Rational alternatives*
To make mistakes reflects the type of person you are.	To make a mistake is evidence you're a human being. It doesn't make you a 'failure' — just a person who sometimes makes mistakes.
I must never do anything which might make others disapprove of me.	I don't like disapproval, but I can stand it. And it's better to base decisions on what I wish rather than on what others may think.
Everyone needs someone stronger than themselves to depend on.	Letting others decide for me only makes me dependent; furthermore, it doesn't get me what I want. Better I seek advice and opinions when I choose to, but then make up my own mind.
What I want doesn't matter. Others should always come first.	What I want is no less important than what others want. To make good decisions, I'd do better to be in touch with my own goals.
Every problem has the ideal solution. It's disastrous when I can't find it.	Problems usually have many possible solutions. It makes sense to select the best available and get on with it. If I make a mistake, it might be unpleasant — but it isn't the end of the world.
Some problems are insoluble, so a decision is impossible.	Sometimes all the options are less than ideal, but there's almost always a choice. At times like these, indecision is the real problem.

18 Changing your circumstances

So far this book has emphasised personal change; but as most chapters demonstrate, becoming strong on the inside can be the first step to improving things on the outside. Now we are going to look at a structured method for changing external circumstances. At first glance the procedure may appear drawn-out, but that is because each step is explained in detail. In practice, it doesn't take long to carry out with most problems.

This chapter, by the way, will make more sense if you have read the preceding one on decision-making.

Adopt a problem-solving attitude

You are more likely to solve external problems when you are feeling strong in yourself, so the first step is to get into the right frame of mind.

Keep your problems in perspective
Remind yourself that you can cope with external problems, but avoid demanding that you resolve them perfectly. Take the example of Karen, whom we met in the previous chapter:

She was having trouble with the care of her two preschool children. She saw no hope of relief, and also believed things shouldn't be that way, which left her feeling hopeless and angry. Then she reminded herself that there was no reason reality should be different (though many reasons why she'd *like* it to be). Her disabling anger subsided. She realised that while her problem was uncomfortable, she had stood it thus far — and could continue to stand it while looking for a solution.

If you find yourself blocked at this stage, do a self-analysis to free up your thinking.

Identify problems when they occur
It is easier to drift along feeling bad than to stop and analyse what you are feeling bad about; so use emotional upset as an aid, a signal that it is time to focus on the problem which has triggered it. Take Karen again:

Soon after the birth of her second child, she began feeling tense, easily flustered and angry towards the baby. Uncomfortable with the thought that she might resent one of her own children, she ignored these emotional warning signs. As a result, the problem grew. When she finally stopped to listen to her feelings, she was able to pinpoint the problem and get to work on it.

Stop yourself doing the first thing you think of
One block to effective problem-solving is to panic and do the first thing that comes to mind — then give up when it doesn't work. *Stop and think.*

Karen saw her children's behaviour as the problem, and reacted by hitting them more and more. She felt bad about it, but kept repeating the process whenever she felt under stress. This became a vicious circle that increased her belief that things were hopeless. Then she realised this was getting her nowhere and stopped to rethink.

Eight steps to a solution

Once you have got into a problem-solving frame of mind, you are ready for the step-by-step method below. Here is a tip: *write down* your thoughts at each step, especially if the problem you are working on is a difficult or complex one.

Step 1: spell out the problem
State the problem in concrete terms. What exactly is happening that you don't like? Be specific:

Not:	*But rather:*
I have bad habits.	I can't seem to stop smoking.
Work's bad.	There's too much to do.

Not:	But rather:
I'm lonely.	I'm afraid to commit myself to a long-term relationship.
Things aren't right at home.	We don't spend enough time together as a family.

In addition, break the problem down into its various parts. This will help you to see it more clearly and to work on it in small chunks. Karen first defined her problem as 'I can't cope.' This was too vague, so she asked herself, 'In exactly what ways am I not coping?' She listed:

> I get tired in the early afternoon.
> I lose my temper when the children are noisy, make a mess or don't do as they're told.
> I want some time to myself each day, but I don't have anyone to look after the children.
> I've always found it hard to relax.

Step 2: set specific goals

Set yourself a direction to go in by expressing your problems in terms of goals. Make these as specific as possible.

Karen decided she wanted:

1. To organise some time for myself each day.
2. To feel better.

She realised the second goal was too ill-defined, so refined it into a couple that were more specific:

2. To be able to relax.
3. To be able to stay calm even when two or three things are happening at once.

Step 3: think up alternative solution strategies

Draw up a range of strategies to achieve your goals. Use the brainstorming procedure: write down every possible solution you can think of, no matter how way-out any of them may seem. The idea is to generate the greatest number of options you can. Don't criticise any or attempt to analyse how workable they are — at this stage, just go for quantity.

For her first goal — getting time to herself — Karen came up with the following strategies:

a) Send the children to a daycare centre.
b) Enrol them at a kindergarten.
c) Divorce and have them live with their father.
d) Move back to where my parents live so they can baby-sit.
e) Leave the children alone for two hours a day.
f) Tranquillise them.

Step 4: decide which strategies to pursue

Examine carefully all the options you have written down, then decide which ones you will use. Ask three key questions:

1. What are the likely *consequences* of each course of action:
    a) both negative and positive?
    b) for myself and significant others?
    c) both long and short term?
2. How does each *fit* with my personal *value system*?
3. How *useful* would each be in helping me achieve the goal I have set?

The idea is to select those strategies most likely to help you achieve your goals while avoiding undesirable consequences. Start by culling any unsuitable options.

Karen decided that although (e) and (f) would 'work', the consequences would be undesirable and both options were at odds with her values. Strategy (c) she threw out as she didn't want a divorce. She also rejected (d), as her husband, Don, would have to give up a very good job and, anyway, it was unrealistic to expect her parents to baby-sit every day. She was uncertain about strategy (a). Although using daycare would achieve the goal, it would cost more money than she and Don could afford. She decided strategy (b) would work only partially. Kindergarten was affordable and involved no undesirable consequences, but only her older child would be able to attend.

Once you start thinking creatively in this way, all sorts of ideas come to mind. You may find yourself returning to earlier stages of the process.

After talking with some friends, Karen thought of a further option:

g) Organise a parents' group.

Each parent would take a turn at caring for everyone's children while the others had a break. She felt too run-down to cope with other children as well as her own, but decided to review this idea later.

Karen finally decided to modify and combine two of the strategies on her list: she would send her older child to kindergarten and the younger one to daycare, which would mean finding the fees for one only.

A single strategy may be enough with which to achieve a goal, but often you will need to follow several courses of action before you feel satisfied. Sometimes, of course, there won't be any solution that is desirable. Take the case in which your only options are divorce or putting up with an unhappy marriage in which your partner won't change. In situations like this, your best approach is to work out what would be the least unsatisfactory option. It is of little use looking for the ideal, because there isn't one.

Step 5: identify any blocks to your strategies

Are there any potential obstacles to the strategies you have chosen? Identify them now, then you can take them into account when it is time to act.

For the daycare option, Karen could identify two possible blocks:

1. There might not be enough money.
2. Don might resist diverting finance from our already tight budget.

Step 6: think up specific tactics

By now you will have selected one or more strategies for achieving your goal. View the successful application of each strategy as a subgoal. It is now time to come up with some tactics — that is, specific ways of achieving your subgoals. In other words, think about what you are actually going to do. Once again, use the brainstorming method as described in step 3. Go for the maximum quantity of ideas without, at this stage, considering their quality.

When she looked at the daycare strategy, Karen thought of the following tactics:

a) Talk to Don tonight and just tell him what's going to happen.
b) Find out the costs of various daycare options.
c) Look at the family budget to see if we can cut down anywhere.
d) Explain to Don how I've been feeling lately. Go through all the strategies with him and explain why I think some are better than others. Then give him the chance to say what he thinks.

Step 7: select your tactics

Select the tactics to put into action. Be guided in your selection by questions similar to those in step 4:

1. What are the likely *consequences* of each one?
2. How does each *fit* with my personal value system?
3. Will this tactic be *useful* in enacting the strategy concerned?
4. Will it get around the potential *blocks* I have identified?

Karen deleted tactic (a), as she thought Don might reject the idea if she didn't explain why she wanted to divert some of their already tight finances. It was also at odds with her belief that consultation was a good thing. Tactics (b) and (c) seemed as if they would help without any undesirable consequences. Tactic (d) seemed likely to ensure Don's cooperation.

Karen decided to carry out (b), (c) and (d).

Step 8: put your tactics into practice and observe the results

Now put the tactics you have chosen to the test. If you don't get the results you want, don't give up. Go back to an earlier stage of the process and start again from that point.

Karen phoned some daycare centres for details and costs. She couldn't locate any spare money in the family budget to cover fees, so she went back to step 6 (thinking up tactics). She came up with a new tactic:

e) Get a part-time job to pay for the daycare.

This appealed to her. She would get the space she wanted, plus the stimulation of mixing with other people.

Karen talked to Don and showed him how important it was to have time away from the children. They agreed that any money she earned would go towards the daycare rather than into the main family budget.

The eight steps summarised

By now you might be saying 'Phew! Do I have to go through all that every time I make a decision?' Don't worry — it isn't as burdensome as it appears at first. Often you will be able to skip some stages. Even the whole process won't take long for many problems. The mere act of stopping to think may even give you a solution.

For major decisions — like moving to another area, getting a divorce or changing jobs — you may choose to spread the process over days or even weeks. Your problem-solving actions might then include collecting information and sounding out other people on various options.

While you are learning the method, go through all the steps when working on a problem. Once you have had some practice, you can modify and shorten the process to suit yourself. Here is the whole thing at a glance:

1. Spell out your problems in concrete, specific terms.
2. Express your problems in terms of *goals*.
3. Brainstorm alternative *strategies*.
4. Consider each strategy (possible results, how it fits with your values, usefulness), then decide which to pursue.
5. Identify any blocks to carrying out your chosen strategies.
6. Brainstorm specific *tactics* for carrying out your strategies.
7. Select the tactics to use.
8. Put your tactics into practice, i.e. get into *action*. Observe the results. If you don't get the outcome you want, go through the steps again.

Remember: goals — strategies — tactics — action.

19 Managing stress

People have always endured stress. However, the subject of stress has assumed a far greater importance in recent years than it has ever done before.[1] Much attention is currently being given to workplace stress in particular.[2] There are a number of reasons for this new emphasis, including an increased awareness of the cost of stress to people and the economy. Probably the main reason, though, is simply that more people feel stressed these days. This prompts another question: why does stress seem to be on the increase?

Stress has two main causes, and to understand these it will help if we begin by defining stress. The word *stress*, as applied to human beings, means two things:

1. *External pressures* — the stress triggers or 'stressors', i.e. events or circumstances that exert pressure, such as an accident, a bereavement or the accumulation of debt.
2. *Internal symptoms* — the stress reaction, e.g. the heart beating faster, quicker breathing, excessive sweating, that occurs when the entire mental and physical system gears up to deal with the challenge of external pressures.

In some respects, life is easier in modern industrialised societies than in other kinds of society and at other times in history. We have pills to ease headaches, for example, and machines to do heavy work. But we also live among unrelenting change, the pace of which is constantly growing. We can feel overwhelmed by the huge amount of information now available via the Internet and other forms of mass media. Values are changing so rapidly it becomes ever harder to make decisions about how to direct our lives.

One key area of value change concerns expectations. Increasingly we demand that modern science solve all our problems — including relieving us of negative emotions. As a result, we are prone to overreact to our own negative feelings and become 'stressed about being stressed'.[3]

It is clear, then, that the current high level of stress has two causes: increased external pressure, and internal self-talk about this pressure.

Some basics about stress

Stress occurs when our view of an event upsets our equilibrium and exerts pressure on us to adjust. Note that pleasant as well as unpleasant events can act as stressors, because all events require some degree of adjustment. Furthermore, a particular event may not by itself trigger the stress reaction, but a number of events can have a cumulative effect and so set it off.

Whatever the activating event(s), stress occurs when we perceive there is a strain on our coping resources. This explains why people react to stress differently from one another. Some people are able to laugh off problems, or otherwise to take them in their stride. Either (1) they don't perceive there is a problem at all, or (2) they do perceive a problem but believe they can cope with it, or (3) they start by believing they can't cope but evaluate their belief rationally and get the situation into perspective (for example, they come to see the situation as 'unfortunate' rather than 'catastrophic'). How we think about stress and its triggers determines how much distress we experience.

If we view stress as a bad thing, we predispose ourselves to overreact to it. But the reality is, not all stress is bad. In fact, some stress is essential to survival: we need it to motivate ourselves and to keep ourselves alert as circumstances require. It is a problem only when we become overloaded by it — when we experience emotional upset, dysfunctional behaviour and physical problems to the extent that they hinder us from coping effectively.

Twelve strategies for managing stress

Effective stress management is generally regarded as depending on a number of basic strategies. Stress is a huge subject in its own right, so there is room here only for a summary of these. (For a more in-depth exposition, see my book *GoodStress*.[4]) Some of the following items will be familiar from earlier in this book.

1. *Have clear, realistic goals and know what your values are.* This comes at the top of the list because it affects how the 11 other strategies are utilised. If you are clear about what you want out of life, you will be better able to make wise day-to-day decisions in keeping with your goals and values. See chapter 17 for detailed coverage of goal-setting.
2. *Care for your body.* Stress-proof your body, e.g. eat a balanced diet, use caffeine and alcohol in moderation, avoid harmful drugs and maintain a regular exercise programme appropriate to your health, age and level of fitness.
3. *Be able to relax your body and mind.* Learn a technique for letting go of tension when your body is tightening up excessively. It is best if you can implement this while going about your daily activities, even while you are with other people. I have found the *three-stage relaxation training* method to be effective with most of my clients over the years.[5] This takes three weeks to work through, using two tape recordings. At the end of this period you will no longer require the tapes, as you will be able to relax instantly in any situation, even while you are busy or with other people. (Tapes and instructions are available via the Internet at www.rational.org.nz/public/relaxtape.htm.) Another helpful technique is *breathing focus.* This is a simple way of freeing up the mind and relaxing the body in order to obtain both physical and mental respite.[6]
4. *Sleep well.* Poor sleep can be a stressor in itself as well as exacerbating other triggers. The solution depends on the type of sleep problem. An important tip: don't rely on sleeping pills – prolonged use can make things worse. You will do better to apply effective self-help behavioural strategies.[7]
5. *Maintain a helpful support system, including family and friends* Talking problems over can ease emotional tension. You can unload annoyances before they become big emotional issues

clarify concerns and get others' opinions. It can also help just to know you are not alone. Support may come from a partner, a close friend, an acquaintance, a relative or a co-worker. You may find support at such places as a social club, a church group, a special-interest club or society, an adult-education class or a local neighbourhood-support group, or at work.

6. *Act assertively in your dealings with other people.* You will be better able to use support from others, and manage your life generally, if you can communicate to others what you want (and don't want) in a clear and appropriately assertive manner. See chapter 15 for help with this.

7. *Keep stimulation and variety in your life.* Lack of variety and stimulation can lead to boredom — a state of weariness and discontent that in turn can lead to frustration and even depression. To stay mentally healthy, humans need a degree of challenge and stimulation. Try to keep some variety in your work routine, cultivate interests outside work, take planned holidays and from time to time find new things to do.

8. *Manage your time effectively to achieve your goals.* Unattended or unfinished jobs can mount up and become overwhelming, which is stressful. Furthermore, other stress-management strategies require time. Consequently, effective stress management requires effective time management. How to manage your time? First, be clear about what is important to you. Categorise things to be done according to the following:

   a) Important and urgent.
   b) Important but not urgent.
   c) Urgent but not important.
   d) Not important and not urgent.

Give most of your time to (a) and (b). Plan how you are going to use your time in advance, keeping your priorities in mind. Break large tasks into smaller subtasks. Avoid perfectionism (see chapter 16). Create extra time by avoiding time-wasting activities, such as low-importance tasks, jobs you can delegate, unnecessary travel and low-priority interruptions.

Make quicker, more effective decisions (see chapter 17).
9. *Manage your financial and material resources.* Having adequate money can help you achieve your goals and therefore avoid stress. Use your money purposefully, always with your goals and values in mind. Have a financial plan, or budget. Make your money go further by using credit judiciously (or not at all), planning any shopping trips and sticking to the plan, shopping around for the best deals, learning how to do your own maintenance, and so on.
10. *Manage the changes in your life.* While stimulation and variety are important, it is possible to have too much of a good thing, so anticipate and manage change as best you can. Plan and prepare for major changes, such as moving house or retirement. Stagger multiple changes; for example, if you are about to start a new job, delay changing your car until you've settled in at work. When you feel overloaded, stick to familiar routines for a while. Make use of support from others when facing change.
11. *Know how to solve problems.* Have a structured process to follow whenever you are faced with a significant problem that does not have an obvious or satisfactory solution. See chapter 18 for advice on this.
12. *Ask for help when you need it.* There may come a time when you need to look beyond your own resources and seek assistance from an appropriate professional. See chapter 22 for guidance.

While stress management alone will not always be enough to deal with severe emotional difficulties, reducing the various pressures in your life will almost certainly help.

References
1. European Agency for Safety and Health at Work. (2000). *Research on Work-Related Stress.* Luxembourg: Office for Official Publications of the European Communities.
2. European Agency for Safety and Health at Work. (2002). *Prevention of Psychosocial Risks and Stress at Work in Practice.* Luxembourg: Office for Official Publications of the European Communities.

3. Froggatt, W., (2003). *FearLess: Your guide to overcoming anxiety*. Auckland: HarperCollins.
4. Froggatt, W., (1997). *GoodStress: The life that can be yours*. Auckland: HarperCollins.
5. Froggatt (1997, 2003).
6. Froggatt (1997, 2003).
7. Froggatt (1997, 2003).

20 Putting it all together: twelve principles for rational living

From 12 strategies for managing stress, we move in this chapter to 12 principles — or ways of *thinking* — that summarise the rational ideas explored in this book. The following is a condensed version of the fuller presentation in my book *GoodStress*.

1. Self-knowledge

Self-knowledge — on which the other principles build — involves knowing your capabilities and your limits, your personal temperament and typical coping style, and your values and goals.

Though you may share many ideals with others in your social group, every person has a unique system of values and goals. In addition, everyone has certain abilities — and limits. Do you recognise your abilities and make the most of them? Do you also acknowledge your limits and know when to stop?

Everyone has their own temperament, style of managing stress and value system. The coping strategies most likely to be effective for you will be relevant to your personal style and compatible with your personal values.

2. Self-acceptance and confidence

To *accept yourself* is to acknowledge three things:

1. You exist.
2. There is no reason why you should be any different from how you are.
3. You are neither worthy nor unworthy.

Self-acceptance involves rejection of any *demand* that you be different. You may sensibly *prefer* to be different and decide to change some things. But keep the desire to change as a preference — there is no 'Law of the Universe' that says you 'have' to change.

Instead of evaluating your 'self', use your energy and time to evaluate:

1. Your behaviour.
2. The quality of your existence.

Check your behaviour to see whether it helps you enjoy your life and achieve your goals. Evaluate the quality of your existence to see whether you are enjoying your life rather than worrying about whether you are a 'worthwhile' person.

Confidence involves three things:

1. Know what you can and can't do.
2. Being prepared to try things to the limit of your ability.
3. Regularly working at extending your capabilities.

Self-confidence implies perfection — that you, as a *total person*, are able to do everything well. Confidence in your *abilities* is more realistic, so instead of self-confidence, aim for ability-confidence[1] — social confidence, work confidence, driving confidence, house-care confidence, examination confidence, relationship confidence and so on.

3. Enlightened self-interest

It is important to your survival and happiness that you are able to act in your own interest. But is also important to keep in mind that your interests will be best served if you take into account the interests of others. In other words, ensure your self-interest is *enlightened*.

Individual interests are best served by mutual cooperation. Self-interest without social interest is misguided; so is social interest without self-interest. Knowing what is in your interest will help you get what is best for you and avoid what is harmful, and keep you moving towards your goals. But you are most likely to achieve your aims if you consider other people. Treat them well and there is a good chance they will reciprocate. Contribute to their welfare and they will be encouraged to contribute to yours. Contributing to the society in which you live will create a better environment in which to pursue your interests.

4. Tolerance for frustration and discomfort

High tolerance will keep you from overreacting to things you dislike. It will help you tackle problems and issues rather than avoid them. It will enable you to take risks and try new experiences. How come? Because high tolerance involves accepting the reality of frustration and discomfort, and keeping the badness of events and circumstances in perspective.

To accept frustration and discomfort is to acknowledge that, while you may dislike them, they are realities. They exist, and there is no 'Law of the Universe' that says they 'shouldn't' exist (although you may *prefer* they didn't). You expect to experience *appropriate* negative emotions such as concern, remorse, regret, sadness, annoyance and disappointment; but you avoid exaggerating these emotions (by telling yourself you 'can't stand' them) into anxiety, guilt, shame, depression, hostile anger, hurt or self-pity.

5. Long-range enjoyment

Like most people, you probably want to enjoy life. As well as avoiding distress, you want to experience pleasure. And you probably want pleasure now, not tomorrow. But there are times when it is in your interests to forgo immediate pleasure in order to obtain greater enjoyment in the longer term.

Seek enjoyment in each and every present moment, rather than putting off pleasure until 'tomorrow' or dwelling on the past. However, to enjoy a continuation of enjoyable present moments, it is sometimes necessary to postpone pleasure. For example, you may wish to drink more alcohol now, but by restricting your intake today you will keep your body in shape for further consumption in ten years' time. Or you may wish to buy a new stereo, but instead make do with the one you already have and save the money for the greater pleasure of an overseas trip. To sum up: *remember the lessons of the past, prepare for the future — but live now.*

6. Risk-taking

It is human nature to seek safety, predictability and freedom from fear. But a totally secure life would be a boring one. To grow as a person and improve one's quality of life means being prepared to take some chances.

Be willing to take sensible risks in order to get more out of life and avoid the distress of boredom, listlessness and dissatisfaction. Learn new things that may challenge existing beliefs; tackle tasks without the guarantee of success; try new relationships; do things even though there is a risk others may disapprove.

7. Moderation

Sensible risk-taking recognises the innate human desire for safety and security. The principle of moderation will help you avoid extremes in thinking, feeling and behaving.

Extreme expectations — those that are too high or too low — will set you up for either constant failure or a life of boredom. Addictive or obsessional behaviour can take control of you. Unrestrained eating, drinking or exercising will stress your body and lead to long-term health complications. Obsessive habits can damage relationships as well as your body.

Take a moderate approach to your whole life, from ultimate goals to daily activities. Develop long-term goals, short-term objectives and tasks that will challenge you and move you forwards, but ensure these are achievable so you do not set yourself up for failure and disillusionment.

Moderation does not preclude risk-taking; in fact, it will help you avoid taking the pursuit of security too far. But you can take risks without being foolhardy.

8. Emotional and behavioural responsibility

People who view their emotions and behaviours as under their control are less prone to distress than people who see themselves as controlled by external forces.[2] To be *emotionally responsible* is to believe that you create your own emotions, and to avoid blaming other people for how you feel. *Behavioural responsibility* involves accepting you cause your own actions and behaviours, and are not compelled to behave in any particular way.

Note that responsibility is not the same thing as blame. Blame is *moralistic*. It seeks to damn and condemn. Responsibility, on the other hand, is *practical*. It seeks either to identify a cause so it can be dealt with, or to identify who needs to take action for a problem to be solved. It is concerned not with moralising, but with finding solutions.

9. Self-direction and commitment

Self-direction involves:

1. Choosing your goals — making sure they are your own.
2. Making your own decisions, even though you may seek opinions from others.

Self-direction does not entail noncooperation with others. You can keep it on the right track by balancing it with other principles, such as enlightened self-interest and moderation (see above) and flexibility (see below).

Commitment is composed of two elements.

1. *Perseverance* is the ability to bind oneself emotionally and intellectually to a course of action. It involves a willingness to do the necessary work (and tolerate any discomfort this might entail) to effect personal change and achieve goals.
2. *Deep involvement* is the ability to enjoy and become absorbed in (but not addicted to) other people, activities and interests — to get pleasure from the *doing*, irrespective of the final result. It applies in all areas — work, sports, hobbies, creative activities and the world of ideas.

10. Flexibility

Flexible people can bend with the storm rather than be broken by it. They know how to *adapt* and adjust to new circumstances that call for fresh ways of thinking and behaving. They have *resilience* — the capacity to bounce back from adversity.

Be open to change in yourself and in the world. As circumstances alter, modify your plans and behaviour. Adopt new ways of thinking that help you cope with a changing world. Let others hold their own beliefs and do things in ways appropriate to them while you do what is right for you.

Be flexible in your *thinking*. Ensure your values are preferences rather than demands. Be prepared to change your opinions in the light of new information and evidence. View change as a challenge rather than a threat.

Be flexible in your *behaviour*. Be able to change direction when it is in your interests, and be willing to try new ways of dealing with problems and frustrations. Let others do things their way, and avoid distressing yourself when they think or act in ways you dislike.

11. Objective thinking

All of the other principles presented here require freedom from ways of thinking that are narrow-minded, sectarian, bigoted or fanatical, or that rely on uncritical acceptance of dogmatic beliefs or 'magical' explanations of the world and what happens in it.

Objective thinking is scientific in nature. It is based on evidence gained from observation and experience rather than on subjective feelings or uncritical belief. It reaches conclusions that follow validly from the evidence. It is pragmatic, i.e. it involves assessing whether a belief is *functional*, whether it creates emotions and behaviours that help the achievement of goals.

To the objective thinker, nothing is absolute or the last word on a matter. Beliefs are theories that are subject to change as new evidence comes to hand. Objectivity encourages a continuing search for explanations that are more accurate and useful than the ones in current use.

12. Acceptance of reality

It makes sense, wherever possible, to change things you dislike. But there will always be some things you will not be able to change. You then have two choices: rail against fate and remain distressed; or accept reality and move on.

To accept something is to do three things:

1. *To admit that reality, including unpleasant reality, exists.* It is inevitable that many things will not be to your liking. Uncertainty, frustration and disappointment are aspects of normal life.
2. *To avoid any demand that reality 'should not' be.* To acknowledge there is no 'Law of the Universe' that says you, other people, things or circumstances 'should' or 'must' be different from how they are even though you may prefer them to be (and may even work at changing them).
3. *To keep unwanted realities in perspective.* To avoid catastrophising things you dislike into 'horrible' or 'unbearable'.

Many people have trouble with the concept of acceptance. They think that to accept something means having to like it, agree with it, justify it, be indifferent to it or at least resign themselves to it. But acceptance is none of these things. You can dislike something, see it as unjustified and prefer that it not be a fact. You can be concerned about it, and take action to change it if change is possible. But you can still accept it by rejecting the idea that it 'should not' be and that it absolutely 'must' be changed.

To paraphrase a well-known saying,[3] the most effective way to achieve happiness is to strive for:

1. The courage to change the things you can.
2. The serenity to accept the things you can't.
3. The wisdom to know the difference.

One last thing. Don't let these principles become demands. They are ideals. Probably no-one could practise them all consistently. Rather than see them as absolute *musts* for managing your life, use them as *guidelines* to a better one.

References

1. Hauck, P.A., (1992). *Overcoming the Rating Game: Beyond self-love – beyond self-esteem.* Louisville, Ken.: Westminster/John Knox.
2. Kobasa, S.C., (1979). Stressful life events, personality, and health: an inquiry into hardiness. *Journal of Personality and Social Psychology,* 37:1, 1–11.
3. Neiders, G., (retrieved 14 Jan. 2003 from the Worldwide Web: http://www.halcyon.com/neiders/conquest/conquest.htm). *The Conquest of Happiness: A rational approach.* The saying was coined by a Taoist monk, then popularised by Reinhold Niebuhr, adopted by Alcoholics Anonymous and paraphrased by Neiders. It has been further paraphrased by this author.

21 Overcoming blocks to change

As you work to increase your happiness you may come up against symptoms that make it hard to get into action, and ways of thinking that keep you immobilised. Both blocks can be overcome.

Symptom blocks

Most people have downers from time to time. The best way to deal with them is to get physically and mentally active, but there is an all-too-common state known as *clinical depression* — described in chapter 12 — which can make it hard to get moving. If you are depressed, you may feel unmotivated and have trouble concentrating on self-help work.

Given time, many depressions will come right of their own accord. There are two good reasons, though, for taking some action. First, you will hasten your recovery. Second, by addressing the underlying cause, you can reduce the chance of a repeat. Most people will be able to help themselves, though some will benefit from outside assistance. There are a few symptoms that, if you experience them, will require professional help as soon as possible:

1. You wish to harm yourself, and make plans to do so.
2. You lose a lot of weight, or stop eating entirely.
3. You have thoughts that are out of touch with reality. For example, you think you are responsible for some natural disaster, that your body is full of disease and will contaminate others, that people can hear what you are thinking, that your mind is under the control of external powers, that you receive messages directed at you from the radio or television, or that you hear voices speaking when no one else is there.
4. You become highly agitated and cannot settle; or you become extremely apathetic and almost immobile.

5. You feel depressed for a time, then suddenly swing into a feeling of elation. You feel high, become hyperactive and hardly sleep.

These symptoms are all treatable, so don't put off getting help. Certain disorders may require medication, even hospitalisation, and regular contact with a professional helper will be necessary to monitor any periods when your thoughts lose touch with reality.

Irrational-thinking blocks

The more common blocks to self-help efforts are ways of thinking. Like most people who seek personal growth, you will probably find it is painful in the short term. It may seem easier to forget the long-term benefits and simply drift along with things as they are. It isn't that you are lazy or unmotivated — you probably do want to change — but let's face it, most of us don't want to spend the time, do the work or experience the pain of change right *now*. The immediate gain from avoidance can get in the way of achieving long-term goals.

Low discomfort tolerance

No one likes pain. Unfortunately, many people turn this into a demand: 'Discomfort and pain are unbearable and I must avoid them at all costs.' If you think this way, you are unlikely to do much changing. Why? Because self-analysis will be uncomfortable in the short term.

For a start, it means confronting the negative labels you apply to yourself. Few people want to admit to their self-ratings of 'worthless', 'useless', 'rotten' and so forth. It also means challenging your demands. To admit that the world doesn't have to be the way you think it should — and accept the reality that it isn't — will be hard at first.

Taking responsibility for your own emotions instead of blaming others won't be easy. Neither will making yourself do the things you have been avoiding through fear.

Wanting versus doing

Fear of discomfort may reveal itself in the 'I don't want to' block. You probably see it is a good idea to work on yourself, but you may not *want* to take the required action right now. Unfortunately, many people think that before they can do something they have to want to.

Jane, for instance, wants to lose weight and feel better about her body. She plans to achieve this by going on a diet and avoiding junk foods; but when confronted with a delicious-looking piece of cake, right there and then she doesn't want to deprive herself. In other words, in the short term she doesn't want to stick to her diet. She pretends that while she knows it would be better to avoid the cake, she simply 'can't help' herself. The real reason, though, is that she doesn't want to experience the pain of self-denial right now.

Craig has the same problem. In the long term he wants to feel more confident in social situations. He has decided it would help him towards this goal to attend a party — but he's anxious. He sees it turning out like many others he has been to in the past — sitting by the wall, feeling uncomfortable, scared to talk to anyone in case he doesn't know what to say. As a result, he doesn't want to go — so doesn't.

Jane and Craig are both making the same mistake: they believe that before they can do something, they must 'want' to. But Jane isn't going to *want* to resist tempting food until she has been doing it for a while and gets the urge for junk food out of her system. Craig won't *want* to attend or enjoy parties until he has been to a few and practised mixing with other people.

You *can* do things you don't want to: not by telling yourself you have to or that you should, but by *choosing* to — then doing them.

I don't enjoy washing the dishes, but I do it anyway — because I dislike even more the idea of eating off dirty plates. Jane could do what she does not want to do — deny herself the cake — by choosing to work towards a long-term goal rather than enjoying a short-term indulgence. Craig could choose to go to the party — even though he doesn't want to — for the same reason.

You can choose to feel unwanted discomfort now in order to make progress towards something better in the future. Wanting does not have to come before doing.

Myths about change
There are other irrational ideas about change that can hinder your

self-help programme. Here is a list of the more common ones to watch out for:

- *Somewhere there is a magic key.* This myth asserts that somewhere, deep down in your unconscious or your dark distant past, there is a full explanation of the origin or real cause of your problems. You think that you cannot change unless you discover this 'key'. You will find plenty of support for this myth. Many psychotherapists still work on what is called the 'insight principle', and it appears in many popular media portrayals of therapy. It makes for exciting drama to discover that your wicked, uncaring parents are the cause of all your problems — but it won't change anything (except, perhaps, to add resentment to the list).
- *Humans cannot change.* Do you believe you have been made the way you are and cannot, or should not, change? This belief doesn't stand up to the evidence. People do change — through maturing, and sometimes by deliberately choosing to.
- *It is too late to change.* This is a subtle version of 'humans cannot change'. It is based on the notion that as people get older, they become more fixed in their ways. But this isn't necessarily true. As people age, their experience of life usually broadens. As they discover how much there is to learn, they may become more open to change and growth.
- *I have little control over my problems.* Some people pay lip service to the idea that they cause their own reactions, while underneath continuing to believe they are not really responsible — other people and their circumstances are.
- *There is a quick solution somewhere.* This myth keeps people searching and searching for a 'magic' therapy — one that will zap them into emotional wellness in a flash, without all this nonsense about hard work and long-term change. They go from therapist to therapist, latching on to the latest fad, but giving up after a short try when the magic cure doesn't materialise.
- *I won't be a real person.* Do you avoid change through fear of becoming 'artificial'? You might think that learning self-control

will make you cold, unemotional and unfeeling. In reality, though, self-control will give you confidence to experience a greater range of emotions. Furthermore, giving up your emotional defences will free you to reveal aspects of yourself you have always kept hidden.

All these obstacles to change are nothing more than irrational beliefs. You can change them, as you can any others.

Strategies for overcoming blocks

Here are some tips and techniques to help you get on with making effective changes:

- *Do a self-analysis whenever you feel blocked.* Dispute vigorously any myths like those listed above. Watch out for catastrophising about how you will feel if you try to tackle things you have been avoiding. Put an end to any self-rating about being 'useless' and therefore incapable of improving yourself. Deal with any fears about what others will think if you change or take steps to achieve your goals. Dispute the belief that you cannot stand or shouldn't have to experience discomfort. Be prepared to tolerate a short-term increase in discomfort in order to better yourself in the long term.

  If you find yourself avoiding self-analyses, see the section on troubleshooting in chapter 8.
- *Ask for help.* A friend can join you in developing self-help skills. You can share and discuss ideas about the principles of rational thinking and remind each other to put into practice what you have learned. If you are depressed, a friend can help by making bargains with you to do things that involve getting active and mixing with other people.

  An appropriate professional can help you identify blocks and find ways to overcome them, as well as structure a treatment programme. Chapter 22 provides advice on seeking professional help.

Finally, if you feel suicidal, tell anyone: a doctor, a friend, a church minister, a neighbour, a telephone counselling service, someone at the Citizens' Advice Bureau — just make contact.

- *Using medication*. Mood-altering drugs are sometimes used for problems such as depression and anxiety. Properly prescribed medication can be helpful in some circumstances — antidepressants, for example. Usually these are given only for a limited period, and they seem to blend well with psychotherapy and self-help work. Make sure, though, that you don't use them to avoid dealing with the underlying causes of your problem.

  The drugs used to treat anxiety — tranquillisers, the most common of which are benzodiazepines, such as diazepam (Valium), alprazolam (Xanax) and lorazepam (Ativan) — are a different story. They can be problematic if used over a long period. Some people become addicted, and there can be undesirable side effects. For example, one of the most commonly used sedatives interferes with memory formation for up to six hours after a normal dose is taken. That isn't going to help you cope with examinations or job interviews. Furthermore, the relief provided by tranquillisers usually doesn't last. Anxiety creeps back, along with the temptation to increase the dose. I have worked with many people hooked on tranquillisers who still get anxious. If you are on a tranquilliser for longer than a week or so, it may be wise to ask for a second opinion.

  Medication is tempting: it promises immediate relief without effort. Use it only when prescribed by a competent medical practitioner, and to help you look beyond the relief of your symptoms and to work on their underlying causes.

- *Be alert to behaviours that suggest low discomfort tolerance*. Watch out for inertia, putting things off, drifting along with continuing bad feelings, demanding perfection before you do anything, getting angry because you 'have' to make the effort, and similar reactions. Use self-analyses to dispute the thinking involved and design strategies to act against it.

- *Act before you feel ready*. You can do something even when you don't feel like it. For instance, if you are afraid of facing certain things, go ahead and face them anyway. See chapter 10 for advice on this. If depression is making it hard to get moving, see chapter 12.

- *What if you aren't sure what to do?* If there is a problem you don't know how to tackle, see chapters 17 and 18 for advice on decision-making and structured problem-solving. Don't forget, also, that using another person as a sounding board or source of advice can help in finding new solutions.
- *Learn to manage your time.* Is finding time to do self-help work a problem? Ask yourself, 'Could feeling better be more important than some of the things I am treating as priorities?' Note, too, that emotional problems make you less efficient in your use of time anyway.
- *Make sure you are not expecting perfection.* If you tend to put things off because you are afraid you won't be able to get them absolutely right, reduce the performance level you expect of yourself. This will help you feel more motivated. See chapter 16 for suggestions. Make sure, also, that demanding a perfect solution isn't an excuse for inaction. In the real world, perfect solutions are rare. Settle for the best you can obtain under the circumstances and get on with it.
- *Develop a system of rewards.* Rewards can help you carry out self-help tasks. They can be either internal or external. *Internal rewards* are reminders to yourself about why you are doing all the work. Achieving your short- and long-term goals will bring intrinsic satisfaction and other benefits, but you may need to remind yourself of these from time to time. *External rewards* are things you find enjoyable, such as reading a novel, having coffee with a friend, watching a movie on TV or buying something you want. Use your imagination in thinking them up: ensure they are things you wouldn't have allowed yourself anyway. Plan them in advance, and make sure you give yourself a reward only when you have earned it by carrying out the prescribed task.
- *Develop a system of prompts to remind you to carry out self-help tasks.* Write your reminders on small cards and place them

where you can't miss them — on the bathroom mirror, in your briefcase or handbag, on the cupboard door, in the car, etc. Think up key words that will remind you to stop and analyse what is happening when you are feeling or acting in ways you don't like, such as 'stop', 'think', 'dispute', and write them somewhere where you will often see them — for example, on a label attached to your key-ring or watch strap.
- *Consider organising a group.* Do you know other people who also want to change and to help each other? Why not get together? You can discuss the principles of rational thinking and undertake with each other to put them into practice.

Everyone is different. Some things will work better than others for you. Try out the suggestions in this chapter (and in the rest of the book), develop some of your own and note the ones that help the most. Then continue to use them. Don't expect instant cures: using a technique once won't make much difference. Put it into frequent practice.

Maintaining change

Continue to re-educate yourself. Be on the lookout for literature that will expose you to new ways of looking at yourself, your problems and the world. (See, for instance, the list of further reading at the back of this book.) Talk to other people. Find out how they view the things that tend to bother you. Remember, though, that other people will have their own irrational beliefs, so don't accept everything you hear without thinking it through for yourself.

Watch out for the most likely way to slip back into the old ways of thinking and behaving — thinking that once you start to feel better, you will always feel like that. This will lead you to stop working on yourself. Things may be all right for a while, but old habits die hard. Sooner or later the problems will start creeping in again, and because it will then seem as if you are back where you started, you will think all the hard work was in vain.

Bear in mind there is no permanent 'cure' for many of life's problems. This book describes strategies for helping yourself feel and act in new ways, but they will only work if you *use* them.

Of course, as you chip away at your irrational beliefs, over time you will need to use these techniques less and less, and to some extent you will be able to avoid being disturbed in the first place. But you are a human being, not a machine, and you will always have ups and downs — so keep on the lookout for irrational thinking. Don't just drift along, with the undesirable consequences — *act*.

22 Getting help

Most of the strategies and techniques presented in this book you will be able to use on yourself throughout your life. However, from time to time you may face situations that are unfamiliar and beyond your experience. This is when it makes sense to ask for help.

Types of help

Help can range from informal support from a friend or neighbour to professional assistance with a complex problem.

Most of your support will probably come from *informal sources*: partners, relatives, friends, neighbours and co-workers. It may involve nothing more than a sympathetic ear and some simple advice.

Sometimes people who have similar problems get together to share support and advice. *Self-help groups* of this sort, when well run, can be very helpful. Beware, though, of groups that focus on whining about a problem rather than dealing with it. Before joining a group, check it out to ensure it is devoted either to developing solutions or to helping people reach acceptance. Talk to others who have had involvement with the group, or attend a session, before making a commitment.

Skills training aimed at developing assertiveness and communication ability is often most effectively carried out in groups. These may be organised by polytechnics, adult education classes or social-service organisations.

Sometimes, because of the difficulty or complexity of a problem, *professional help* is called for. Counselling and psychotherapy can help in many ways, from assisting with problem-solving to helping an individual make long-term changes in how they typically react to life. Here are some of the more common sources of professional help:

- Your family doctor.
- A health-service social worker or psychologist.
- A private counsellor/psychotherapist.
- A culturally based health service.
- Marriage Guidance.
- An alcohol or drug addiction service.
- A church social service.

Do not worry too much about a particular helping professional's label; rather, go on recommendations from an adviser you trust or someone who has actually consulted the professional concerned.

Sometimes there will be a problem that requires immediate help. Support in a crisis can be obtained from services such as a mental health crisis team, Victim Support, Women's Refuge, Rape Crisis and the Lifeline telephone counselling service.

If you are unsure where to go for help, consider consulting your family doctor, pastor or local Citizens' Advice Bureau, or some other service listed in your phone book.

Before you see a counsellor

You will increase the chance that counselling will be a satisfying experience if you do some advance checking and monitor your on-going contact with the counsellor. The following suggestions are drawn from the check list developed by Stephen Palmer and Kasia Szymanska[1], as well as from my own experience.

Here are some questions to consider in advance of or soon after starting counselling:

- Does the counsellor have relevant qualifications and experience?
- Does the counsellor receive supervision from another professional counsellor or supervision group? Most professional bodies consider supervision to be mandatory.
- Is the counsellor a member of a professional body with a clear code of ethics? Obtain a copy of the code if possible.
- What type of approach does the counsellor use and how does

it relate to your problem? Note that Cognitive-Behaviour Therapy (CBT) is the recommended approach for most emotional and behavioural problems. This book is based on CBT; consider showing it to a potential counsellor to see whether his or her approach is compatible.
- Discuss with the counsellor your goals and what you expect to get from counselling.
- Ask about fees, if any, and discuss the frequency and estimated duration of your counselling.
- Finally, do not enter into a long-term counselling contract unless you are satisfied this is *necessary* and *beneficial* to you. If in doubt, get a second opinion.

Bear the following points in mind while seeing a counsellor:

- *Regular reviews*. Ask for periodic evaluations of progress towards your specified goals.
- *Keep the focus on your problems.* Self-disclosure by the counsellor can sometimes be therapeutically useful, but speak up if the sessions are dominated by the counsellor discussing his or her own problems.
- *Maintain appropriate boundaries between yourself and your counsellor.* Do not accept significant gifts (apart from relevant therapeutic material, such as reading), or social invitations (unless they are part of the therapeutic work itself — for instance, facing social anxiety by going with your counsellor to a busy café). If your counsellor proposes a change in venue for your sessions — for example, from a centre to his or her own home — without good reason, do not agree. It is not beneficial — in fact, it is usually damaging — for clients to have sexual contact with their counsellor, and it is unethical for counsellors to engage in any such contact with their clients.
- *Express any concerns.* If at any time you feel discounted, undermined or manipulated, or have any doubts about the counselling you are receiving, discuss this with your counsellor. Try to resolve issues as they arise rather than sit on them. If

you are still uncertain, seek advice. Talk to a friend, your doctor, your local Citizens' Advice Bureau, the professional body to which your counsellor belongs, or the agency, if any, that employs him or her.

Be realistic about change

Finally, watch out for any internal demand that you be able to change anything and everything you dislike. This may lead to potentially dangerous behaviour (such as radical dieting) and, finally, to disillusionment. Some things you can change, some you cannot.[2] Desire change — just hold your desire as a preference, not a demand.

References
1. Palmer, S., & Szymanska, K., (1994). A checklist for clients interested in receiving counselling, psychotherapy or hypnosis. *The Rational Emotive Behaviour Therapist*, 2:1, 28–31.
2. Seligman, M.E.P., (1994). *What You Can Change and What You Can't: The complete guide to successful self-improvement.* Sydney: Random House.

Further reading

There are many books and articles — based, like this volume, on the principles of Cognitive-Behaviour Therapy — that could help you expand your understanding of yourself and improve your self-help skills. The first list below is of titles aimed primarily at a general readership, while the second is of publications most likely to be of interest to professionals.

General literature

Multiple self-help topics

Bernard, M.E. (1986). *Staying Rational in an Irrational World: Albert Ellis and Rational-Emotive Therapy.* New York, N.Y.: Lyle Stuart.

Dyer, W. (1976). *Your Erroneous Zones.* London: Sphere Books.

Ellis, A. (1988). *How to Stubbornly Refuse to Make Yourself Miserable About Anything.* New York, N.Y.: Lyle Stuart.

Self-acceptance, self-change and anger management

Birkedahl, N. (1990). *The Habit Control Workbook.* Oakland, Cal.: New Harbinger.

Dryden, W. (1996). *Overcoming Anger.* London: Sheldon Press.

Ellis, A. (1977). *Anger — How to Live with and without It.* New York, N.Y.: Carol Publishing.

Ellis, A. & Knaus, W.J. (1977). *Overcoming Procrastination.* New York, N.Y.: Signet: New American Library.

Hauck, P.A. (1992). *Overcoming the Rating Game: Beyond self-love — beyond self-esteem.* Louisville, Ken.: Westminster/John Knox.

Stress management

Burns, D. (1980). The perfectionist's script for self-defeat. *Psychology Today* (Nov.), 34–52.

Cooper, C.L., & Palmer, S. (2000). *Conquer Your Stress*. London: Chartered Institute of Personnel and Development.

Davis, M., Eshelman, E.R. & McKay, M. (1988). *The Relaxation and Stress Reduction Workbook*. Oakland, Cal.: New Harbinger.

Froggatt, W. (1997). *GoodStress: The life that can be yours*. Auckland: HarperCollins.

Anxiety

Borkovec, T.D. (1985). What's the use of worrying? *Psychology Today* (Dec.), 59–64.

Bourne, E.J. (1995). *The Anxiety & Phobia Workbook*, 2nd edn. Oakland, Cal.: New Harbinger.

Copeland, M.E. (1998). *The Worry Control Workbook*. Oakland, Cal.: New Harbinger.

Dumont, R. (1997). *The Sky Is Falling: Understanding and coping with phobias, panic, and obsessive-compulsive disorders*. New York, N.Y.: Norton.

Ellis, A. (1972). *How to Master Your Fear of Flying*. New York, N.Y.: Institute for Rational Living.

Froggatt, W. (2003). *FearLess: Your guide to overcoming anxiety*. Auckland: HarperCollins.

Hauck, P. (1975). *Why Be Afraid?* London: Sheldon Press.

Robin, M.W. & Balter, R. (1995). *Performance Anxiety*. Holbrook, Mass.: Adams Publishing.

Steketee, G. & White, K. (1990). *When Once Is Not Enough: Help for obsessive-compulsives*. Oakland, Cal: New Harbinger.

Depression

Burns, D. (1989). *The Feeling Good Handbook*. New York, N.Y.: Plume/Penguin.

Burns, D.M. (1980). *Feeling Good: The new mood therapy*. New York, N.Y.: Signet/New American Library.

Hauck, P. (1976). *Overcoming Depression*. Philadelphia, Pa.: The Westminster Press.

Smith, G. (1996). *Sharing the Load: What to do when someone you love is depressed*. Auckland: Random House.

Assertiveness, relationships and family

Beck, A. (1988). *Love Is Never Enough*. New York, N.Y.: Harper & Row.

Ellis, A., & Lange, A. (1994). *How to Keep People from Pushing Your Buttons*. New York, N.Y.: Citadel Press.

Hauck, P. (1967). *How to Bring Up Your Child Successfully*. London: Sheldon Press.

Hauck, P. (1967). *The Rational Management of Children*. New York, N.Y.: Libra.

Hauck, P. (1977). *Making Marriage Work*. London: Sheldon Press.

Jakubowski, P. & Lange, A.J. (1978). *The Assertive Option: Your rights and responsibilities*. Champaign, Ill.: Research Press.

Montgomery, R., & Evans, L. (1982). *Living & Loving Together: A practical step-by-step manual to help you make and keep better relationships*. Ringwood, Vic.: Viking O'Neil.

Pittman, F. (1994). How to manage Mom & Dad. *Psychology Today*, 27:6 (Nov.–Dec.), 44–49 and 74.

Wolfe, J. (1992). *What to Do When He Has a Headache: How to rekindle your man's desire*. London: Thorson's.

Physical health

Catalano, E. (1987). *The Chronic Pain Control Workbook*. Oakland, Cal.: New Harbinger.

Deardorff, W.W., & Reeves, J.L. (1997). *Preparing for Surgery: A mind–body approach to enhance healing and recovery*. Oakland, Cal.: New Harbinger.

Ellis, A., & Abrams, M. (1994). *How to Cope with a Fatal Illness: The rational management of death and dying*. New York, N.Y.: Barricade Books.

Miscellaneous

Dryden, W. (1998). *Overcoming Jealousy*. London: Sheldon Press.

Dryden, W. (1997). *Overcoming Shame*. London: Sheldon Press.

Dryden, W. & Gordon, J. (1993). *Beating the Comfort Trap*. London: Sheldon Press.

Ellis, A., Abrams, M., & Dengelegi, L. (1992). *The Art & Science of*

Rational Eating. Fort Lee, N.J.: Barricade Books.

Ellis, T.T. & Newman, C.F. (1996). *Choosing to Live: How to defeat suicide through cognitive therapy.* Oakland: New Harbinger.

Robb, H.B. (1988). *How to Stop Driving Yourself Crazy with Help from the Bible.* New York: Institute for Rational-Emotive Therapy.

Sandbek, T.J. (1993). *The Deadly Diet: Recovering from anorexia and bulimia.* Oakland, Cal.: New Harbinger.

Seligman, M.E.P. (1994). *What You Can Change and What You Can't: The complete guide to successful self-improvement.* Sydney: Random House.

Other self-help resources

A good selection of audiotapes on rational self-help topics is obtainable from the Albert Ellis Institute, 45 East 65th Street, New York, NY 10021-6593, USA. Phone 001-212-535-0822, fax 001-212-249-3582, Internet: http://www.rebt.org/

A growing selection of tapes is also available from the Australian Institute for Rational-Emotive Therapy, 45 Balcombe Road, Mentone, Vic. 3194, Australia. Phone/fax 0061-613-9585-1881, Internet: http://www.rational.org.nz/rebt.htm

Professional literature

Addiction

Ellis, A., *et al.* (1988). *Rational-Emotive Therapy with Alcoholics and Substance Abusers.* New York: Pergamon Press.

Ferstein, M.E. & Whiston, S.C. (1991). Utilizing RET for effective treatment of adult children of alcoholics. *Journal of Rational-Emotive & Cognitive-Behavior Therapy,* 9:1, 39-49.

Oei, J.P.S. & Jackson, P.R. (1994). Some effective therapeutic factors in group Cognitive-Behavioural Therapy with problem drinkers. *Journal of Studies on Alcohol,* 45:2, 119–23.

Toneatto T. & Sobell L.C. (1990). Pathological gambling treated with Cognitive-Behavior Therapy: a case report. *Addictive Behaviors.* 15:5, 497–501.

Anger

Blackburn, J. (2001). Anger, chronic pain and Rational-Emotive-Behaviour Therapy. *The Rational-Emotive-Behaviour Therapist*. 9:1, 23–8.

Nelson, W.M., Hart, K.J. & Finch, A.J. (1993). Anger in children: a cognitive-behavioral view of the assessment-therapy connection. *Journal of Rational-Emotive & Cognitive-Behavior Therapy*, 11:3, 135–50.

Novaco, R. (1975). *Anger Control*. Lexington, Mass.: Lexington Books.

Novaco, R.W. (1977). Stress inoculation: a cognitive therapy for anger. *Journal of Consulting & Clinical Psychology*, 45, 600–608.

Wilde, J. (1995). Anger Management in Education: Alternatives to student violence. Lancaster, Pa.: Technomic Publishing.

Wilde, J. (2001). Interventions for children with anger problems. *Journal of Rational-Emotive & Cognitive-Behavior Therapy*, 19:3, 191–7

Anxiety

Beck, A.T. & Emery, G. (1985). *Anxiety Disorders*. New York, N.Y.: Basic Books.

van Oppen, P. & Arntz, A. (1994). Cognitive therapy for obsessive-compulsive disorder. *Behaviour Research & Therapy*, 32:1, 79–87.

Walen, S. (1982). Phrenophobia. *Cognitive Therapy & Research*, 6, 399–408.

Warren, R. & Zgourides, G. (1991). *Anxiety Disorders: A rational-emotive approach*. New York, N.Y.: Pergamon Press.

Crisis work

Dattilio, F.M. & Freeman, A. (eds.), (1994). *Cognitive-Behavioural Strategies in Crisis Intervention*. New York, N.Y.: Guilford.

Resick, P.A. & Schnicke, M.K. (1992). Cognitive processing therapy for sexual assault victims. *Journal of Consulting and Clinical Psychology*, 60, 748–56.

Depression

Covi, L., Roth, D. & Lipman, R.S. (1982). Cognitive group psychotherapy of depression: the close-ended group. *American Journal of Psychotherapy*, 36, 459–69.

Ellis, A. (1987). A sadly neglected cognitive element in depression. *Cognitive Therapy & Research*, 11, 121–46.

Yost, E.B. *et al.* (1986). *Group Cognitive Therapy: A treatment approach for depressed older adults.* New York, N.Y.: Pergamon.

Eating disorders

Sandbek, T.J. (1993). *The Deadly Diet.* Oakland, Cal.: New Harbinger.

Mines, R.A. & Merrill, C.A. (1986). The group treatment of bulimia: assumptions and recommendations. *American Mental Health Counsellors Association Journal*, 8, 229–36.

Grief

Kavanagh, D.J. (1990). Towards a cognitive-behavioural intervention for adult grief reactions [review]. *British Journal of Psychiatry*, 157, 373–83.

Malkinson, R. (1996). Cognitive-behavioural grief therapy. *Journal of Rational-Emotive & Cognitive-Behaviour Therapy*, 14:3, 155–71.

Intellectual disability

Lindsay, W.R., Howells, L. & Pitcaithly, D. (1993). Cognitive therapy for depression with individuals with intellectual disabilities. *British Journal of Medical Psychology*, 66 (pt 2), 135–41.

Zeitlin, S. & Williamson, G. (1987). The coping with stress model: families with a handicapped child. *Journal of Counselling & Development.* 65:8, 443–6.

Personality disorders

Beck, A.T., Freeman, A. & associates (1990). *Cognitive Therapy of Personality Disorders.* New York, N.Y.: Guilford.

Kiehn, B. & Swales, M. (1995) An overview of dialectical behaviour therapy in the treatment of borderline personality disorder. *Psychiatry Online.* Retrieved 13 Jan. 2003 from: www.priory.com/dbt.htm

Layden, M.A. *et al.* (1993). Cognitive Therapy of Borderline Personality Disorder. Needham Heights, Mass.: Allyn & Bacon.

Linehan, M.M. (1992). *Cognitive-Behavioural Treatment of Border-*

line Personality Disorder. New York, N.Y.: Guilford Press.

Salkovskis, P.M., Atha, C. & Storer, D. (1990). Cognitive-behavioural problem-solving in the treatment of patients who repeatedly attempt suicide: a controlled trial. *British Journal of Psychiatry*, 157, 871–6.

Physical health

Butler, S. *et al.* (1991). Cognitive-Behaviour Therapy in chronic fatigue syndrome. *Journal of Neurology, Neurosurgery & Psychiatry*, 54:2, 153–8.

Girido, M. & Wood, D. (1979). Talking yourself out of pain: the importance of believing that you can. *Cognitive Therapy & Research*, 3, 23–33.

Kongstvedt, S.J. (1987). Cognitive approaches to pain control: common factors. *Journal of Counselling & Development*. 65:10, 538–41.

Psychosis, inpatients and severe mental disorders

Chadwick, P., Birchwood, M. & Trower, P. (1996). *Cognitive Therapy for Delusions, Voices and Paranoia*. Chichester: Wiley.

Davis, M.H. & Casey, D.A. (1990). Utilizing cognitive therapy on the short-term psychiatric inpatient unit. *General Hospital Psychiatry*, 12:3, 170–76.

Kopec, A.M. (1995). Rational-Emotive-Behaviour Therapy in a forensic setting: practical issues. *Journal of Rational-Emotive & Cognitive-Behavior Therapy*, 13:4, 243–53.

Wright, J.H. *et al.* (1993). *Cognitive Therapy with Inpatients: Developing a cognitive milieu*. New York, N.Y.: Guilford Press.

Stress management

Ellis, A. *et al.* (1997). *Stress Counselling: A rational-emotive behavioural approach*. London: Cassell (also published 1998, New York, N.Y.: Springer).

Froggatt, W. (1997). *GoodStress: The life that can be yours*. Auckland: HarperCollins.

Palmer, S. & Dryden, W. (1991). A multimodal approach to stress management. *Stress News*, 3:1, 2–10.

Suicide
Dattilio, F.M. & Freeman, A. (eds.), (1994). *Cognitive-Behavioural Strategies in Crisis Intervention*. New York, N.Y.: Guilford.

Scott, J., Williams, J. M.G. & Beck, A.T. (1989). *Cognitive Therapy in Clinical Practice*. London: Routledge.

The workplace
DiMattia, D. & Ijzermans, T. (1996). *Reaching Their Minds: A trainer's manual for rational effectiveness training*. New York, N.Y.: Institute for Rational-Emotive Therapy.

Nucci, C. (2002). The rational teacher: Rational-Emotive-Behaviour Therapy in teacher education. *Journal of Rational-Emotive & Cognitive-Behavior Therapy*, 20:1, 15–32

Wilde, J. (1995). *Anger Management in Education: Alternatives to student violence*. Lancaster, Pa.: Technomic Publishing.

Miscellaneous
Gibbs, J.C., Potter, G.B. & Goldstein, A.P. (1995). *The Equip Program: Teaching youth to think and act responsibly through a peer-helping approach*. Champaign, Ill.: Research Press.

Lange, A., & Jakubowski, P. (1976). *Responsible Assertive Behaviour: Cognitive-behavioural procedures for trainers*. Champaign, Ill.: Research Press.

Rieckert, J. & Möller, A. (2000). Rational-Emotive Behaviour Therapy in the treatment of adult victims of childhood sexual abuse. *Journal of Rational-Emotive & Cognitive-Behavior Therapy*, 18:2, 87–102.

Sloan, E.P. *et al.* (1993). The nuts and bolts of behavioral therapy for insomnia. *Journal of Psychosomatic Research*, 37 (supp.1), 19–37.

Multiple applications
Cigno, K. & Bourn, D. (eds.), (1998). *Cognitive-Behavioural Social Work in Practice*. Aldershot: Ashgate.

Ellis, A. & Bernard, M.E. (eds.), (1985). *Clinical Applications of Rational-Emotive Therapy*. New York, N.Y.: Plenum.

France, R. & Robson, M. (1997). *Cognitive-Behavioural Therapy in*

Primary Care. London: Jessica Kingsley.
Hawton, K. *et al.* (1989). *Cognitive-Behaviour Therapy for Psychiatric Problems*. Oxford: Oxford University Press.
Treatment Protocol Project (1997). Management of Mental Disorders, 2nd edn. Sydney: World Health Organisation.

Children and adolescents

Bernard, M.E. & Joyce, M. (1984). *Rational-Emotive Therapy with Children and Adolescents*. New York, N.Y.: Wiley.

Deblinger, E., McLeer, S.V. & Henry, D. (1990). Cognitive-behavioral treatment for sexually abused children suffering post-traumatic stress: preliminary findings. *Journal of the American Academy of Child & Adolescent Psychiatry*. 29:5, 747–52.

Kinney, A. (1991). Cognitive-Behavior Therapy with children: developmental reconsiderations. *Journal of Rational-Emotive & Cognitive-Behavior Therapy*, 9:1, 51–61.

Morris, G.B. (1993). A rational-emotive treatment program with conduct disorder and attention-deficit hyperactivity disorder in adolescents. *Journal of Rational-Emotive & Cognitive-Behavior Therapy*, 11:3, 123–34.

Nelson, W.M. *et al.* (1993). Anger in children: a cognitive-behavioral view of the assessment-therapy connection. *Journal of Rational-Emotive & Cognitive-Behavior Therapy*, 11:3, 135–50.

Ronan, K.R. & Kendall, P.C. (1990). Non-self-controlled adolescents: applications of Cognitive-Behavioral Therapy. *Adolescent Psychiatry*, 17, 479–505.

Seasock, J.P. (1995). Identification of adolescent sex offenders: An REBT model. *Journal of Rational-Emotive & Cognitive-Behavior Therapy*, 13:4, 261–71.

Whitford, R. & Parr, V. (1995). Uses of Rational-Emotive-Behaviour Therapy with juvenile sex offenders. *Journal of Rational-Emotive & Cognitive-Behavior Therapy*. 13:4, 273–82.

Wilde, J. (2001). Interventions for children with anger problems. *Journal of Rational-Emotive & Cognitive-Behavior Therapy*, 19:3, 191–7.

Older adults

Ellis, A. (1999). Rational-Emotive-Behaviour Therapy and Cognitive-Behaviour Therapy for elderly people. *Journal of Rational-Emotive & Cognitive-Behaviour Therapy*, 17:1, 5–18.

Hitch, S. (1994). Cognitive therapy as a tool for caring for the elderly confused person. *Journal of Clinical Nursing*, 3:1, 49–55.

Morin, C.M. *et al.* (1993). Cognitive-Behavior Therapy for late-life insomnia. *Journal of Consulting & Clinical Psychology*, 61:1, 137–46.

Oliver, R. & Bock, F.A. (1990). Alleviating the distress of caregivers of Alzheimer's disease patients: a Rational-Emotive Therapy model. *Journal of Rational-Emotive & Cognitive-Behavior Therapy*, 8:1, 53–69.

Zerhusen, J.D., Boyle, K. & Wilson, W. (1991). Out of the darkness: group cognitive therapy for depressed elderly. *Journal of Psychosocial Nursing & Mental Health Services*, 29:9, 16–21.

Specific cultural groups

Chen, C.P. (1995). Counselling applications of RET in a Chinese cultural context. *Journal of Rational-Emotive & Cognitive-Behavior Therapy*, 13:2, 117–29.

La Fromboise, T.D. & Rowe, W. (1983). Skills training for bicultural competence: rationale and application. *Journal of Counselling Psychology*, 30:4, 589–95.

McFarlane-Nathan, G.H. (1994). Cognitive-Behaviour Therapy and the Maori client. Unpublished paper, Psychological Services Division Annual Conference, New Zealand.

Renfrey, G.S. (1992). Cognitive-Behaviour Therapy and the Native American client. *Behavior Therapy*, 23, 321–40.

Religious clients

Johnson, W. (1993). Christian Rational-Emotive Therapy: a treatment protocol. *Journal of Psychology and Christianity*, 12:13, 254–61.

Mathews, T.J. (2000). The Cross and the Christian client. *The Rational Emotive Behaviour Therapist*, 8:1, 10–14.

Rob, H.B. (2001). Can Rational-Emotive-Behavior Therapy lead to spiritual transformation? Yes, sometimes! *Journal of Rational-Emotive & Cognitive-Behavior Therapy*, 19:3, 153–61.

Warnock, S. (1989). Rational-Emotive Therapy and the Christian client. *Journal of Rational-Emotive & Cognitive-Behavior Therapy*. 7:4, 263–80.

Group work

Ellis, A. (1992). Group Rational-Emotive and Cognitive-Behavioral Therapy. *International Journal of Group Psychotherapy*, 42:1, 63–80.

Free, M.L. (1999). *Cognitive Therapy in Groups: Guidelines and resources for practice*. Chichester: John Wiley.

Family and couples

Ellis, A. *et al.* (1989). *Rational-Emotive Couples' Therapy*. New York, N.Y.: Pergamon.

Epstein, N., Schlesinger, S.E. & Dryden, W. (1988). *Cognitive-Behavioral Therapy with Families*. New York, N.Y.: Brunner/Mazel.

General CBT theory and practice

Dryden, W. & Golden, W.L. (eds.), (1987). *Cognitive-Behavioural Approaches to Psychotherapy*. New York, N.Y.: Hemisphere.

Safran, J.D. & Segal, Z.V. (1990). *Interpersonal Process in Cognitive Therapy*. New York, N.Y.: Basic Books.

Ziegler, D.J. (2000). Basic assumptions concerning human nature underlying Rational-Emotive-Behaviour Therapy (REBT) personality theory. *Journal of Rational-Emotive & Cognitive-Behavior Therapy*, 18:2, 67–85.

Learning to use CBT

Bernard, M. (1991). *Using Rational-Emotive Therapy Effectively: A practitioner's guide*. New York, N.Y.: Plenum Press.

Dryden, W. (1995). *Brief Rational-Emotive-Behaviour Therapy*. Chichester: John Wiley.

Lazarus, A.A. (1990). The Practice of Multimodal Therapy. Baltimore: Johns Hopkins University Press.

Scott, M.J., Stradling, S.G. & Dryden, W. (1995). *Developing Cognitive-Behavioural Counselling*. London: Sage Publications.

Walen, S.R., Digiuseppe, R. & Dryden, W. (1992). *A Practitioner's Guide to Rational-Emotive Therapy*, 2nd edn. New York, N.Y.: Oxford University Press.

CBT techniques

Bernard, M.E. & Wolfe, J.L. (2000). *The REBT Resource Book for Practitioners* 2nd edn. New York, N.Y.: Albert Ellis Institute.

McMullin, R.E. (2000). *The New Handbook of Cognitive Therapy Techniques*. New York, N.Y.: Norton.

Index

ABC model of causation, 18–21
    examples, 39–40
    see also
        causation
        rational self-analysis
Acceptance
    of problems as a part of life, 226
    of reality, 57, 250
    of self, *see* people-rating: self-acceptance
Action strategies, *see* behavioural strategies
Activity scheduling, 89–90, 155–9
Aggression, *see*
    anger
    assertiveness
Analysis, *see* rational self-analysis
Anger, 162–79
    causes, 166–9
    changing anger thoughts, 170–2
    constructive anger, 164, 175
    costs of a., 163–4
    destructive anger, 163–4
    identifying a., 163–4, 165–6
    interrupting anger, 172–3
Anxiety, 120–36
    discomfort anxiety, 122
    fear of anxiety,
    identifying fears, 125–6
    inappropriate anxiety, 120–1
    overcoming, 126–36
    phobias, 121
    relationship to fear, 120
    self-devaluation anxiety, 123–4
    worrying, 129–30
Approval-seeking
    combating, 183
    identifying, 181–2
    problems with, 180
    reasons for, 180–1, 182–3
    see also, criticism: handling
Assertiveness, 174–5, 193–207
    and stress, 241
    causes, 195–7
    combating unassertive thinking, 197–9
    cultural differences, 207
    identifying, 193–4
    responsible assertiveness, 200–1, 206–7
    self-directed behaviour, 201–4, 248
    see also
        criticism: handling
        enlightened self-interest
        manipulation by others
Awfulising, *see* catastrophising

Behaviour
    evaluating b. rather than self, 69, 144
Behavioural responsibility, 248
Behavioural strategies
    designing, 108–9
    see also
        activity scheduling
        contradictory behaviour
        exposure
        in-vivo disputing
        self-treating
        stimulus control
        time-out
Beliefs, *see* thinking
Biochemistry, *see* causation
Black and white thinking, 44–5, 85
Blame, *see* responsibility
Blocks to change, *see* motivation
Broken-record technique, 201–3

Can't-stand-it-itis, *see* catastrophising
Catastrophe scale, 84
Catastrophising

awfulising, 59
can't-stand-it-itis, 60, 85
causes, 60–1, 85
identifying, 104
overcoming, 63, 84, 85
rational alternative, 61–2

Causation
biochemical changes, 28
biological susceptibility, 22, 48, 66, 210
learning, 22–3, 47–8
myths about, 23–4
technological change
thinking, 16–18
see also
 circumstances
 control: internal v. external

Change
changing self, *see* thinking: changing
maintaining, 259–60
managing in one's life, 242
myths about, 255–6
realistic expectations of, 264

Circumstances
influence of, 27–8
myth of control by, 24
taking action on, 131, 174–5
see also problem-solving

Compulsiveness, 211, 216–17

Concern
and assertiveness, 197–8
as alternative to anxiety, 130, 135
as alternative to guilt, 142–6

Confidence, 244–5

Contradictory behaviour, 88

Control
controlling others, 67, 198–9
internal v. external, 25–6
sense of, 29
see also
 causation
 circumstances

Core beliefs, *see* thinking: core beliefs

Counsellor, seeing one, 262–4

Criticism, handling, 184–5, 187–9

Cultural differences and assertiveness, 207

Decision-making, 220–30

Demanding
and anger, 166
and approval, 183–4
and catastrophising, 61
and guilt, 141–2
changing, 55–7, 84, 85
changing to preferences, 53, 55–8, 85, 170–1, 224–5
consequences of, 51–2, 53–4
identifying, 103–4
nature of, 52–3
origins of, 54–5

Depression, 147–61, 252
causes, 148–9, 149–52
changing depressive thinking, 152–5
description, 147–8

Diaries, 98, 100–1, 107, 121, 141, 165–6

Disapproval, *see* approval-seeking

Discomfort
and anger, 167–8
fear of, 122, 210, 212
increasing tolerance for, 126–8, 246, 253–5
low-intolerance for 29–30, 60, 253, 257
see also catastrophising

Disputation, *see* thinking: disputing

Distorting reality, *see* interpretations

Double-standard technique, 84

Drugs, 28

Education, of self, 86–7

Emotional and behavioural responsibility, 248

Emotional reasoning, 46–7, 85

Emotions
accepting own emotions, 155
causes of, *see* causation
fear of own emotions, 121, 124
list of, 76–7

Enlightened self-interest, 199–200, 206–7, 245–6

Evaluations
changing, 83
see also
 catastrophising
 demanding
 people-rating

Excellence, *see* perfectionism

INDEX

Existence, valuing your own, 69
Exposure, 88–9, 127–8, 133–4, 186

Fear, *see* anxiety
Feelings, *see* emotions
Filtering, 45, 85
Finances, managing, 242
Flexibility, 249
Fortune-telling, 46, 85
Frustration, tolerance for, 246

Goals, 220–30
    acting on, 229
    and problem-solving, 233
    and stress management, 240
    importance for assertiveness, 203–4
    importance of keeping realistic, 216
    knowing your own, 227–9
    see also
        indecision
        values
Groups, self-help, 259, 261
Guilt, 137–46
    causes of, 139–40, 141–2
    changing to concern, 142–6
    consequences of, 138
    description of, 137
    how to recognize, 141

Help, asking for, 256–7, 261–4
Hostility, *see* anger

Indecision, 220–30
    causes of, 221–4
    consequences of, 220
    overcoming, 224–9
    see also
        goals
        values
Interpretations, 35–8
    alternatives to, 49–50
    and anger, 168–9, 171
    changing, 48–9, 82–3
    checking out, 129, 172
    identifying, 102–3
    types of, 44–7
    see also
        black and white thinking
        emotional reasoning
        filtering
        fortune-telling
        mind-reading
        overgeneralising
        personalising
Intuition, 224, 226–7
In-vivo
    disputing 'on-the-spot', 84
    exposure, *see* exposure
Irrational, *see* thinking: irrational thinking

Logical thinking, 226–7
Long-range enjoyment, 246–7
Low discomfort-tolerance, *see* discomfort: low tolerance for

Manipulation by others, 194–5, 204
Medication
    effects of, 28
    using, 257
Mental health statistics, 16
Mind-reading, 46, 85
Mistakes
    fear of, 225–6
    necessity of, 214
Moderation, 247
Moralising, *see* demanding
Motivation
    and depression 160
    demanding, effect of on motivation, 55
    overcoming blocks to using self-help, 92–3, 160
    overcoming obstacles to change, 29–30, 178–9, 252–60
Musturbation, *see* demanding

Needs, *see* demanding

Objective thinking, 249
Obstacles, *see* motivation
Overgeneralising, 46, 85

Past, influence of, 23–4
People-rating
    and anger, 168

and guilt, 139, 142
and unassertiveness, 196
causes, 66–7
description of, 64–6
identifying, 104–5
overcoming, 71–2, 84, 85, 172
rational alternative, 68–9, 70
self-acceptance, 68–9, 128–9, 244–5
self-devaluation anxiety, 123–4, 210, 212
Perfectionism, 208–19
acting against, 216–17
causes, 210, 211–13
consequences of, 208–9
excellence as alternative to, 213–14
identifying, 210, 258
Personalising, 47, 85
Phobias, *see* anxiety: phobias
Positive thinking, 40–1, 85–6
Preferential thinking, *see* demanding: changing: to preferences
Prevention, 160–1
Principles,
acceptance of reality, 250
emotional and behavioural responsibility, 248
enlightened self-interest, 245–6
flexibility, 249
long-range enjoyment, 246–7
moderation, 247
objective thinking, 249
risk-taking, 247
self-acceptance and confidence, 244–5
self-direction, 248
self-knowledge, 244
tolerance for frustration and discomfort, 246
twelve rational, 244–51
Problem-solving, 90, 131–2, 225, 231–7
Productivity
increasing, 215–16
perfectionism a block to, 209

Rational cards, 87–8
Rational self-analysis
checklist for, 94–6
description of, 73–5
examples of, 90–1, 110–12
how to carry out, 75–91,
A, 75–6
B, 77–81
C, 76–7
D, 82–6
E, 81–2
F, 90
practice exercises for, 97–115
troubleshooting, 92–4
when to carry out, 91–2
Rational thinking, *see* thinking: rational thinking
Reality, *see* acceptance: of reality
Relationships
and perfectionism, 209
see also, assertiveness
Relaxation training, 132, 240
Responsibility
different to blame, 24–5
emotional and behavioural responsibility, 248
responsible assertiveness, 200–1
Risk-taking, 247

Scientific thinking, 249
Self-acceptance, *see* people-rating: self-acceptance
Self-analysis, *see* rational self-analysis
Self-care, 132, 173, 240
Self-change, *see* thinking: changing
Self-direction, *see* assertiveness
Self-esteem, *see* people-rating
Self-interest, *see* enlightened self-interest
Selfishness, 198
see also, enlightened self-interest
Self-knowledge, 244
Self-rating, *see* people-rating
Self-treating, 145, 158–9
Sleep, 240
'So what if' technique, 129
Stimulus control, 89
Stress
definition of, 238, 239
reasons for increase in, 238–9
see also, stress management
Stress management, 238–43
twelve strategies, 240–2

INDEX

see also
   relaxation training
   self-care
   time-management
Subconscious
   subconscious gains, 48
   see also, thinking: subconscious
Suicide, what to do, 252–3
Support from others, 240–1

Techniques
   assertiveness, *see* broken-record
   behavioural, *see* behavioural strategies
      miscellaneous, *see*
      education: of self
      relaxation training
      self-care
      time-out
      rethinking, *see*
   diaries
   double-standard
   rational cards
   'so what if' technique
   thinking: disputation
   stress, *see* stress management
Thinking
   causes, *see* causation
   changing, 31–2
   evaluations, 83
   interpretations, 48–50, 82–3
   core beliefs
      examples, 38
      identifying, 105–7

   nature of, 34
   twelve irrational beliefs, 33–4
   twelve rational beliefs, 41–2
   disputing, 82–4, 107–8
   evaluations, 35–8
      see also
      catastrophising
      demanding
      people-rating
   identifying, 77–81, 98–107
   interpretations, *see* interpretations
   irrational thinking, nature of, 33
   objective thinking, 249
   rational thinking
      examples, 41–2
      nature of, 40–1, 249
   replacing old beliefs, 85–6
   subconscious, 21–2
Time management, 132–3, 241–2
Time out, 173
Tolerance for frustration and discomfort, 246

Values
   confusion about, 223–4
   held as preferences, 56–7
   knowing your own, 227–9
   see also
      goals
      indecision

Worrying, *see* anxiety: worrying